Praise for *The Financial Times Guide to Sustainable Business*

The Financial Times Guide to Sustainable Business has inspired me to work with boards of directors and executive management to showcase the financial opportunities of sustainability. Barker and Johnstone-Louis powerfully assert that sustainability is not just an aspirational goal but a critical business imperative. The book serves as a blueprint for improved profitability. It sets out how sustainability – when integrated into corporate strategy – drives innovation, unlocks value, and builds resilience. We're all looking for strategic advantage in today's complex economic landscape. This book tells us how.

> — Rebekah Cheney, Climate governance expert and graduate of the Oxford Leading Sustainable Corporations Programme

I've been waiting for this book. It beautifully strikes that hard-to-find balance that recognizes the responsibility companies have for the natural and social systems upon which they depend while at the same time recognizing their responsibility to create value for shareholders. It is both practical and inspirational. I wish every leader would read this book. They'd all be better for it."

> Professor Robert G. Eccles, Founding Chair, Sustainability Accounting Standards Board, co-founder, founding Chair of KKR Sustainability Expert Advisory Group

Business leaders confront a once-in-a-generation polycrisis—and a once-in-a-career nexus of market opportunities. For those rising to the challenge, *The Financial Times Guide to Sustainable Business* will be an invaluable guide.

> John Elkington, co-founder of ENDS, SustainAbility and Volans and author of 21 books, most recently *Green Swans: The Coming Boom In Regenerative Capitalism* (2021) and *Tickling Sharks: How We Sold Business On Sustainability* (2024)

"Throughout history, our biggest leaps in understanding have come from wrestling with paradox, from realizing that light can be both wave and particle, to learning that freedom sometimes requires structure. In business, we've too often been boxed in linear thinking or in false choices: profit or purpose, efficiency or equity, growth or sustainability.

Reading Barker and Johnstone-Louis's book, I felt a kind of intellectual relief. They give language and structure to what many of us in social innovation and impact investing have seen for a long time: that the real breakthroughs happen when we stop seeing social and environmental value as trade-offs and start treating them as dynamic tensions to be navigated.

This book doesn't fall into the trap of prescribing easy "win-win" fixes. Instead, it gives you the tools to work through complexity without flinching and without defaulting to business-as-usual. It's rigorous, grounded, and refreshingly honest.

The authors' systems-based framework doesn't just challenge conventional wisdom, it provides the analytical tools necessary to discover new forms of value creation that were invisible under old paradigms.

If you're leading a business, funding change, or trying to design systems that actually work for people and for the planet, this is a book that will help you think more clearly, act more courageously, and see value where others might not even be looking."

Professor Vanina Faber, elea Professor of Social Innovation and Dean of the EMBA, IMD Business School

On Oxford Leading Sustainable Corporations, the programme on which this book is based: "PPG chose to collaborate with the Oxford Saïd Business School as the key partner for our internal sustainability leadership program. As our inaugural program of this size and scale, we wanted to ensure that we could rely on a partner to provide a strong backbone for understanding sustainability... The programme... ultimately gave PPG employees a deep dive into sustainability trends, risks and opportunities, as well as a greater appreciation for its strategic necessity for business growth. This programme will ultimately equip our leaders to leverage sustainability in their day-to-day roles and expand the reach of our core sustainability team.

Mats Hägerström, Head of Sustainability EMEA, PPG

Richard and Mary have produced a timely and vital guide for business leaders navigating the sustainability transition. With clarity and depth, they show that profitability and the regeneration of social and environmental systems can go hand in hand. Their call to build strong businesses in strong systems aligns closely with my own belief that business must become a force for renewal, not extraction. What sets this book apart is its pragmatism: it offers real strategies, not rhetoric. In an era of short-term thinking, this book offers long-term vision and practical action.

André Hoffmann, Vice-Chairman of the Board of Directors, Roche, Supervisory Board Chair, Capitals Coalition, author *The New Nature of Business* (2024)

Mary and Richard have put together an essential guide to help leaders sharpen their thinking on how to operate sustainable businesses. I had the pleasure of working with Mary, Richard and the team at Oxford Said Business School to create an in-depth, high-impact programme that we took the entire global leadership group through at Diageo. The framing of what sustainability really means from a societal and environmental perspective and the practical advice on how to create tangible plans for your business are invaluable. If you really want to figure this out for you and your company, then get your hands on this book.

John Kennedy, President, Europe, Diageo

"This book is a call to action. Far from fads and easy shortcuts, Mary Johnstone-Louis and Richard Barker combine depth of analysis and practical experience to guide us in building more resilient businesses, aligned with nature and people."

Guilherme Leal, co-founder and co-chair of Natura, Most Sustainable Brand in the World, Kantar, 2025

"This is the definitive guide on how to build sustainable businesses. It is essential reading for anyone interested in the subject. Written by two of the most authoritative leaders in the field, it provides a clear, comprehensive and practical description of how to put sustainability into practice."

Professor Colin Mayer CBE FBA, author of Firm Commitment (2014), Prosperity (2021), and Capitalism and Crises (2024)

An important and timely guide from authors ideally placed to bring together business and academic perspectives.

Arunma Oteh, former Treasurer and Vice President of the World Bank, author of *All Hands On Deck* **(2025)**

"Knowing Richard and Mary, I expected a thoughtful, evidence-filled, action-oriented book for executives seeking to make sustainability core to their businesses. The book far exceeds my high expectations. It is an important and clear-eyed guide for leaders in a time when opportunities to build sustainable business are great, social and planetary needs are even greater, but headwinds around the world are strong."

Professor Peter Tufano, Baker Foundation Professor at Harvard Business School and Senior Advisor to the Harvard Salata Institute for Climate and Sustainability

"This timely and insightful guide highlights precisely why – and how – businesses can transform to address pressing environmental and social risks and identify opportunities in the process. Mary Johnstone-Louis and Richard Barker deliver essential reading for leaders committed to creating lasting value and genuine sustainability. A must-have resource for leaders navigating an increasingly complex landscape."

Keith Tuffley, CEO, Race to Belém, former Global Co-Head of Sustainability & Corporate Transitions, Citibank, former CEO, the B Team

"This book dives into the heart of what it takes to run a company successfully long term. Companies have an impact and have a responsibility to be transparent about impact and a moral duty to improve and reduce impact. Ultimately, demonstrating real progress in sustainability improves the company's social licence and ability to develop new business."

Jakob Stausholm, CEO of Rio Tinto

THE FINANCIAL TIMES GUIDE TO SUSTAINABLE BUSINESS

⟫Pearson

At Pearson, we believe in learning – all kinds of learning for all kinds of people. Whether it's at home, in the classroom or in the workplace, learning is the key to improving our life chances.

That's why we're working with leading authors to bring you the latest thinking and best practices, so you can get better at the things that are important to you. You can learn on the page or on the move, and with content that's always crafted to help you understand quickly and apply what you've learned.

If you want to upgrade your personal skills or accelerate your career, become a more effective leader or more powerful communicator, discover new opportunities or simply find more inspiration, we can help you make progress in your work and life.

Every day our work helps learning flourish, and wherever learning flourishes, so do people.

To learn more, please visit us at **www.pearson.com**

The Financial Times

With a worldwide network of highly respected journalists, *The Financial Times* provides global business news, insightful opinion and expert analysis of business, finance and politics. With over 500 journalists reporting from 50 countries worldwide, our in-depth coverage of international news is objectively reported and analysed from an independent, global perspective.

To find out more, visit **www.ft.com**

THE FINANCIAL TIMES GUIDE TO SUSTAINABLE BUSINESS

RICHARD BARKER AND MARY JOHNSTONE-LOUIS

Harlow, England • London • New York • Boston • San Francisco • Toronto • Sydney
Dubai • Singapore • Hong Kong • Tokyo • Seoul • Taipei • New Delhi
Cape Town • São Paulo • Mexico City • Madrid • Amsterdam • Munich • Paris • Milan

PEARSON EDUCATION LIMITED
KAO Two
KAO Park
Harlow CM17 9NA
United Kingdom
Tel: +44 (0)1279 623623
Web: www.pearson.com

First edition published 2026 (print and electronic)
© Pearson Education Limited 2026 (print and electronic)

The right of Richard Barker and Mary Johnstone-Louis to be identified as authors of this work has been asserted by them in accordance with the Copyright, Designs and Patents Act 1988.

The print publication is protected by copyright. Prior to any prohibited reproduction, storage in a retrieval system, distribution or transmission in any form or by any means, electronic, mechanical, recording or otherwise, permission should be obtained from the publisher or, where applicable, a licence permitting restricted copying in the United Kingdom should be obtained from the Copyright Licensing Agency Ltd, Barnard's Inn, 86 Fetter Lane, London EC4A 1EN.

The ePublication is protected by copyright and must not be copied, reproduced, transferred, distributed, leased, licensed or publicly performed or used in any way except as specifically permitted in writing by the publishers, as allowed under the terms and conditions under which it was purchased, or as strictly permitted by applicable copyright law. Any unauthorised distribution or use of this text may be a direct infringement of the author's and the publisher's rights and those responsible may be liable in law accordingly.

All trademarks used herein are the property of their respective owners. The use of any trademark in this text does not vest in the author or publisher any trademark ownership rights in such trademarks, nor does the use of such trademarks imply any affiliation with or endorsement of this book by such owners.

Pearson Education is not responsible for the content of third-party internet sites.

ISBN: 978-1-292-43558-9 (print)
        978-1-292-43556-5 (ePub)

British Library Cataloguing-in-Publication Data
A catalogue record for the print edition is available from the British Library

Library of Congress Cataloging-in-Publication Data
A catalog record for the print edition is available from the Library of Congress

10 9 8 7 6 5 4 3 2 1
30 29 28 27 26

Cover design by Michelle Morgan
Cover credit: ssguy/Shutterstock

Print edition typeset in 9.5/14pt Stone Serif ITC Pro by Straive
Printed by Bell & Bain Ltd, Glasgow

NOTE THAT ANY PAGE CROSS REFERENCES REFER TO THE PRINT EDITION

CONTENTS

Author Bios — xiii
Acknowledgements — xv

1 Why sustainability matters to you as a leader — 1
- Making sense of leadership and sustainability — 8
- Sustainability: a word on language and perspective — 12
- Focusing sustainability efforts — 15
- What it means to lead a business sustainably — 17
- Making sense of this book: a word from the authors — 18
- How to use this book — 21
- Recommended reading — 24
- Notes — 25

2 What purpose do corporations serve? — 31
- Corporations are legal structures that create economic value, and more — 31
- Who controls the corporation, and to what end? — 36
- The corporation: what can go wrong? — 41
- What is a sustainable corporation? — 45
- Reflection questions — 53
- Recommended reading — 54
- Notes — 54

3 Climate crisis: the leadership challenge of our time — 57
- What is the issue? — 57
- Why does climate change matter to corporations? — 64
- Corporations and climate change — 69
- What are a corporation's carbon emissions? — 70
- Emissions: decision relevance — 78
- Lifecycle analysis — 80
- Net zero: the role of carbon offsets — 81
- Climate transition — 83

Reflection questions	84
Recommended reading	84
Note 3.1 CO_2 equivalents	85
Note 3.2 Lifecycle analysis	86
Notes	88

4 Why nature matters to business, and what to do about it — 91

Natural capital	98
Why are natural systems being degraded?	100
The role of business	111
Why should companies care?	113
Re-framing business and nature	115
Evaluating nature and your business	123
Action on nature as a business	126
Reflection questions	128
Recommended reading	129
Notes	130

5 What is social sustainability and why does it matter to business? — 133

Business and social licence to operate	135
Business and human rights	141
Business, human rights and the United Nations Sustainable Development Goals	146
Re-framing business and social systems	151
Evaluating social systems and your business	154
Action on social systems as a business	158
Reflection questions	161
Recommended reading	162
Notes	163

6 How and why to embed sustainability into corporate reporting — 171

Financial accounting	173
Corporate governance	177
Why sustainability reporting matters	178

Reporting to other stakeholders	186
Transition plans	188
Evaluate sustainability reporting in your own business	191
Reflection questions	194
Recommended reading	195
Appendix 6.1 Overview of IFRS Sustainability Disclosure Standards	195
Notes	198

7 How to build your sustainability Action Plan and lead change 201

Introduction	201
Maintaining vision while rethinking the trade-off mindset	202
Long-term orientation and adaptive leadership	207
Building your Action Plan: three steps	211
Conclusion	221
Kicking off your Action Plan	222
Recommended reading	223
Notes	224

Index	**227**

AUTHOR BIOS

Richard Barker is Professor of Accounting and formerly Deputy Dean at Saïd Business School, University of Oxford. He is also Senior Associate Research Fellow at Christ Church, Oxford. Richard has served as Chair of the Expert Panel of Accounting for Sustainability, Fellow of Chapter Zero, as a member of the Climate Governance Expert Community, World Economic Forum, and as Director of the MBA at both Oxford and Cambridge. He is a recipient of several teaching awards, including 'Most Acclaimed Lecturer' in the Social Sciences Division, awarded by Oxford University Student Union.

Mary Johnstone-Louis is Senior Fellow in Management Practice at Saïd Business School, University of Oxford and a member of the University of Oxford's St. Cross College. She is Fellow and Advisory Board Member at Oxford's Skoll Centre, Senior Associate of Oxford Net Zero, Chair of B Lab UK, Board Member of Blueprint for Better Business, and Senior Fellow of the Business Fights Poverty Institute. She is a regular speaker and panellist and has served on multiple awards juries, including Oxford's Vice Chancellor's Awards, the WE Empower SDG Challenge, and the IMD-Pictet Sustainability in Family Business Award. She has also served as a Fellow of the World Economic Forum's Global Future Council on New Agendas for Economic Growth and is a regular contributor to Forbes.com.

ACKNOWLEDGEMENTS

This book is based on *Leading Sustainable Corporations*, an online executive programme at Saïd Business School, University of Oxford, which has so far trained thousands of participants from across the globe, including by means of in-house adoption by several major corporations.

Having designed and launched the programme, Richard would like to acknowledge those who made it possible, including the following expert contributors, from across Oxford University and beyond: Myles Allen, Matt Amengual, Ladi Balogun, Marcelo Behar, Marya Besharov, Aoife Brophy, Tor Burrows, Bob Eccles, Dominic Emery, Liz Fisher, Al Gore, Moya Greene, Andrea Harris, Cameron Hepburn, Dieter Helm, Rodney Irwin, Mary Johnstone-Louis, Charmian Love, Colin Mayer, Malcom McCulloch, Anette Mikes, Hiro Mizuno, Alan Morrison, Russell Picot, Paul Polman, Veronica Poole, Rafael Ramirez, Caroline Rees, Fiona Reynolds, Martin Rich, Marc Thompson, Shriti Vadera, Marc Ventresca, Bettina Wittneben, Kathy Willis and Rupert Younger.

Richard is also very grateful to Peter Tufano for initiating Oxford Saïd's online programmes, to the team members who ensured that *Leading Sustainable Corporations* came to life, including Jovana Mandic, Lauren O'Brien, Brad Peaston, Matt Richards, Daniel Rom and Josie Thurston, and to Mary for her catalysing role across all aspects of the programme and for taking on the role of co-director.

Richard and Mary are hugely grateful to the programme's wonderful team of tutors, in particular Cyrus Suntook, Alexandra Ewing and Lisa Plit; they have worked tirelessly with participants to craft individual action plans, which are designed as the key outcome of the programme and the vehicle for enabling innovation and change.

Beyond the programme, many others have also contributed in one way or another to Richard's work on the book, though rather than including some and failing to include others, he would just like to add a dedication: Amy and Andrew, this book is for you.

Mary would like to express appreciation to those who generously provided their insights and feedback on parts of this manuscript: Colin Mayer, Bob Eccles, Laura Spence, Marya Besharov, James Ashall, Marike Westra, Marcela Manubens, Tom Lawrence, Paulo Savaget, and Rehema Msulwa. Your reflections have made this a better book, and your friendship and inspiration are deeply appreciated.

Mary's heartfelt thanks also go to Adriaan Louis, Abeni Johnstone-Louis, Naila Johnstone-Louis, Kate Kirkpatrick, Juliane Reinecke, and Charmian Love, whose support and encouragement have been invaluable throughout the writing process.

We would also like to thank our publisher at Pearson, Eloise Cook, for unfailing support.

Any remaining errors or oversights remain, of course, solely our responsibility.

While we work hard to present unbiased, fully accessible content, we want to hear from you about any concerns or needs with this Pearson product so that we can investigate and address them:

- Please contact us with concerns about any potential bias at https://www.pearson.com/report-bias.html
- For accessibility-related issues, such as using assistive technology with Pearson products, alternative text requests, or accessibility documentation, email the Pearson Disability Support team at disability.support@pearson.com

CHAPTER 1
WHY SUSTAINABILITY MATTERS TO YOU AS A LEADER

We wrote this book because the shift towards sustainable value creation presents a once-in-a-generation opportunity for leaders who can prepare their companies to grasp it. This leadership is crucial given the significant pressure our environmental and social systems are under today. Our goal is to equip you, as a corporate leader, to effectively understand and navigate the opportunities and challenges that sustainability introduces.

The insights in this book draw heavily from our experience in designing and delivering the Oxford *Leading Sustainable Corporations* programme, an online course that has trained over 6,000 leaders from across sectors and over 60 countries to date. As part of this programme, participants design an Action Plan to bring their lessons to life in their organisations. This book follows the same approach: it is not intended for passive readership. It is an invitation for you, as a leader, to design a plan to take action.

Inevitably, each reader of this book will be at a unique stage. Your organisation may be deeply engaged in a well-resourced sustainability change process. Or, your company may have made initial gestures towards sustainability but lost confidence on whether or how to proceed. Just as likely, your company may be in an initial phase, unsure how to define the scope of this critical work. This book is designed to enable every reader to find their company's place in what we believe to be an ongoing and iterative process. The scale of the sustainability transition means risks and opportunities are present for every company and industry. Regardless of where your company is today, this book aims to provide you with the guidance needed to design a plan to bring action in to your organisation.

We start from the premise that a two-way relationship exists between business and the natural and social environment. Companies depend on natural and social systems to generate value and, in turn, their actions influence the health of these systems. At a fundamental level, instability in natural and social systems leads to higher costs and risks for businesses. Unfortunately, examples abound: by 2024, intensified wildfires in California – the largest economy in the United States – have driven major insurers to exit the state. Similarly, record-low rainfall in Western Europe has drastically reduced water levels in Germany's Rhine River, a vital industrial transport route, causing disruptions that ultimately affect companies, investors, and consumers.

In their best form, businesses create economic value by meeting society's needs. As environmental and social conditions evolve, so too do these needs. This shift presents new opportunities for businesses that adapt and lead, as well as increased risks for those that do not. Acknowledging the interdependent relationship between business and its context, we define a sustainable corporation in this book as follows:[1]

> **Definition**
>
> A sustainable corporation creates profitable products and services as it strengthens natural and social systems.

Few of today's companies and industries were designed with such a view of sustainability in mind. The design principles associated with modern economic growth include scale, cost savings and speed. These, and an emphasis on the financial performance of individual companies, are associated with systematic failure to note the environmental and social systems in which companies operate. Yet as those systems come increasingly under strain, the economic prospects for companies change and, for this reason, there will be increasing financial benefit to companies that offer solutions to environmental and social challenges, while also diminishing returns to those adding to the problem. The prospect of the sustainable corporation therefore represents either an immense

---

[1] Similar to our definition, Mayer (2018) defines the purpose of business as being to 'produce profitable solutions to the problems of people and planet – and not to profit from problems,' while Polman and Winston (2021) ask simply: 'Is the world better off because your business is in it?' These perspectives focus on business doing what it does best: innovation, problem solving and generating value. They do not ask business to take over the role of civil society or become a social enterprise or charity, yet they also emphasise that leaders face choices about how they generate value.

innovation opportunity or a substantial risk, or perhaps both. In this book, we argue that sustainability leadership means enabling your company to better evaluate how it creates value by identifying its impacts and dependencies on environmental and social systems. A company's financial performance is as sustainable as the systems on which it impacts and depends. This is a key insight, and a significant mindset shift for leaders.

The business case for the planet

By Richard Barker

The greatest change we face is the sustainability-related transformation of the global economy. We can either figure out a way to make economic activity sustainable, or the system starts to break down. There are two alternative outcomes. The first is that global warming remains within the Paris Agreement target of 1.5C. This will mean the change in how we power and operate our economy will be fast and dramatic, and will create winners and losers. The second is if we maintain our trajectory of global warming beyond Paris limits, where the transition to a sustainable economy will be too slow to prevent unprecedented disruption. Winners would be outweighed by losers. Either way, there is change and uncertainty, and thereby opportunity and risk. A lead indicator of this change is the auto industry, where the transition to electric vehicles has already been disruptive. Tesla is a relatively new entrant, yet its market capitalisation is now roughly equal to the rest of the global top 10 automakers combined. This disruption continues. A truly zero-carbon vehicle is also carbon-free in production. Porsche set a target of (net) carbon neutrality throughout its value chain for new vehicles from 2030. Others will follow.

Inevitably, the implication is that Porsche's suppliers must decarbonise. An example is Norway's Hydro, which is investing in recycling to produce aluminium with a carbon footprint 30 times lower than the industry average. In turn, there are implications for mining and other industries. Transitions such as these are not philanthropic, but business decisions, to enhance economic value. The case for decarbonising arises because a sustainable economy is more valuable than one heading for collapse. As this becomes increasingly evident, companies that better manage climate-related risks and opportunities will be the suppliers of choice. There will be more regulation (and taxes or subsidies), changes in consumer preference and greater social pressure on the licence to operate.

This enhances the business case for sustainability, increasing the opportunities for innovation and the risks from business as usual. One example is in electricity generation, where solar and wind have become economically competitive and are gaining market share.

▶

While the climate-driven transition is under way, other transitions will follow. Climate change is one of nine "planetary boundaries" that economic activity cannot sustainably exceed. Others include biodiversity loss, water use, change in land use (like deforestation), and pollution. With water, withdrawals already exceed sustainable levels in several regions. This problem is set to grow as the effects of climate change reduce flow in glacier-fed rivers. Non-dairy milk is growing, given that oat milk uses 600 litres less water per litre of milk than its dairy alternative. Likewise, the market in second-hand clothing is increasing, reflecting the fact that a cotton T-shirt takes 2,700 litres of water to make.

Land use is integral to food and other renewable natural resources, manufacturing and construction, waste management, climate mitigation and access to critical minerals. All economic activity depends in one way or another upon the resources of nature. Companies that finance, insure, advise or provide other services to industries are indirectly dependent on natural resources, creating risks and opportunities. In the 2024 World Economic Forum ranking of global risks over a 10-year horizon, the top four are all environmental: extreme weather events; critical change to Earth systems; biodiversity loss and ecosystem collapse; and natural resource shortages.

Your business might be exposed even if its environmental impact is low, such as through vulnerability to climate-related weather events. State Farm, the largest property insurer in the US, stopped offering homeowner insurance in California in 2023, declaring it "necessary...to improve the company's financial strength". These outcomes have repercussions: the college graduate who can't get a home loan because she can't get insurance has an effect on retail banking and on the employer seeking to hire her. Disruption of systems can have widespread consequences, many of them not immediately apparent.

One illustration is pandemic risk, which increases as economic growth causes deforestation and other changes in land use, especially as livestock and wildlife come into closer contact. Preparing for the next Covid-19 might feel like normal business practice in risk management and strategic planning. It should. Global economic activity has reached a scale where a stable climate and an abundance of natural resources can no longer be taken for granted. Viewed in terms of share price performance and access to capital, investors want to understand how any business is responding to these risks and opportunities. Reporting on sustainability to investors is not a compliance exercise, it is a communication of value creation and business resilience. IFRS Accounting Standards are now complemented by IFRS Sustainability Disclosure Standards, which are being adopted across global jurisdictions. Both enhance financial reporting, and help companies communicate value-relevant information in the transition to a sustainable economy.

Source: Richard Barker (2024) 'The business case for the planet', Financial Times, 09 Oct. © The Financial Times Limited 2025. All Rights Reserved.

Modern industry has raised living standards for billions of people across the globe. It has been a source of innovation and solutions on a scale without precedent in human history. In this sense, today's corporations are doing exactly what they were designed to do: deliver goods including food, housing, clothing, transport and a wide range of services to the greatest possible number of people. However, these gains have been achieved at significant environmental and social cost. Sometimes called 'negative externalities', these are costs resulting from a company's activities that are not borne by that company itself. Examples are present across industries: modern food production has dramatically increased the percentage of the global population that can reliably afford a nutritious diet, yet it also contributes around a quarter of global GHG emissions as well as using 50 per cent of habitable land and 70 per cent of available fresh water across the globe.[i] Single-use plastic, now a ubiquitous material, is a cheap, reliable means to store and transport food and medicines, and dramatically reduces the cost of many goods to consumers as a result. At the same time, the material has generated substantial levels of pollution, including toxic by-products, which increasingly impact biodiversity and human health.[ii] Some studies suggest that more than 50 per cent of single-use plastic waste globally can be traced to a small subset of companies, many the same firms responsible for substantial GHG emissions.[iii]

As we will discuss in Chapter 2, the vast majority of externalities are generated without companies breaking the law or violating regulations. Some externalities, of course, result from lawbreaking. When such cases can be proven, a company may pay some form of penalty. More important for this book is that negative externalities are typically a feature of law-abiding business-as-usual; their costs are simply not reflected in the company's income statement. A classic example comes from the garment sector. Scarce and highly valued for clothing and shelter through the ages, textiles have been transformed into a global fashion industry estimated to be responsible for 10 per cent of global carbon emissions annually.[iv] While clothing is now affordable for more people across the world than ever in history, the means of delivering this benefit has brought its own set of significant risks and disadvantages. Take cotton, which makes up close to half of all manufactured textiles. While cotton production provides income for more than 250 million people across the globe,[v] it is also associated with severe negative environmental impacts. Extremely high water use, pollution and profound soil degradation are all closely associated with global cotton production. The results are water scarcity, danger to human and animal health, soil erosion, and a range of other upstream externalities.[vi] Downstream, more than 80 per cent of clothing is eventually incinerated or placed in landfill, and many communities across the globe experience severe detrimental effects due to the oversupply of waste textiles.[vii]

This example offers a truism for much of corporate sustainability: today's problems are often the direct result of yesterday's solutions.[viii] Indeed, a key reason that externalities persist is that mainstream value creation models and business strategy represent a 'linear economy'. In a linear economy, products are designed under a 'take, make, use and lose'[ix] model in which resources are extracted to be used and then discarded. This is highly inefficient. On a planet with finite resources, it is also impossible to sustain. Sustainability invites you as a leader to innovate on design and business models to move from a linear, 'cradle to grave' approach towards a 'cradle to cradle' value proposition in which companies create value in ways that are robust, holistic and elegant.[x] Leaders who enable the culture, processes and resources for this kind of innovation in their businesses are poised to generate value as they build strong businesses in strong natural and social systems.

Crucial to achieving this is your ability to move from a focus on your company alone to also think in terms of the environmental and social systems in which your company operates. Systems are a 'set of things ... interconnected in such a way that they produce their own pattern of behaviour over time'.[xi] An obvious example is social media networks, which comprise a set of interacting and interdependent parts that form a whole from which (often unanticipated) properties can emerge. Systems are characterised by common features including feedback mechanisms (in which actions in one part of the system impact the behaviour of other parts) and emergent properties (characteristics or behaviours that surface from the interaction between components of the system, but are not necessarily present in any one of those components independently).

It is essential for you to see your company as embedded in natural and social systems, and as an agent within these systems. This is the inescapable fact of corporate existence: companies have an impact on the natural and social environment, and a dependency on those systems, whether or not they describe their business as 'responsible' or 'purposeful', concerned with 'impact', or anything similar. As we will discuss in Chapters 3, 4 and 5, social and natural systems are de facto part of your company's value generation. The question is what your company's impacts and dependencies may be, and how well the company understands them.

When you take this perspective, you can unleash the creativity and innovation required to deliver strong businesses in strong systems. Such an approach also avoids a range of all-too-familiar pitfalls. These include PR-driven sustainability commitments, through which companies attempt to burnish their credentials in public while protecting incumbent business models.[xii] The US 2019 Business Roundtable statement, initially much vaunted for its claim that signatories committed their companies to pivot from 'serving shareholders' to 'delivering value to all stakeholders',[xiii] appeared rather less newsworthy when scholars pointed out that only 2 per cent of the 181 CEO signatories[xiv] sought board approval before signing the statement.[xv] For the obvious reason that corporate boards sign off on major shifts in strategic direction, it is hardly credible that these CEOs envisioned their signatures to signal a substantial modification in their businesses.

For customers and employees, the result of inauthentic 'commitment' is an observable loss of trust in business.[xvi] What appears to be missing is business integrity, in the original sense of the word. 'Integrity' is rooted in the Latin *integer*, meaning whole, complete, or undivided. The perspective we offer in this book – leadership grounded in mutually reinforcing links between natural and social systems and corporate value creation – is a much-needed antidote to fragmented approaches that not only introduce risk but also leave significant value on the table. We say this without any suggestion that business should act as a charity – profit is not the enemy of this view of sustainability. On the contrary, our view is firmly rooted in value creation: strong businesses in strong environmental and social systems.

Why is this a challenge? One reason is clear: it is impossible for business to completely avoid all forms of 'harm'.[xvii] Currently, there are evident trade-offs between low prices for consumers and quality of work and compensation for employees, between affordable, reliable energy provision and greenhouse gas emissions, between packaging required to preserve food and medicines and generation of plastic and other waste. A distributor that sells bottled water has a carbon footprint, likely contributes to global plastic pollution, potentially competes with public provision of potable water yet, at the same time, may enable residents of informal urban settlements across the globe to hydrate themselves and their children safely in the context of their current constraints. A manufacturer that provides hospitals and clinics with life-saving equipment for premature babies may generate significant medical waste that is later incinerated or sent to landfill. Each of these situations represents a norm for business, not an exception. It is precisely the existence of trade-offs that makes leadership so important for sustainability.

For example, implicit within any robust definition of sustainability is the company's ability to commit over time. As the landmark report of the United Nations Brundtland Commission emphasised in 1987, sustainability refers to 'meeting the needs of the present without compromising the ability of future generations to meet their own needs'. Leading a sustainable corporation does not mean being all things to all people at all times. Far from it. Your board and executive team make choices about which issues they prioritise in light of current or future strategies for value creation. Trade-offs must be clearly and comprehensively identified, weighted and discussed in an open, transparent manner, including with those who stand to be most affected by a business' activities. Investors need to understand how a business is addressing both risks and opportunities, how resilient the business is and how it plans to sustain and grow value.

This book is timely because expectations of business on this score are mounting rapidly. In 2021, the International Financial Reporting Standards foundation (IFRS), the entity that sets global standards for financial reporting, launched the International Sustainability Standards Board (ISSB) with the remit to develop a mandatory set of corporate sustainability standards characterised by a global baseline of 'decision-useful' information for investors.[xviii] This, alongside regional and national initiatives in markets from China to the European Union, is creating the norm that companies understand and report on their sustainability in a way that is transparent, consistent and meaningful. Expectations around transparent disclosure are increasing not just from investors but also from other stakeholders, including employees, customers, regulators and the media. The 2025 Net Zero Tracker showed that two-thirds (63%) of the Forbes Global 2000 have net zero targets, with commitments by U.S. companies increasing overall by 9% between 2024–25. Businesses built on sustainable strategies are better positioned to adapt to changing market conditions, anticipate emerging trends and thrive as industry leaders in a rapidly evolving world.

Making sense of leadership and sustainability

Investors and other stakeholders share a common interest in a future economy that is vibrant, resilient and sustainable, as opposed to one in which the potential for profitability and growth is compromised by the collapse of natural and social systems. It follows that the shift to sustainable business offers extraordinary opportunities for value creation. Yet the changes required by individual companies to realise these gains typically also require short-to-medium term investment. In 2023, an estimated one in five cars sold were electric, double the share from just two years previous. This share is expected to rise to at least 60 per cent of new cars sold by 2030.[xix] And yet this growth reflects significant up-front cost for individual fleet owners as they tally up expenditure to acquire, maintain, insure and run new vehicles, decisions which might themselves depend upon major recharging infrastructure investment. Across much of Europe,[xx] electric vehicles (EVs) are already equally or more cost effective than their diesel or petrol equivalents, but the initial (public and private) capital investment required to transition to EVs remains a barrier. Energy presents a similar dilemma: sun- and wind-rich geographies, including the Middle East and much of Africa, remain economically dependent on domestic use of fossil fuel or fossil fuel export. This generates significant exposure and risk: more than half of African oil and gas-producing nations rely on these products for more than 50 per cent of their total export revenues.[xxi] These economies are ostensibly well-positioned to lead on the transition to renewable energy, but the need for investment in infrastructure, reskilling and transition plans too often remains prohibitive. The result is staggering lost opportunity.

To build a value proposition that balances costs and benefits, you need a clear understanding of the set of incentives and constraints in which your current business operates. In turn, this requires the ability to identify and manage not just trade-offs but also paradox. By paradox, we refer to 'interdependent, persistent contradictions'[xxii] inherent in dilemmas we face. For you as a leader, this speaks to your ability to identify where two seemingly opposing goals must coexist and be managed in tandem. This is powerful when elements may appear contradictory, but are continually present in your organisation, and may not necessarily be in conflict.[xxiii] For instance, rather than seeing short-term profit and investing for the long term as incompatible, a paradox mindset enables you to be more specific, identifying when and how sustainable practices contribute to profitability by building brand loyalty, reducing regulatory risk, or fostering innovation over time.

In this view, your board and executive team may become convinced that such investment is key to long-term success. Similarly, instead of choosing between product affordability and ethical sourcing, your company may innovate to identify ways to make ethical sourcing affordable, perhaps by improved supply chain data or practices that strengthen your relationship with your suppliers. In short, challenging yourself and your teams to be specific about when and why trade-offs can actually be examples of paradox enables you to identify areas where your strategy can move from an 'either-or' towards 'both-and'.[xxiv] As we have acknowledged, this will not always be immediately possible. The discipline of testing what really is a trade-off (and what is not) nevertheless encourages your business to find innovative, creative solutions where sustainability and performance goals evolve together. For you as a leader, a key skill is identifying what is a true trade-off and where the potential for paradox exists.

Insurers embrace climate change investments as catastrophe costs mount

By Brooke Masters

Virtually all global insurers now include at least one low-carbon transition goal within their investment plans, a sharp change from two years ago when only 2 per cent of them had actual commitments, BlackRock's latest survey of the industry has found.

The survey of 410 senior executives at companies with a collective $27tn in assets highlights the importance insurance companies place on getting to grips with climate change and the long-term opportunities they see in financing the transition.

Most insurers, 57 per cent, attributed their interest in transition investing to a need to manage and mitigate climate risks. Global insured losses from natural catastrophes exceeded $100bn for the fourth consecutive year in 2023, and Moody's has estimated that the recent US hurricanes Helene and Milton will drive up to $55bn in losses.

Despite significant political backlash against green initiatives, particularly in the US, two-thirds of global insurers told BlackRock they had more conviction in transition investing than they did a year ago. The share with increased enthusiasm for transition investing was highest in North America at 73 per cent, while Latin America came in lowest at 58 per cent.

"For insurers, separate to the political aspect, they have to look at climate and transition risk from a liability and an asset perspective," said Mark Erickson, global head of BlackRock's financial institutions group. "If you are a [property and casualty] insurer you're dealing with the effects of wildfires and hurricanes."

Ninety-nine per cent of insurers have at least one low-carbon objective, with net zero emissions by a particular date being the most common globally, while year-on-year emission reduction targets are most popular in North and Latin America. Fifty-four per cent of insurers globally said they were responding to shareholder and policyholder interests.

Many money managers, including BlackRock, are talking less about investing based on environmental, social and governance factors, while at the same time stepping up their offerings in green energy and low carbon infrastructure.

1 WHY SUSTAINABILITY MATTERS TO YOU AS A LEADER 11

> The insurers' commitment to addressing climate change comes as individual investors are becoming more sceptical of ESG. A new survey by the Association of Investment Companies found that the share of investors who considered ESG as part of their investing process had fallen for the third straight year, to 48 per cent, from a high of 65 per cent in 2021 and 53 per cent last year.
>
> The proportion who thought ESG investing was likely to deliver improved performance had dropped to 17 per cent from a peak of 33 per cent in 2021, the survey found.
>
> BlackRock's survey also found significant regional differences in insurers' macroeconomic outlook. More than 85 per cent of North American and European insurers expected a "soft landing", which would see inflation ease and growth slow, while 75 per cent of Asian insurers expected continued high inflation and economic resilience.
>
> Across the board, insurers were expecting to increase their allocations to cash, in part because deposit rates were higher, and in part because they needed to be able to meet cash calls for their commitments to private equity and private debt.

Source: Brooke Masters (2024) 'Insurers embrace climate change investments as catastrophe costs mount', Financial Times, 15 Oct. © The Financial Times Limited 2025. All Rights Reserved.

Two leadership traits are essential for your work in sustainability: adaptive leadership[xxv] and a long-term perspective. Adaptive leadership contains a strong emphasis on the leader's ability to move their organisations and teams from the known to the unknown. In the case of sustainability, the 'known' focus on value creation is established and embedded in 'business as usual' and the challenge is to move mindsets and practices to an alternative, sustainable business model. The adaptation is how to understand the here and now and how to realise the move to the future. By long term, we refer to your ability to refer to a time horizon that extends beyond immediate quarterly profits and incremental gains in the current business model, moving towards a view in which the evolving links between impacts and dependencies on environmental and social systems and corporate value creation become more evident. This extended view is essential for sustainability because it enables you to identify strategic choices that account for risks such as climate change, resource scarcity and social or regulatory shifts, positioning your company to lead and thrive over time. Leadership characterised by a long-term mindset also fosters innovation, allowing you to develop products, processes and business models that are adaptable and resilient.

As you read this book, be aware that a central leadership task is to develop clarity on opportunities and risks presented by the interface between natural and social systems and current business models, supply chains, energy sources, waste management and product lifecycles. When you are quick to identify how incumbent design principles curtail your organisation's ability to deliver sustainable value propositions, you position your company for industry leadership. While arguments for a straightforward causal link between sustainable practices and financial performance are unlikely to hold for all companies and industries (if they did, this book would not need to be written), the data present some green shoots. One study showed that companies in the '100 Best Companies to Work For', a ranking of employee satisfaction produced by Fortune, outperformed matched peer companies on stock returns by 2.3–3.8 per cent across a 28-year period.[xxvi] Another suggested that the sales value of consumer products marketed as 'sustainable' in the United States grew market share at twice the rate of 'conventional' offerings between 2013–22.[xxvii] The World Economic Forum has made the case that $44 trillion of economic value, which they point out is over 50 per cent of global GDP, is 'moderately' or 'highly' dependent on nature.[xxviii] Ultimately, of course, 100 per cent of economic activity has this dependency, which is easily overlooked with a 'business as usual' mindset, yet which, at a time when environmental systems are under unprecedented strain, is worthy of serious reflection.[xxix]

At the same time, in complex systems, it is essential to understand that easy 'win-win' outcomes tend to be rare.[xxx] Yet the work required is rewarding, urgent and worthwhile. Just as the economic prospects for the corporate sector depend upon sustainable natural and social systems, so too the economic well-being of society depends upon the presence of financially prosperous corporations. When companies fail, jobs are lost. Investment and R&D falters. The consequences are widely felt. The scale of the transition from linear, extractive value propositions to sustainable value creation represents an unparalleled opportunity for companies with the courage and creativity to master it. In any case, as systems scientist Peter Senge sagely cautions, the 'easy' way out of complex challenges usually charts a path right back into them.[xxxi] This is why sustainable leadership matters, and matters right now.

Sustainability: a word on language and perspective

To effectively navigate transition to a sustainable corporation, you need a clear working definition of sustainability. Unfortunately, language around sustainability is often cluttered and imprecise. The terms 'ESG' (environmental, social, and governance) and 'sustainability' are often used interchangeably, alongside references to 'responsible business' or 'business ethics', which in turn appear to sit alongside specific frameworks such as 'shared value'[xxxii] or the 'triple bottom line'.[xxxiii] On the one hand, the proliferation of terms to describe the relationship between business, society and the environment has increased awareness and enlivened the debate about business' role and responsibilities. On the other hand, it has contributed to a rising sense of confusion and fatigue as leaders, investors, regulators and consumers try to make sense of a growing cacophony of sustainability-related lingo. Importantly, some of these terms also appear to fudge or avoid the need for leaders to clearly understand and navigate the incentives and trade-offs associated with the shifts required of their companies.

The practice of 'corporate social responsibility' (CSR) has long been a feature of corporate life. We understand CSR to refer to corporate activities that are undertaken for a social or environmental benefit. Some CSR activities may have a direct or indirect impact on financial value creation, and some may not. Crucially, CSR is voluntary, sometimes simply philanthropic. Within a corporation, CSR activities may be housed within the marketing, PR or external relations business functions. While often worthy efforts, when this activity is not core to business strategy and value creation, it does not meet the definition of sustainability we offer in this book. Similarly, we understand ESG to be a concept designed for investors and capital markets, intended to cover metrics related to financial prospects.[xxxiv] Yet ESG metrics are currently diverse and wide-ranging, may poorly correlate with each other,[xxxv] and do not necessarily capture either impact or financial performance.[xxxvi] ESG has also found itself in political crosshairs as its limitations have led it to be contested in some jurisdictions: in 2023, for example, legislation against inclusion of ESG considerations in investment of public funds were put forward in 22 states of the United States. We do not find the term ESG to be helpful and we will avoid using it.

In this book, we will consistently use the word 'sustainability'. Our definition of a sustainable corporation is *one that creates profitable products and services while strengthening natural and social systems*. This goes beyond non-core business and activities associated with marketing, philanthropy or compliance. Sustainability is instead core. It is about fostering innovation that builds successful and profitable businesses, which sit in stronger, more resilient natural and social systems. Delivering this outcome will require you to forge effective collaborations with stakeholders to collectively identify, pilot and scale innovations. The essence of sustainability, as conceptualised in this book, invites you to think beyond your own organisation and understand how it sits as part of multiple systems.

To break this down, you may find it helpful to start by introducing a 'trio' of lenses on sustainability to your company. First is the impact *of* business on sustainability, which concerns how environmental and social systems are affected by the activities of the business. Second is the effect of environmental and social systems *on* business, which concerns how dependencies on natural and social systems create risk for the business. Third is the prospects of environmental and social systems *for* business, which concerns how the development of natural and social systems create opportunities for the business.

For some businesses, the starting place will be gathering data to better understand the impact *of* their operations on the health of natural and social systems. To illustrate, we start with air pollution. Air pollution is a key factor in the current global disease burden. In 2019, it contributed to almost 8.5 million excess deaths across the globe. The effects are disproportionately felt by the elderly and the very young and those in Asia, Africa and Latin America.[xxxvii] It is possible to combine databases on wind conditions and respiratory disease risk to demonstrate the health risk to humans from the air pollution generated by a given company.[xxxviii] Such data help build the 'business case' for companies to invest in cleaner operations as the impact of their activates becomes clearer to their leadership, shareholders and other stakeholders, and raises the opportunity and imperative for innovation.

Other businesses may need to start by better understanding the effects of natural or social systems *on* their business. Coffee, grown in more than 70 countries and supporting the livelihoods of an estimated 125 million people, is an example readers are likely to know well.[xxxix] What may be less widely known is that changes in weather patterns mean coffee farming is under threat: rising temperatures and changes in rainfall patterns mean that more than 50 per cent of coffee farmland could be non-viable by 2050.[xl] This, along with soil degradation due to farming methods, has also introduced uncertainty and cost into coffee supply chains. In response, coffee buyers are testing weather insurance programmes to ensure coffee farms can financially withstand and re-establish their crops post unpredictable weather events. Since 2023, food giant Nestlé has partnered with climate insurance specialist Blue Marble to develop such a programme, in addition to leveraging satellite-based data to assess crop impacts. Companies in the sector including illycaffè, one of the world's largest coffee roasters, have invested[xli] in innovative methods of regenerative agriculture in order to protect yields. When done well, such practices restore soil fertility, boost biodiversity and strengthen coffee supply chains, safeguarding coffee buyers from volatility and sustainability-related risks to their core product. The company has also found that consumer and media response to their efforts has been enthusiastic as their approach differentiates in a highly competitive market.[xlii]

Finally, companies that recognise the importance of sustainability and reorganise their operations accordingly stand to realise opportunities *for* their business. An example is innovations in production of one of the world's most widely consumed food crops: rice. The staple grain, which accounts for an estimated one fifth[xliii] of global calorie consumption, is also highly vulnerable to drought, introducing risk to agricultural business and cost to companies who rely on rice as an input. Rice farming is also water-intensive and emissions-heavy, estimated to be responsible for 12 per cent of methane emissions and as much as 1.5 per cent of GHG emissions globally.[xliv] Corporate buyers including Kellogg[xlv] and Mars[xlvi] have worked with suppliers on innovations in farming methods that reduce emissions and water use associated with rice farming by over 70 per cent and 30 per cent respectively.[xlvii] These innovations have also boosted yields, introduced cost savings,[xlviii] and reduced value chain risk.[xlix] This example from a global staple food is an apt one: from this perspective, sustainability is not a 'nice-to-have', but core to a resilient business. Indeed, from 2015 to 2023, Mars itself achieved a 16 per cent reduction in greenhouse gas emissions across its value chain while growing its business by 60 per cent.[l] This outcome demonstrates the potential for you to decouple emissions from business growth and capture the opportunities that sustainability can bring to operations.

Focusing sustainability efforts

Throughout this book, we will use the United Nations Sustainable Development Goals (SDGs) as a framework to guide our approach to topics on which leadership is needed. The SDGs (Figure 1.1) were developed and adopted by UN member states as a call to cross-sector partnership on pressing issues facing humanity and our natural world. As such, they provide the closest we have to a globally agreed and comprehensive coverage of the core areas of environmental and social sustainability. They have been called The World's To-Do List.[li]

Figure 1.1 The United Nations Sustainable Development Goals

Source: The content of this publication has not been approved by the United Nations and does not reflect the views of the United Nations or its officials or Member States, https://www.un.org/sustainabledevelopment/

The SDGs are grounded in a human rights framework, which we will discuss in Chapter 5 as part of our focus on sustainability in social systems. The scale, resources, skills and impact of the private sector mean that the chances of achieving the SDGs without meaningful collaboration with business are vanishingly slim. At the same time, the SDGs present significant opportunities for business to create value, precisely because they imply demand for the goods and services that the corporate sector provides.

There are 17 SDGs in total. They are designed with the understanding that progress on one goal (e.g. ending poverty) works in tandem with other goals (e.g. clean water and sanitation). Goals with a social emphasis support those with an environmental emphasis, and vice versa. This is a reason for using the language of systems in this book: throughout the text, we will encounter multiple instances of environmental and social outcomes interacting with each other.

No single company has anything close to a flawless track record on all 17 SDGs. Indeed, it is perfectly possible for a company to demonstrate positive contribution on one SDG while their operations undermine progress on others. Yet they represent a core pillar of sustainability, grounded in international

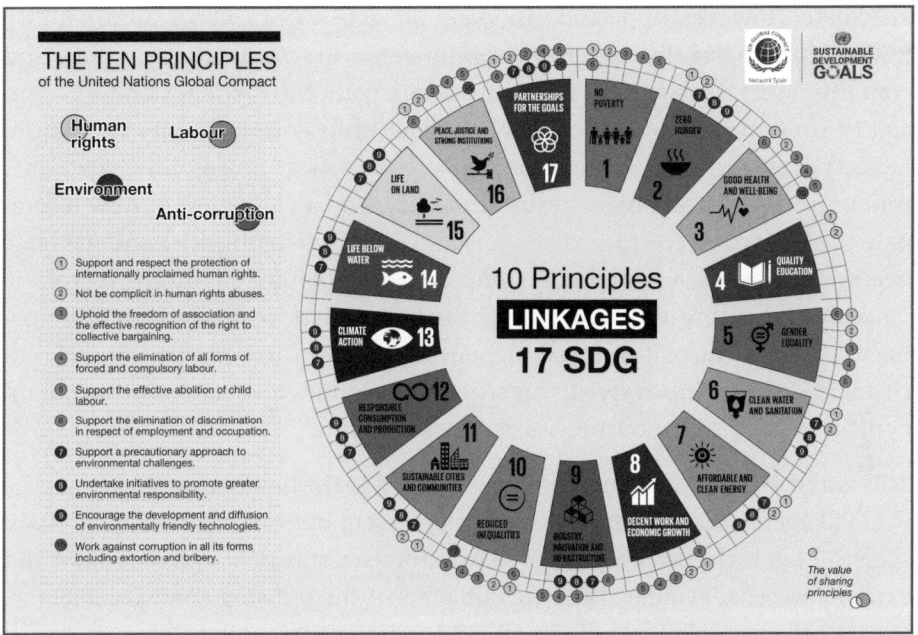

Image/photo: UN Global Compact Spanish Network

Figure 1.2 The Ten Principles of the United Nations Global Compact

collaboration, and with the potential to focus corporate efforts. In support of this, more than 15,000 companies in more than 160 countries have signed a private sector initiative known as the UN Global Compact, committing to uphold Ten Principles of corporate good practice on a range of issues including human rights, workers' rights, transparency and environmental protection. Together with the SDGs, the UN Global Compact offers leaders a high-level framing, as a way in to building on sustainability (Figure 1.2) as part of strategy and value creation.

What it means to lead a business sustainably

'A leader is a dealer in hope'.[lii] This aphorism is apt for our book, albeit incomplete. Sustainability leadership implies commitment to an ambitious vision that will typically require fundamental changes to strategy and business models. This is the 'hope' leaders of sustainable corporations commit to tirelessly articulate. However, hope and vision are far from sufficient for sustainability leadership. Precisely because sustainability refers to system-level outcomes and contains facets that are difficult to measure, rigour, transparency and accountability are as important to sustainability leadership as are creativity and vision. Leaders of sustainable corporations must have a close grasp of the trade-offs inherent to their transition to sustainability, and a clear view of how to prepare their boards, investors, customers and suppliers to prioritise and navigate necessary changes. A sustainable company does not have all the answers at the outset but is committed to a willingness to learn as it develops a dynamic, ongoing understanding of its impacts, dependencies, risks and opportunities. From there, leaders can innovate, discovering new avenues to create value in a manner that creates strong businesses in strong systems.

This is a high bar. Leadership roles are complex at the best of times. Many of the world's largest companies face pressures due to geopolitical conflict, supply chain shocks, high inflation, challenges to workforce recruitment and retention, and extreme weather events. These are but a few of the pressing contextual factors generating what is often called a VUCA landscape in which leaders are tasked to navigate ongoing **v**olatility, **u**ncertainty, **c**omplexity and **a**mbiguity.[liii] And yet sustainability leadership also enables companies to move from volatility to stability, from uncertainty to confidence, from complexity to clarity, and from ambiguity to insight. This vision is both incredibly compelling and very much in reach.

Making sense of this book: a word from the authors

If this book speaks only to corporate leaders who already consider themselves to be deeply committed to their companies' sustainability journey, we will have failed. Rather, our aim is to create a diverse cohort of leaders who will bring their own corporate, geopolitical, and personal perspectives to the issues we present, and who will find creative ways (more creative than we could ever suggest) to deliver in their own contexts. We hope to learn from our readership as this occurs. We share a concern that one of the current weaknesses of discussions about corporate sustainability may be an 'echo chamber' effect. By this, we mean the topic has become, in some cases, partisan to a point that the debate is no longer about business opportunity and risk, but instead about a whole host of adjacent issues that appear to ensure those with opposing views are unlikely to enter constructive debate or, indeed, even ever to meet each other in person. Our hope is that this book can be a place of common ground from which great strategies are generated.

We write as authors with a combined experience of highly global careers and a substantial track record of teaching in some of the most globally diverse business programmes in the world. We nevertheless write from our own point of view and point in time, based in the United Kingdom, with attendant inevitable limitations on our perspectives as a result. And yet we are clear: for us as authors, sustainability is as urgent as it is aspirational, something companies 'will' do in future if they have not already started. A stronger version of this view is that sustainability is something companies 'must' do to endure. Throughout the book, we will substantiate these claims by walking through, in detail, the ways in which companies impact and depend on environmental and social systems. Examining the case of carbon emissions, natural resources and social systems in turn, we identify aspects of the business case associated with corporate engagement with each of these systems, and we frame business challenges and opportunities accordingly.

We also explore macro changes that make sustainability a 'must' for companies. Far from being a corporate nice-to-have or simply an opportunity for CSR or philanthropic largesse, sustainability is not discretionary, and it is not charity. Businesses are, first and foremost, profit-making entities. However, this statement is not as simple as sometimes assumed. From the perspective of data and transparency about corporate behaviour, expectations from law and regulation, pressure from social media and other public outlets, as well as rising existential vulnerabilities in the environmental and social systems on which companies rely, sustainability is a business imperative. Innovators, pioneers and early adopters have the chance to set trends and get ahead of, rather than catch up to, pressures in their contextual environment. Companies who follow face costs to get up to speed but may garner fewer benefits than first movers. And, of course, companies who are slow to act face a costly game of catch up.

It's in companies' own interests to adopt global sustainability standards

By Richard Manley

The writer is chief sustainability officer of CPP Investments and chair emeritus ISSB Investor Advisory Group

Milton Friedman's famous doctrine on the social responsibility of business did not suggest ransacking the environment and abusing labour in the name of corporate profits. He implored companies to maximise the value of the enterprise "while conforming to the basic rules of the society, both those embodied in law and those embodied in ethical custom". The doctrine is as relevant today as it was when drafted more than 50 years ago.

While the basic rules of society in which companies operate have been transformed beyond recognition (thanks to the impact of population growth, digitisation and climate change, to name just three factors), the roles, rights and responsibilities that accrue to owners, boards and executives have not changed. Public company investors should not tell boards how to set company strategy or appoint management, but instead have clear expectations of how directors will discharge their duty to their companies.

In November 2021, the International Financial Reporting Standards Foundation created the International Sustainability Standards Board with a mandate to develop a global baseline for sustainability reporting. The final ISSB standards published in June last year require companies to demonstrate they are managing the most material risks confronting their businesses. Adoption of this global baseline presents an opportunity to consolidate the alphabet soup of voluntary ESG reporting frameworks currently plaguing companies.

Today, jurisdictions representing more than half of global GDP are already taking steps towards adoption. The standards also bring a significant advantage to small and medium-sized businesses through the principle of proportionality, allowing them to report within their capabilities while striving for incremental enhancements over time.

National-level consultations on the adoption of these standards pose a dilemma for board directors. Should they advocate in favour of the ISSB, to ensure they and shareholders have disclosure of these material risks and opportunities? Or should they stand back and allow industry associations to undermine this critical disclosure framework by arguing for extended reliefs or carve-outs?

While the new standards help investors hold boards to account, the insights they generate are as relevant to company success as they are to investors. Investors will benefit from comprehensive reporting of this data, but the primary beneficiary, if used to inform strategy, will always be the board of directors and the companies they oversee.

Has a board discharged its duty to the company if it has not compelled management to identify the material sources of risk and opportunity at the nexus of the business? Is it acting in the long-term interest of the company if it has failed to quantify the carbon footprint of the business when it operates in jurisdictions committed to decarbonising their economy over the coming decades? Can it really be confident that its operations and supply chain will prove resilient to climate risks if an analysis of physical risks has not been done?

Where these risks and opportunities have not been identified, quantified and reflected in strategy and disclosures, shareholders should consider two simple questions. Is the board discharging its duty to the company? And do we have the right directors?

With consultations under way, now is the time for all market participants and issuers to encourage comprehensive adoption of the global sustainability baseline. Many boards have already pushed for disclosure aligned with the ISSB's previous standards. For any still on the fence, reporting on the two sets of standard (S1 and S2), should not be viewed as a concession to investors, but as an act of enlightened self-interest.

Source: Richard Manley (2024) 'It's in companies' own interests to adopt global sustainability standards', Financial Times, 11 Aug. © The Financial Times Limited 2025. All Rights Reserved.

Ahead of us all is a move from an extractive, linear economy to an economy that generates value and delivers quality of life, without degrading natural or social systems, for a global population expected to surpass 10 billion[liv] by the end of the century. Due to its size and scale, this is an industrial transformation unprecedented in human history. The market for new product offerings, new ways of delivering services, leapfrog technologies in logistics and energy, and revolutions in core activities such as agriculture and construction will create entire new industries. Leaders who leverage their organisations in the light of this transition are positioned to generate substantial value. Those who do not, of course, face the risk of obsolescence and the pain of missed opportunity. With this book, we aim to enable you to find a place for your organisation to contribute to this incredibly exciting set of opportunities, and to inspire your peers to do the same.

How to use this book

The aim of this book is to equip you to build strong businesses in strong natural and social systems. To accomplish this, we first set out the purpose of a corporation and who corporations are designed to serve (Chapter 2). This chapter provides the foundation for a clear understanding of the role of shareholders and other stakeholders, including employees, customers, suppliers, communities and the natural and social systems on which the corporation impacts or depends. Chapters 3 and 4 detail the two-way relationship between business and climate systems (Chapter 3) and natural resources (Chapter 4), respectively. Next, Chapter 5 identifies key frameworks through which business can understand its impact and dependency on social systems. Chapter 6 outlines how business can approach meaningful and effective measurement and reporting on sustainability.

At the end of each chapter, we present reflection questions for you to consider in light of your experience or the realities of your current organisation. Chapter 7 builds upon these reflective exercises, exploring how you can develop an Action Plan for your leadership and organisation.

The reflection questions in each chapter are designed both for personal reflection and to work in teams and across your company. At the core of this book are two design principles we think of as the basis of a kind of 'contract' with our readers: first, this is not a textbook designed for passive reference. Rather, you are an active participant in this material. This book provides structure and challenge as you apply your experience and reflect personally, allowing us to co-create your plans with you. Second, the book is designed to enable you to build an Action Plan that is tangible and actionable. You will get more out of this book if you start off by identifying individuals and teams with whom you can work through the questions at the end of each chapter in a workshop format, linking the book content with your corporate setting in real time. When you do this with your team, you employ your own organisation as a site for learning and action. This enables you to navigate the challenges and opportunities we identify in your own context, testing solutions and working towards a set of actions you then bring to your organisation for implementation. As you kick off this book, we suggest you also begin to workshop the following areas together:

1 **How well is sustainability integrated into your corporate assessments of risk *and* opportunity?**

   How closely is sustainability currently integrated into your overall business strategy today? What specific sustainability risks and opportunities have been identified as relevant to your business, and how are you addressing them? As you consider and discuss these questions, remember: sustainable corporations understand the impacts and dependencies of their activities on natural and social systems (their impact *on* these systems, the impact *of* these systems on the company, and opportunities *for* the company from these systems).

2. **Given your understanding of risks and opportunities, is your approach to governance and strategy fit for purpose?**

   As you and your teams start to understand the risks and opportunities associated with sustainability, the next step is to critically assess your company's governance and strategy processes in line with this view of the business. This evaluation involves determining whether the current structures and decision-making mechanisms are suited to effectively address sustainability opportunities and risks, for example whether your governance body has the requisite sustainability-related understanding and oversight, and whether your strategy embeds consideration of alternative decarbonisation pathways and similar projections.

3. **Does your organisation (targets, processes and culture) enable you to demonstrate leadership in how you deliver on your strategy?**

   A good way into this question as you workshop it is this: within your strategy, are there clear growth objectives that are directly tied to innovation in terms of sustainable value creation? Sustainability is closely tied to the core revenue-generating activities and strategic decisions of a corporation. It goes beyond superficial gestures and therefore requires thoughtful integration into company targets.

   Similarly, because impacts and dependencies on natural and social systems may not be immediately evident, an exclusive focus on short-term planning horizons is unlikely to generate credible approaches to sustainability leadership. Sustainable companies require effective mechanisms to ensure planning horizons beyond the short term. Organisational culture must also support the company's goals. Sustainability leadership does not rely on unverifiable or unsubstantiated claims about the benefit of corporate activities. Such claims place companies at heightened reputational and even, in some cases, regulatory or legal risk. By contrast, a sustainable corporation is fundamentally delivered by its people, enabled by its culture: sustainability requires a coherent and consistent commitment to 'walk the talk' on sustainability in which actions align with public-facing goals.

4. **Do your reporting and accountability mechanisms demonstrate leadership in sustainability?**

   Sustainability leadership calls for transparency in how companies communicate their efforts, impacts and lessons learned. Sustainable companies disclose relevant information and metrics to stakeholders on an ongoing basis to create accountability. This includes explaining in what ways your business currently depends upon and impacts the environment and society, and what measures are in place to mitigate risks and realise opportunities. This is not reporting with a mindset of compliance. Instead, transparency helps build trust and credibility in the company. It also creates commitment internally to deliver and makes that commitment more likely to be realised. Because no company can credibly claim to have resolved all potential and actual sustainability concerns, sustainability leadership includes being candid about challenges, setbacks and areas for improvement.

Building on this final point: these four questions are not meant to elicit a simple 'yes' or 'no' response. Corporate sustainability is often described as a journey, a cliché that can raise hackles among those with a well-trained eye for greenwashing, purpose washing or similar forms of corporate double-speak. However, the description is accurate: the transition from an extractive, linear economy to one that is sustainable in the way we describe in this book is no small task. The scale of the challenge will not put leaders off. The size of the opportunity will keep them engaged, creative and resolved. The questions we provide to frame engagement with the book are designed to provoke an ongoing process of evaluation and reflection. By engaging with these questions regularly and at all levels of the organisation, you equip yourself and your teams to contribute to stronger societies on a healthier planet, and stronger, more innovative, more resilient companies.

Recommended reading

Anthony, S.D. (2023) The Hidden Opportunity in Paradoxes. *MIT Sloan Management Review* 65, no. 2, 12 December. Available at: https://sloanreview.mit.edu/article/the-hidden-opportunity-in-paradoxes/.

Berners-Lee, M. (2019) *There Is No Planet B: A Handbook for the Make-or-Break Years*. Cambridge University Press.

Carney, M. (2021) *Value(S): Building a Better World for All*. S.L.: William Collins.

Henderson, R. (2020) *Reimagining Capitalism in a World on Fire*. New York: PublicAffairs, an imprint of Perseus Books, LLC, a subsidiary of Hachette Book Group, Inc..

Johnstone-Louis, M. (2024) *Debates, Metrics, and the Competitive Advantage of ESG, ESG: The Insights You Need from Harvard Business Review*. Harvard Business Press.

Mayer, C. (2018). *Prosperity: Better Business Makes the Greater Good*. Oxford University Press.

Meadows, D.H. (2008) *Thinking in Systems: A Primer*. Illustrated edition. White River Junction, Vermont: Chelsea Green Publishing.

Smith, W.K. and Besharov, M.L. (2017) *Bowing before Dual Gods: How Structured Flexibility Sustains Organizational Hybridity. Administrative Science Quarterly* 64, no. 1, 19 December: 1–44. Available at: https://doi.org/10.1177/0001839217750826

Taylor, A. (2024) *Higher Ground*. Harvard Business Review Press.

Townsend, S. (2023) *The Solutionists*. Kogan Page Publishers.

Notes

[i] Ritchie, H., Roser, M. and Rosado, P. (2022) Environmental Impacts of Food Production. *Our World in Data*. Available at: https://ourworldindata.org/environmental-impacts-of-food.

[ii] Editorial (2022) Prioritizing Plastic Pollution. *Nature Reviews Earth & Environment* 3, no. 11 (9 November): 719–19. Available at: https://doi.org/10.1038/s43017-022-00369-7.

[iii] Rylander, Y. and Gardner, T. (2021) 20 Companies Responsible for Most Single-Use Plastic Waste. *SEI*, 20 May. Available at: https://www.sei.org/features/20-companies-responsible-for-most-single-use-plastic-waste/.

[iv] The World Bank (2019) How Much Do Our Wardrobes Cost to the Environment? The World Bank, 23 September. Available at: https://www.worldbank.org/en/news/feature/2019/09/23/costo-moda-medio-ambiente.

[v] WWF (2022) Can organic cotton help protect tigers? Cotton Industries World Wildlife Fund. Available at: https://www.worldwildlife.org/industries/cotton#:~:text=Production%20and%20processing%20of%20cotton.

[vi] Zhang, Z., *et al*. (2023) Environmental Impacts of Cotton and Opportunities for Improvement. *Nature Reviews Earth & Environment* 4, 5 September: 1–13. Available at: https://doi.org/10.1038/s43017-023-00476-z.

vii Hyde, P. (2023) Rags, Not Riches: Why Ghana Is Fast Fashion's Dumping Ground. www.forbesafrica.com, 18 January. Available at: https://www.forbesafrica.com/fashion/2023/01/18/rags-not-riches-why-ghana-is-fast-fashions-dumping-ground/.

viii Senge, P.M. (1990) *The Fifth Discipline: The Art and Practice of the Learning Organization*. London: Random House Business (repr. 2006).

ix See the discussion in Raworth (2018).

x Braungart, M. and McDonough, M. (2009) *Cradle to Cradle: Remaking the Way We Make Things*. London: Vintage.

xi Meadows, D.H. (2008) *Thinking in Systems: A Primer*. Illustrated edition. White River Junction, Vermont: Chelsea Green Publishing.

xii InfluenceMap (2021) Corporate Climate Policy Footprint, influencemap.org, November. Available at: https://influencemap.org/briefing/Corporate-Climate-Policy-Footprint-20137.

xiii Business Roundtable (2019) Our Commitment – Business Roundtable. Business Roundtable. Available at: https://opportunity.businessroundtable.org/ourcommitment/.

xiv Bebchuk, L.A. and Tallarita, R. (2020) The Illusory Promise of Stakeholder Governance, papers.ssrn.com. Rochester, NY, February. Available at: https://papers.ssrn.com/sol3/papers.cfm?abstract_id=3544978.

xv For further discussion of the context around the 2019 US Business Roundtable statement, see Chapter 8 of Alex Edman's *Grow the Pie*.

xvi Edelman Trust Institute (2023) Special Report – Trust and Climate Change. Edelman, November. Available at: https://www.edelman.com/trust/2023/trust-barometer/special-report-trust-climate.

xvii Thanks are due to Professor Colin Mayer CBE FBA for helpfully developing our thinking on this point.

xviii Richard Barker is a board member of the ISSB. The views represented in this book are expressed in a personal capacity and do not represent official positions of the ISSB.

xix International Energy Agency (2024) Global EV Outlook 2024 Moving towards Increased Affordability. Available at: https://iea.blob.core.windows.net/assets/a9e3544b-0b12-4e15-b407-65f5c8ce1b5f/GlobalEVOutlook2024.pdf.

xx Campbell, P. (2022) Electric Car Costs Draw Level with Petrol and Diesel. *Financial Times*, 11 December. Available at: https://www.ft.com/content/24ae34f9-2d61-45cb-9bbc-158c2e5e26b3.

xxi Leke, A. Gaius-Obaseki, P. and Onyekweli, O. (2022) The Future of African Oil and Gas: Positioning for the Energy Transition, www.

xxii mckinsey.com, 8 June. Available at: https://www.mckinsey.com/za/~/media/mckinsey/industries/oil%20and%20gas/our%20insights/the%20future%20of%20african%20oil%20and%20gas%20positioning%20for%20the%20energy%20transition/the-future-of-african-oil-and-gas-positioning-for-the-energy-transition.pdf.

xxii Smith, W.K. and Besharov, M.L. (2017) Bowing before Dual Gods: How Structured Flexibility Sustains Organizational Hybridity. *Administrative Science Quarterly* 64, no. 1, 19 December: 1–44. Available at: https://doi.org/10.1177/0001839217750826.

xxiii Smith, W., Lewis, M. and Edmondson, A.C. (2022) *Both/and Thinking: Embracing Creative Tensions to Solve Your Toughest Problems*. La Vergne: Harvard Business Review Press.

xxiv Wendy Smith, Marianne Lewis, and Amy C. Edmondson, *Both/and Thinking: Embracing Creative Tensions to Solve Your Toughest Problems* (La Vergne: Harvard Business Review Press, 2022).

xxv Parks, S.D. (2005) *Leadership Can Be Taught: A Bold Approach For a Complex World*. Harvard Business Press, p. 9.

xxvi Edmans, A. (2016) 28 Years of Stock Market Data Shows a Link between Employee Satisfaction and Long-Term Value. *Harvard Business Review*, 24 March. Available at: https://hbr.org/2016/03/28-years-of-stock-market-data-shows-a-link-between-employee-satisfaction-and-long-term-value.

xxvii NYU Stern (2022) Sustainable Market Share Index, www.stern.nyu.edu. Available at: https://www.stern.nyu.edu/experience-stern/about/departments-centers-initiatives/centers-of-research/center-sustainable-business/research/csb-sustainable-market-share-index.

xxviii World Economic Forum (2020) Half of World's GDP Moderately or Highly Dependent on Nature, Says New Report. World Economic Forum, 19 January. Available at: https://www.weforum.org/press/2020/01/half-of-world-s-gdp-moderately-or-highly-dependent-on-nature-says-new-report/#:~:text=Pollination%2C%20water%20quality%20and%20disease.

xxix Craig, D. and Mrema, E. (2024) Why Businesses Must Address Nature-Related Financial Risks. World Economic Forum, 8 January. Available at: https://www.weforum.org/agenda/2024/01/businesses-address-nature-related-financial-risks/.

xxx Hegwood, M., Langendorf, R.E. and Burgess, M.D. (2022) Why Win–Wins Are Rare in Complex Environmental Management. *Nature Sustainability* 5, 24 March. Available at: https://doi.org/10.1038/s41893-022-00866-z.

xxxi Senge, P.M. (1990) *The Fifth Discipline: The Art and Practice of the Learning Organization*. London: Random House Business. Repr. 2006.

xxxii Porter, M.E. and Kramer, M.R. (2011) Creating Shared Value. *Harvard Business Review*. Available at: https://hbr.org/2011/01/the-big-idea-creating-shared-value.

xxxiii Elkington, E. (2018) 25 Years Ago I Coined the Phrase 'Triple Bottom Line'. Here's Why It's Time to Rethink It. *Harvard Business Review*, 25 June. Available at: https://hbr.org/2018/06/25-years-ago-i-coined-the-phrase-triple-bottom-line-heres-why-im-giving-up-on-it.

xxxiv Johnstone-Louis, M. (2024) *Debates, Metrics, and the Competitive Advantage of ESG*, ESG: The Insights You Need from Harvard Business Review. Harvard Business Press).

xxxv Berg, F., Kölbel, J. and Rigobon, R. (2022) Aggregate Confusion: The Divergence of ESG Ratings. *Review of Finance* 26, no. 6. Available at: https://doi.org/10.2139/ssrn.3438533.

xxxvi Edmans, A. (2022) The End of ESG. *Financial Management* 52, no. 1, 21 December. Available at: https://doi.org/10.1111/fima.12413.

xxxvii Ritchie, H. and Roser, M. (2021) Air Pollution. *Our World in Data*, Global Change Data Lab, January. Available at: https://ourworldindata.org/air-pollution.

xxxviii Balch, O. (2021) Big Data Helps Put Numbers on Sustainability' www.ft.com, 25 January. Available at: https://www.ft.com/content/2a405cf6-9592-4de2-960b-4c3e5d0df030.

xxxix *The Economist* (2024) Can Scientists Save Your Morning Cup of Coffee? *The Economist*, 23 June. Available at: https://www.economist.com/science-and-technology/2024/01/23/can-scientists-save-your-morning-cup-of-coffee.

xl *The Economist* (2024) Can Scientists Save Your Morning Cup of Coffee? *The Economist*, 23 June. Available at: https://www.economist.com/science-and-technology/2024/01/23/can-scientists-save-your-morning-cup-of-coffee.

xli 'Illycaffè First Coffee Brand to Achieve Regenagri® Certification — Regenagri' (2023) Regenagri, 29 September. Available at: https://www.forbes.com/sites/christophermarquis/2025/04/17/quality-through-sustainability-how-illys-regenerative-practices-create-award-winning-brazilian-coffee/.

xlii Illy, A. (2022) The Chair of Illycaffè on Creating Virtuous Agricultural Ecosystems. *Harvard Business Review*, 1 September. Available at: https://hbr.org/2022/09/the-chair-of-illycaff-on-creating-virtuous-agricultural-ecosystems.

xliii WWF (2023) To Feed the World, We Need Sustainable Rice. World Wildlife Fund. Available at: https://www.worldwildlife.org/magazine/issues/winter-2023/articles/to-feed-the-world-we-need-sustainable-rice.

xliv Kurnik, J. and Devine, K. (2022) Innovation in Reducing Methane Emissions from the Food Sector. World Wildlife Fund, 12 April. Available at: https://www.worldwildlife.org/blogs/sustainability-works/posts/innovation-in-reducing-methane-emissions-from-the-food-sector-side-of-rice-hold-the-methane.

xlv MultiVu – PR Newswire (2023) Kellogg Helping Rice Farmers Reduce Greenhouse Gas Emissions. MultiVu. Available at: https://newsroom.kellanova.com/2023-01-23-Kellogg-helping-rice-farmers-reduce-greenhouse-gas-emissions.

xlvi BusinessGreen (2024) How Mars Cut Emissions 16 per Cent and Still Grew Its Business by 60 per Cent. BusinessGreen, 9 August. Available at: https://www.businessgreen.com/news/4345173/mars-cut-emissions-cent-grew-business-cent.

xlvii WWF (2023) To Feed the World, We Need Sustainable Rice. World Wildlife Fund. Available at: https://www.worldwildlife.org/magazine/issues/winter-2023/articles/to-feed-the-world-we-need-sustainable-rice.

xlviii WWF (2023) To Feed the World, We Need Sustainable Rice. World Wildlife Fund . Available at: https://www.worldwildlife.org/magazine/issues/winter-2023/articles/to-feed-the-world-we-need-sustainable-rice.

xlix Reed, J. (2020) Thai Rice Farmers Step up to Tackle Carbon Footprint. www.ft.com, 25 June. Available at: https://www.ft.com/content/8ff2b454-9390-11ea-899a-f62a20d54625.

l Mars (2024) Mars Delivers Record Carbon Emissions Reduction. Mars.com. Available at: https://www.mars.com/en-gb/news-and-stories/press-releases-statements/mars-delivers-record-carbon-emissions-reduction.

li Let's Get the #WorldsToDoList Done. World's To Do List, n.d. Available at: https://worldstodolist.org.

lii Often attributed, intriguingly, to Napoleon Bonaparte.

liii Bennett, N. and Lemoine, G.J. (2014) What VUCA Really Means for You. *Harvard Business Review*, February. Available at: https://hbr.org/2014/01/what-vuca-really-means-for-you.

liv Ritchie, H., *et al.* (2023) Population Growth. *Our World in Data*, 11 July. Available at: https://ourworldindata.org/un-population-2024-revision.

CHAPTER 2
WHAT PURPOSE DO CORPORATIONS SERVE?

At the heart of this book is a particular institution, the corporation. We need to understand what the purpose of a corporation is. What is it for? What kind of value does it create, and for whom? What costs does it generate, who bears these costs, and how? In the face of global and local challenges, what role does the corporation play in society? Who controls corporate activity, how is that control applied, and how can corporate activity change over time? The answers to these questions establish the context for the role of the business leader.

In part, these are legal questions because the corporation, at its most basic, is a legal construct. Yet corporations do not derive value independently from natural and social systems. It is therefore the interaction between the *legal entity* of the corporation and its *context* that generates the expectations, risks and opportunities for sustainability we discuss in this book. The purpose of this chapter is to understand how the corporation is structured in law, what it is designed to do and how corporations interact with the context around them. This approach will also highlight what the corporation is *not* designed to do, and the potential unintended consequences of these limitations.

Corporations are legal structures that create economic value, and more

Fundamentally, the corporation is a legal structure that enables and defines various contractual relationships. This structure is simple, yet extraordinarily powerful. It is embedded in political, cultural and natural systems across the world. It enables the creation – and destruction – of enormous economic, social and environmental value. This is why it is so significant.

Given its prevalence in modern life, it is easy to overlook that the corporation is a relatively new entity in human history. Introduced in its current form in the middle of the nineteenth century, the corporation quickly established itself both as a powerful engine of the Industrial Revolution and as fundamental to global economic growth.[i] Today, a striking feature of corporations is the extent to which they share fundamental legal characteristics, no matter the industry in which they operate, no matter where in the world, and no matter whether at the scale of a multinational business, or a small, local firm. This ubiquity suggests an unusually effective design.

The legal characteristics that are shared by most corporations include legal personality, limited liability, transferable shares and a board of directors that is distinct from the managers of the business.[ii] Each of these characteristics operates in combination with one another, together making up the corporation.

First, and particularly important, is that the corporation is recognised as having a legal personality, which enables it to be the counterparty in a contract. This provides economic efficiency because the corporation can act as a single contracting entity, even though it may have many shareholders. Suppose that the company is in the retail business, and that it acquires a new store. If the shareholders needed to act collectively to make this happen, each taking part in writing a contract for the purchase, it would be time-consuming, costly and, perhaps, impracticable. But because the corporation is itself a legal person, it can be the counterparty in a single contract, acting on behalf of all shareholders, without any of them having to take specific action.

Second, the corporation is a mechanism for combining resources, enabling shareholders to benefit by conducting business on a scale that they could not achieve individually. Suppose, for example, that there are economies of scale in operating a large retail store. The pooling of resources, into the hands of a single legal entity, enables that large store to exist and allows each investor to benefit from its existence, in proportion to the extent to which they have provided funds via their investment in the company.

Third, a single legal entity can employ dedicated, specialist managers tasked with maximising the value of shareholders' investments. All shareholders alike can benefit from employing an experienced retail CEO, focused entirely on the business, and able to do the job better than any of the shareholders could themselves. Here, we note the distinct role of directors and of managers within the corporation. In principle, while delegated managers run the business, the board provides governance and oversight on behalf of the shareholders, ensuring that the company acts in a way that their interests are protected.

Further mechanisms in this regard include shareholders' control rights with respect to electing directors, and shareholders' appointment of auditors to provide assurance on the financial record of corporate performance.

Fourth, through the ability to vary their level of investment in a single business, the shareholder can invest across a whole range of businesses, thereby spreading and reducing their individual exposure to risk. In the extreme case, the shareholder can simply withdraw their investment entirely by selling the shares. Notice here how the characteristic of transferable shares benefits not just the owner of the share in question but also other shareholders. The activities of the corporation itself are unaffected by the change in share ownership. This is because selling the shareholder's investment does not imply liquidating part of the business itself (selling assets to pay off the shareholder) but instead is simply a transfer of ownership (with the assets of the business remaining unchanged). It is the corporation itself that has the legal right of control over its business operations, while shareholders have only legal right of control over their own shares. In other words, shareholders do not have full ownership of the business. What they own entitles them to benefit from the wealth created by business operations, but they do not have direct control over the business itself. In this regard, the common perception that shareholders are the 'owners' of the corporation is incorrect. Rather, they have ceded some of the benefits of ownership, in exchange for the benefits derived from corporate structure.

These issues of ownership and control are important. A defining feature of the corporation is that its legal structure enables distinctive, beneficial forms of ownership, both for shareholders and for other stakeholders in the business. To see this, consider first that the concept of ownership subsumes two distinct ideas, a right of control and a right to benefit. If a person owns a car, they get to decide when the car is driven, where it is parked, whether and when it gets maintained and serviced, and so on. The right of control is the right to make such decisions and, correspondingly, the right to prevent others from doing so. The right to benefit, meanwhile, entitles the owner to enjoy the benefits of ownership, most obviously in being able to use the car for the service of getting from one place to another. While ownership commonly brings both control and benefit, either might be constrained in some way or another in practice.[iii] For example, a landlord benefits from the income that a property generates, yet the tenant has a right of control over the property during the tenancy, and benefits from occupancy in that period. A fund manager might have delegated control over an investment portfolio, but the ultimate owner has beneficial rights associated with the value of that portfolio. And in the case of a corporation, shareholders benefit from their unconditional ownership of shares, but their 'ownership' of the business is limited in that they have no direct control over the day-to-day activities of the business, notwithstanding that they have the right to benefit from the financial surplus that those activities generate.

The question of shareholder ownership becomes more nuanced once other creditors are introduced into the analysis. Banks lend to corporations and, consequently, become creditors. If suppliers to the corporation remain unpaid, then they too become creditors. The law provides that creditors have priority over other shareholders with respect to a company's assets. Furthermore, while shareholders can sell their shares, share capital as a whole cannot readily be withdrawn from the corporation itself, thereby providing a permanent degree of security for creditors. Hence, shareholders are simply the 'residual owners' of the corporation in the sense that they are entitled to receive however much value is left once the claims of all creditors have been settled.

These relationships provide the conceptual foundation for the corporate balance sheet.

As Figure 2.1 illustrates, creditors and shareholders have in common a claim on the company's assets, yet while the company has a contractual obligation to repay creditors, it has no such obligation to shareholders. Instead, shareholders are simply entitled to whatever is left after the creditors have been paid. Indeed, this is how equity is defined – as assets less liabilities – and a balance sheet always balances because the shareholders' claim on the company's assets is always equal to this residual.

Given that shareholders have no direct control over the activities of the business and only a residual right to economic benefit, their position appears rather weak. However, this vulnerability is recognised in law, which offers shareholders two forms of compensation. First is the characteristic of 'limited liability', which protects shareholders in the event that creditors' claims against the business exceed the value of its assets. While shareholders in this case lose the whole of the investment that they made in the company, creditors have no claim against personal assets that shareholders own outside of the company. It is for this reason that share prices cannot be negative.[iv] Second, and as will be explored further below, directors have a particular 'fiduciary duty' towards shareholders; in other words, a special duty of care towards shareholders' economic interests.

Assets		Liabilities	
Assets comprise cash, receivables, inventory, buildings, etc. These are sources of economic value, controlled by the company itself, by its directors and managers.		Liabilities comprise payables, debt, etc. They can largely be understood as contractual claims on assets. They are obligations on the company to transfer economic value to contractual counterparties.	
Cash	100	Payables	210
Financial assets	250	Tax due	50
Receivables		Bank loan	800
Inventory	140		
Plant & equipment	180		**1,060**
Land & buildings	540	Equity	
Intangible assets		Equity is simply the difference between assets and liabilities. It makes the balance sheet balance. It the shareholders' claim on assets. It is not contractual but instead residual: shareholders are entitled to whatever is left of the company's assets after liabilities have been settled.	
	700		
	120		
		Share capital	500
		Retained profit	470
	2,030		**970**

Figure 2.1 Corporate balance sheet

Overall, this set of relationships between shareholders, creditors and the corporation itself is designed with value creation in mind.[v] For example, the limits to shareholders' ownership rights are beneficial to creditors, making it more attractive for them to enter a contractual relationship with the corporation. Suppose that a supplier makes a delivery to the retail company, for which payment remains outstanding. Or that a bank makes a loan to the company, which has not yet been paid back. In both cases, the creditors are more likely to enter these transactions knowing that they are protected by the legal priority of their claims on the business over those of shareholders, as well as by restrictions on shareholders being able to withdraw their capital. This protection makes it more likely that suppliers of goods, services and finance will contract with the corporation and do so on terms that reflect low levels of perceived risk. The business activities of the corporation benefit accordingly and so, too, in due course, do the shareholders because the residual surplus from those business activities accrues to them.

In this way, it is not only the shareholders who benefit from the corporate form, but also the suppliers and bank, and so too employees and customers.

In principle, all of these stakeholders enter mutually beneficial exchange relationships with the corporation because its underlying legal structure makes it aligned with their own interests to do so. To the extent that such activities enable the corporation to exist, grow and create economic value, all stakeholders are enabled to benefit. This careful balancing of different interests, enabling the whole to be greater than the sum of its parts, is the 'unusually effective design' we referred to earlier.

Who controls the corporation, and to what end?

A central theme in the above discussion is that shareholders, in the interests of economic efficiency, cede a significant degree of control over their investment to the corporation. Moreover, once ceded, that control is remarkably hard to take back. Suppose, for example, that a company has one thousand shareholders, and that a few of these are unhappy with how the company is being run. These individuals can, in theory, 'exit' the investment easily, by means of selling shares. Yet the directors remain in control. The alternative is to exercise one of the limited instruments of direct control, such as voting the directors out of office, yet this can be employed only by acting together with a majority of other shareholders (and incurring the costs of so doing).

The power to engage is therefore significantly weaker than the power to walk away. In this way, legal personality gives the corporation, in practice, something of a life of its own, independent of its shareholders and other contractual counterparties.[vi] Moreover, while those holding shares in the company can (and will) change over time, there is no reason why the company itself cannot, at least in principle, continue indefinitely. In this sense, a corporation is not just a legal person; it can also 'live forever' unless legally dissolved.

If, then, shareholders have ceded control, and in effect have done so indefinitely, who has assumed control, and to what end are they likely to direct the corporation's activities? Here, again, corporate law intervenes. It does so by first recognising that a corporation's economic relationship with its shareholders differs in substance from those with its contractual counterparties, such as employees, customers, suppliers and banks. A standard assumption with these stakeholders is that they and the company voluntarily enter into a contract because of the expectation of mutual gain. In this narrative, contractors take for granted (a significant assumption, in some cases) that they are protected by a fair and functioning legal system. An employee should be able to turn to employment law, for example, should the need arise. In contrast, shareholders have no such protection, because theirs is not a contractual relationship. For this reason, corporate law tends to treat shareholders as a special case, parties to whom the directors of the corporation have a distinct duty.

While directors' duties vary by jurisdiction, similarities between jurisdictions are considerable on this point. And, while the precise nature of those duties is a matter for ongoing debate, it is hard to find an interpretation of directors' duties in which shareholders do not feature prominently.[vii] To illustrate, the following is the extract from United Kingdom corporate law that, while headed 'Duty to promote the success of the company', can be seen to correspond to a primary duty towards shareholders (referred to here as 'members').[viii]

> (1) A director of a company must act in the way he considers, in good faith, would be most likely to promote the success of the company for the benefit of its members as a whole, and in doing so have regard (amongst other matters) to—
>
> (a) the likely consequences of any decision in the long term,
> (b) the interests of the company's employees,
> (c) the need to foster the company's business relationships with suppliers, customers and others,
> (d) the impact of the company's operations on the community and the environment,
> (e) the desirability of the company maintaining a reputation for high standards of business conduct, and
> (f) the need to act fairly as between members of the company.

Aside from the anachronism that UK corporate law is not yet gender neutral, notice three things about the above. Most important, the success of the company is explicitly instrumental to the benefit of its members. This is what is commonly known as 'shareholder primacy'. Ultimately, what the directors 'must' do is act in a way intended to benefit shareholders, for which a successful company is a means to an end. Moreover, in the typical situation in which directors' remuneration is aligned with the achievement of profit, and with stock market performance, directors have not only the duty to further shareholders' interests but, perhaps more consequentially, the motivation to do so.

Second, notice that corporate law does not intervene regarding how 'success' might be achieved. While directors must act 'in good faith', the legal system is careful to steer clear of ruling on whether judgements made by directors, under conditions of uncertainty, were the 'right' decisions or not. In this regard, the board is a collective, deliberative, decision-making body. The shareholders might disagree with the directors about the 'right' course of action, but the power to decide belongs with the directors.

Third, while the law requires directors to 'have regard' to various other matters, this is again typically interpreted as instrumental to acting in the interests of shareholders. The argument is that if, for example, there is disregard for 'the interests of the company's employees' or of 'the need to bolster the company's business relationships with suppliers, customers, and others', then there is likely also disregard for the success of the company. Importantly, there is not an explicit legal requirement for directors to prioritise (nor even to balance) the interests of other stakeholders in relation to those of shareholders. There is instead simply a 'reminder' for directors to consider their company's 'licence to operate', a concept we explore in detail in Chapter 5. If, for example, a company engages in business activity that, while not strictly illegal, is decidedly antisocial and adversely affects community and environment, then – not least through reputational damage – the risk is one of adverse economic consequences for the business itself, and thereby also for its shareholders. What these provisions are not doing, however, is explicitly 'authorising' directors to serve the interests of stakeholders when such is not also in the interests of shareholders. The thinking here is that investing in the community and the environment can be interpreted as a contravention of directors' duties unless it can be argued that shareholders ultimately benefit.

Alternative corporate legal forms such as 'benefit corporations' have been created in response to the dominant form we have described here.[ix] In general, the legal form of a benefit corporation requires it to generate profits in tandem with 'public benefit', a material positive impact on the environment or society.[1]

---

1   The first legislation permitting benefit corporation incorporation was passed in the state of Maryland in the United States in 2010. Since then, 36 US states, Washington DC and Puerto Rico have passed benefit corporation statutes. Similar legislation has been passed in multiple jurisdictions across the globe including Italy, France, Colombia, Ecuador and Peru. In the United States, directors of benefit corporations are required to consider the impact of their decisions on shareholders and other stakeholders, including employees, customers and the environment, and to publish an annual report of the public benefit achieved.

This corporate form also permits companies to specify one or more specific stakeholders whose benefit they seek to advance, i.e. a legally defined set of stakeholders beyond shareholders. Yet such structures remain the exception rather than the norm and, of course, they do not exempt corporations from market competition and the associated pressure to avoid operating at a loss. For most business leaders, therefore, the importance of directors' duties to shareholders cannot be sidelined. For all companies, the ongoing ability to generate a profit for shareholders (or at least to avoid loss) must, instead, be understood as a critical constraint in evaluating whether and how the business can operate sustainably.

The UK should pin down what it means by corporate purpose

By Helen Thomas

It's a bad week if you don't have a purpose. Or if you roll your eyes at the very mention of the word.

First, the British Academy has published the final report in its four-year project investigating the place of business in society and how to improve it: "purposeful" business, it argues, creates profitable solutions for problems experienced by people and the planet (and doesn't profit from the creation of problems).

Second, London is set to get its first listed B Corp, or benefit corporation, an accreditation of commitment to putting social and environmental concerns on an equal footing with financial ones. Shareholders in Kin + Carta, the digital consultancy whose shares have quadrupled over the past year, voted overwhelmingly to change the company's articles of association to that effect.

The two events are coming at the same issue from slightly different directions, namely that companies have obligations to a broader range of groups than just their shareholders. But there is also a tension here, one the UK government could usefully resolve.

Proponents of corporate purpose or stakeholder capitalism (and a well-defined example of the first should result in the second) argue that this is coming to boardrooms whether companies like it or not. "The zeitgeist has changed dramatically since 2018," said Colin Mayer, the Saïd Business School professor who leads the British Academy project.

Greater transparency and social media help individuals or groups make themselves heard more than ever. Polling last year, commissioned by the non-profit behind B Corps, found 72 per cent of the UK public thought businesses should have a legal responsibility to people and the planet alongside investors. That would be easy to dismiss were it not for an Institute of Directors survey of its members that found similar: three-fifths believed businesses shouldn't exist purely to make money and half thought companies should have a stated social purpose.

The B Corp model addresses some of the British Academy's priorities for how this should be taken forward: it comes with in-built accountability and measurement in the form of external vetting, which helps address cynicism about just how much of corporate purpose amounts to puff. But it is also at odds with the idea that this should apply to everyone: as Mayer puts it, this "can't be a subset of the corporate sector. It has to be regarded as mainstream."

And that tension sits within UK corporate law. Section 172 of the Companies Act 2006 says companies are run for the benefit of their members, aka shareholders, but should "have regard ... to" employees, customers, suppliers or indeed long-term consequences (which you'd hope didn't need saying).

The next paragraph, though, specifies that companies can adopt a purpose beyond its members if (the suggestion seems to be) they are the strange, altruistic folk that choose to do so.

The good news is that UK companies have the tools there that they need. But quite what weight section 172 generally requires boards to give factors besides, say, the price on offer in a takeover situation is a subject of hot debate among lawyers, not least surrounding the Wm Morrison and Vectura bidding this year. The message from deal practitioners is that often shareholders and price ultimately carry the day.

The 2006 Act embedded shareholder primacy, said one person intricately involved in its formulation. More broadly, "it set out to find a new basis for companies and it didn't", they added, not least thanks to opposition from within the government of the day.

There may not be an easy fix – the 2006 Act was years in the making. But today's government is currently lobbying the largest UK companies to sign up to net-zero commitments where cost or even feasibility may be unknown. It should pick up proposals from the Better Business Act campaign to ensure the law underpins the idea that wider obligations apply to all companies, not just a select few.

A looming opportunity is the expansive audit and corporate governance reforms slated for this autumn. The government and society is increasingly asking all companies to subscribe to a more purposeful way of doing business. The law must match that ambition.

Source: Helen Thomas (2021) 'The UK should pin down what it means by corporate purpose, Financial Times, 22 Sep. © The Financial Times Limited 2025. All Rights Reserved.

Taken together, these issues of purpose and control paint a subtle, nuanced picture. While shareholder primacy is critically important, directors' duties towards shareholders should not be evaluated in isolation. They form part of a larger body of legal structure, in which different stakeholders are protected in different ways. Corporate law is emphatically *not* designed to pursue the single purpose of providing benefit to shareholders, even though a hasty reading of either directors' duties alone, or of a conventional finance textbook, might lead to that conclusion. From the public interest perspective of the lawmaker, it would be an indefensible starting point to declare shareholders' interests to dominate those of any other sector of society and to then design corporate structure to that end.[x] Instead, the corporation is designed to meet the public interest by acting as a vehicle for the creation of economic value. To this end follows a legal structure in which shareholders enjoy the right to benefit from the residual claims to a business and where, given the vulnerable nature of those claims in relation to contractual claims of other stakeholders, they are afforded an additional degree of legal protection. Alternatively stated, the maximisation of profit is not the purpose of corporate law, notwithstanding that the achievement of profit is a measure of corporate success.

The corporation: what can go wrong?

There is, of course, a difference between what any law is intended to achieve and what it actually achieves in practice. In this regard, at least two critical weaknesses exist in a system that is anchored in protecting the residual claims of shareholders and that assumes that other relationships are protected either by contract or by some other legally enforceable action. The implication of these weaknesses is that special protection for shareholders in company law might, and often does, lead to benefit for shareholders accruing at the expense of other stakeholders.

The first weakness is that the contractual rights of stakeholders might not, in practice, be adequately protected. An example might be an employee whose rights are protected by contract and theoretically enforceable in law, but who experiences significant personal or professional cost in the pursuit of that enforcement, perhaps to the extent that the law offers no meaningful safeguard.

The second weakness is that some interests might not be protected by contract at all. This is the case when the activities of a corporation impose external costs on third parties, who are not counterparties in contracts with the company. A classic example would be degradation of a community's air quality as a result of pollution from corporate activities, the case of externalities we mentioned in Chapter 1. This is not a breach of contract. Neither the community nor its members are likely to have any contractual relationship with the company or companies in question. In an ideal scenario, government mediates to offset or reduce this impact or else the community has some form of effective legal redress. But such resolution is often not possible or practical.

Yet externalities represent real costs, imposed on society, on the environment and often, in particular, on future generations. This means that directors, acting in shareholders' economic interests, are incentivised to contribute to problems such as carbon emissions and, thereby, climate change (which we will explore in Chapter 3). The economics of this are simple: if the imposition of external costs generates economic benefit for the company, then the company has a financial incentive to undertake the activities that impose those costs. This is not a problem with which the legal structure of the corporation is designed to cope.

How to build a more responsible corporate capitalism

By The editorial board

When the US Business Roundtable recast its statement on the "purpose of a corporation" in August, the Financial Times cautiously endorsed the shift from shareholder primacy to a broader commitment to all stakeholders. We also urged businesses to practise what they preached. Our series on companies that are forging purpose-led strategies that will sustain them into the future shows how difficult that can be.

Many signatories to the BRT statement still seem to believe it was merely catching up with progress they had already made at their own companies. They are in for a rude shock. There are clear reasons why further action is necessary. They include the rising tide of protest about failure to tackle climate change, the commitment of younger workers and customers to purpose-led businesses (and their disquiet about companies that fall short), and tensions over the fact that wages continue to lag overall economic growth.

As Paul Polman, former chief executive of Unilever, put it at a recent forum on progress towards the UN's sustainable development goals, the cost of inaction is rapidly becoming significantly higher than the cost of action.

At the least, enlightened self-interest ought to prompt companies — and shareholders — to keep employees happy, communities healthy and governments funded. Otherwise, they will succumb to a tragedy of the corporate commons, in which each company's pursuit of its narrow short-term interests will undermine the long-term survival of the whole group.

The question is how to encourage chief executives and business owners to do the right thing. The evidence of the FT series suggests three important areas of action to encourage long-term sustainable growth.

One is to align asset managers' and owners' goals more closely with those of the purpose-led companies in which they invest. Danone's chief executive told the FT individual fund managers' short-term horizons were often at odds with the long-termism their bosses have begun to advocate.

A second, linked imperative is to accelerate improvements in non-financial measures that assess the impact companies have on society and the environment. Consensus on such measures would provide solid new benchmarks for progress and allow regulators, investors and staff to hold executives to account — and reward them accordingly.

Finally, there is a need for structural and regulatory solutions. These should include a more relaxed attitude to two-tier shareholder structures, such as time-limited supervoting shares for anchor shareholders that protect long-term strategy-making. Regulators need, too, to explore ways to discourage companies and investors' nearsighted focus on quarterly earnings.

Governments must co-operate to ensure multinational companies pay their fair share of tax. Policymakers should promote a diversity of corporate models, from the foundation and trust control common in some northern European countries, to employee-owned companies and cooperatives, through to private equity ownership and public listing.

It was clear already after the financial crisis that crude maximisation of the share price was a management goal that jeopardised sustained corporate growth. The BRT's recognition of this fact is welcome, if overdue. No company will achieve its long-term goals, however worthy, without achieving short-term success. But to prosper well into the future, managers, and those who oversee them, need to take account of the wider health of the societies in which they operate.

 Source: The editorial board (2019) 'How to build a more responsible corporate capitalism', Financial Times, 13 Oct. © The Financial Times Limited 2025. All Rights Reserved.

The scale of these two critical weaknesses should not be underestimated. Figure 2.2 illustrates that GDP is correlated with energy use – not surprisingly, given that economic activity requires energy. Given our historical reliance on fossil fuel as a source of energy, the implication is that, while the corporation has been an extraordinarily effective vehicle for the creation of economic wealth, it is has proved equally effective in generating negative externalities. Figure 2.3 lays out the challenge further: if all countries pursued a lifestyle equivalent in generating CO_2 emissions to that of the average American, the world's emissions would be more than treble their current levels.

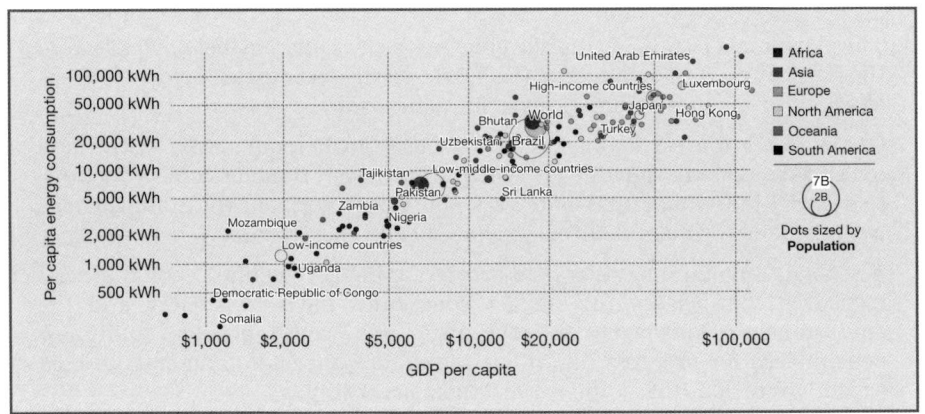

Figure 2.2 Energy use per person vs GDP per capita, 2021

Source: US Energy Information Administration (EIA); Energy Institute Statistical Review of World Energy (2023); Data compiled from ultiple sources by World Bank.

Note: Energy refers to primary energy – the energy input before the transformation to forms of energy for end use (such as electricity or petrol for transport).

OurWorldinData.org/energy

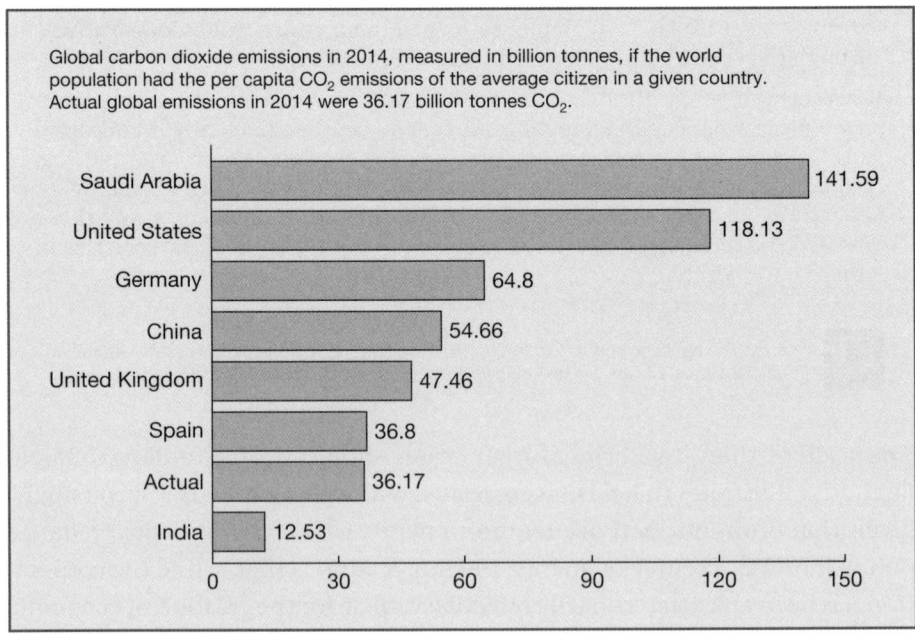

Figure 2.3 Global CO_2 emissions if everyone lived like the average citizen in a given country

Source: CDIAC; UN Population Prospects.

Note: Emissions data is based on CO_2 production (rather than CO_2 consumption) as a result of poorer estimates on national consumption figures through time.

When it comes to incentives created by the current corporate form, therefore, the question is not so much 'What *can* go wrong?' but instead 'What *has* gone wrong?' Alongside the immense economic benefits that corporations bring, there also comes significant damage to environmental and social systems, which current structures are not designed to alleviate. This is not just consequential but also existential because (on the one hand) corporations are so effective in enabling consumption and growth and (on the other hand) the resources of the planet are finite.

What is a sustainable corporation?

A sustainable corporation creates profitable products and services as it strengthens natural and social systems. The opportunity of sustainable business, therefore, is to expand the benefits of value creation while (at minimum) avoiding negative effects and (at best) generating positive effects on people and planet. This is illustrated in Figure 2.4.

If a company fails financially, it ceases to exist. No company can remain indefinitely loss-making. A precondition for a sustainable business is, therefore, that financial performance is sufficiently strong to keep the business alive. In short, and allowing for annual variation, the company must, on balance, be profitable. Meanwhile, if profit is earned at the expense of natural or social systems, then the criterion for sustainability is not met. We call this the 'shareholder-sustainable corporation' because the shareholders are made better off by the activities of the company, while negative externalities are imposed on other stakeholders and future generations. We reserve the term 'sustainable corporation' for the special case in which a business is profitable and where it generates benefit, not harm, to the systems on which it impacts and depends.

		Corporate activity strengthens natural and social systems?	
		Yes	No
Financial profitability achieved?	Yes	Sustainable corporation	Shareholder-sustainable corporation
	No	Philanthropic entity	Failing entity

Figure 2.4 A sustainable corporation?

Earlier in this chapter, we outlined why the generation of profit for shareholders is central to the design of the corporate form. Yet if profitability is the aim for business leaders, what happens if the pursuit of that aim conflicts with the welfare of natural or social systems? If being a shareholder-sustainable corporation works for shareholders, then what incentive is there to become a sustainable corporation? Current corporations exist neither to protect the environment nor to promote social benefit as ends in themselves. Instead, they make use of both natural and social resources to provide products and services for human consumption. And, by so doing, they aim to make a profit, increasing financial capital for the benefit of their shareholders. By design, it is the sustainability of financial performance for which corporate directors are accountable, and not the sustainability of planet and people.

Such is the perspective famously associated with Milton Friedman, a Nobel Laureate in Economic Sciences.[xi] His oft-quoted dictum is that 'the business of business is business' and that, within the capitalist system, the role that falls to the corporate sector is to generate profit for shareholders. The argument is a simple one. Economic efficiency means generating the greatest value from the resources we have available. If market-based incentives are the best means to efficiency, then, in principle, these are the optimal way to organise economic activity. Within this system, the role of the corporation is to advance the efficient operation of markets, while the corresponding role of government is to ensure that those markets are designed and regulated in a way that benefits society and the environment. In well-functioning markets, the achievement of profit, for the private benefit of shareholders, is an achievement of social progress. This is Adam Smith's 'invisible hand' at work. What is profit, after all, in this view, if not a measure of the extent to which the value provided to consumers (revenue) outweighs the cost of resources consumed to generate that value (expense)? Friedman argues that business leaders should not do the job that belongs to governments but should instead focus on the 'business of business'. He even adds that this is their moral obligation. They have been entrusted with capital that belongs to shareholders, and their corresponding duty is to invest that capital in the shareholders' best interests.

Critically, this perspective does not allow room for the corporate pursuit of environmental or social benefit as an end in itself. A company serves its customers, provides work for its employees and innovates in the creation of new products and services *in order* to make money for its shareholders. Those activities serve a social purpose in the form of providing consumers with goods and services, individuals with employment and governments with tax revenues, yet these provisions are entirely instrumental to the profit motive with which the shareholders created the company in the first place. It follows that a business should not be credited with the moral label of 'acting responsibly' if, by using natural resources more efficiently, it reduces operating expenses and increases profit; it is instead simply controlling costs. Similarly, if the customers of a given business prefer to pay more for goods that are sourced in a 'sustainable' way, then sustainable sourcing is profitable for the shareholders of that business. But if, as is more common, customers are unwilling to pay a 'green' premium, then management's obligation to shareholders is to avoid incurring the extra cost. In short, the Friedman argument is that business leaders *should* maximise profits but in order to 'do well' not to 'do good'. The latter is simply a *non sequitur*.

It is also critical to recognise that a corporation exists because markets allow it to survive. The Darwinian logic is that individual corporations must adapt to survive or else they are replaced. If a business leader is distracted by a purpose that conflicts with the generation of profit, then their corporation risks failure. In much the same way that ethics play no role in Darwin's account of natural selection, the argument is that there is no sentimental role for corporations 'doing the right thing' whenever that thing is not priced by the market. Friedman understands this, which is why he is careful to presume that governments will take care of regulating markets in the public interest.

It has become fashionable to criticise Friedman, and to assert that his defence of capitalism is somehow no longer relevant. Such criticism is typically flawed. Friedman's argument is logically coherent and it remains the most concise and deductively consistent defence of shareholder capitalism. His supporters find the argument irrefutable and they have a point. The counterargument is not that Friedman's reasoning is flawed but instead that it relies on multiple stylised facts, each of which is open to substantial challenge. The implication is that he can be understood as 'right' in principle, yet 'wrong' if applied in practice in guiding the role of business in society.

Friedman's argument is not premised on a convincing depiction of the reality of corporate context, for at least three reasons. First, corporations are deeply embedded in environmental and social systems and depend on these systems to create value. This includes dependency on natural resources, as we discuss in Chapter 4, and on a healthy, working age and appropriately skilled population, as we discuss in Chapter 5. In the process of accruing private benefit to shareholders, it is not possible for corporations to avoid impact or dependency on natural and environmental systems. In this sense, Friedman's argument falters in that it offers on an incomplete account of corporate profitmaking.

Even if this were corrected, a second concern remains: it is not necessarily with respect to corporate activity that Friedman's argument fails in practice, but instead with respect to his rather naïve faith in national governments, which enables him to claim an over-riding 'moral' responsibility to shareholders. This is because any moral obligation to other stakeholders is assumed to be in the safe hands of governments, for example by means of legislation that protects consumers' and employees' rights, that taxes or prohibits pollution, and that disallows bribery and corruption. The reality, however, is that governments are imperfect regulators of markets and that, as a practical matter, the law cannot be presumed to adequately protect all stakeholders, nor the health of natural and social systems on which business depends.

Friedman's argument fails in practice for a third related reason – markets, and natural and social systems, exist across the boundaries of nation-states. A national government lacks mandate to regulate outside its borders. International law and multilateral agencies may have mandate, but not always the ability to enforce. International coordination and collaboration, while crucial, cannot be taken for granted as a mechanism through which to regulate on transnational concerns in a timely and effective manner.

The point here is that the moral and even legal obligations of corporations are more subtle than Friedman's argument often appears to suggest. Challenges facing the United Kingdom's water sector illustrate this point. A 2023 UK Government investigation found that UK regulator Ofwat had failed to provide sufficient guardrails to prevent UK water companies (which are not publicly owned) from dumping large amounts of untreated sewage into UK waterways. Multiple UK water companies had prioritised return to shareholders at the expense of environmental sustainability. Despite the critical need for investment in water infrastructure, the report argued that Ofwat's emphasis on keeping bills low discouraged necessary spending on water infrastructure, a perverse outcome from a regulator. At the same time, multiple water companies continued to award executives bonuses, even as they missed performance targets. In this case, the report finds, the UK Government failed to implement a cohesive strategy to address pollution, secure water supply and support the sector. The example provides insight into how Friedman's argument breaks down at the national level if his assumptions about government do not hold.

At the transnational level, similar challenges exist. Garment factories producing for major fashion brands operate in highly globalised and fragmented supply chains, with minimal levels of transparency available regarding Tier 2 suppliers and below. Exploitative labour conditions and unsafe work environments persist in many areas of the sector despite decades of attempts to overcome these challenges. Despite some progress, as we will discuss in Chapter 5, fast fashion companies frequently fail to implement or enforce meaningful reforms. The transnational nature of the challenge means that the issue is difficult to address via regulation. In short, governments are frequently unwilling or unable to fulfil the role Friedman ideologically ascribes to them. It is therefore more than a little fanciful to design an economic system that requires, in order to function, that obstacles to unencumbered government effectiveness will miraculously vanish. The persistent 'failure' of government to enact the role so neatly ascribed to it in the Friedman model means conventional wisdom associated with Friedman is mostly incomplete as a guide to the practical challenges of business embedded in natural and social systems.

Fast fashion: 'We aren't doing enough to fix the problem'

By Silvia Sciorilli Borrelli

Italy's verdant Veneto region is home to luxury fashion brands and world-class textile suppliers, but it has also been plagued by environmental pollution with its watercourses poisoned by "forever chemicals".

In the 1960s, textile group Marzotto installed a research centre in the town of Trissino, where it began to produce the chemicals known as perfluoroalkyl and polyfluoroalkyl substances, or PFAS, to waterproof garments. The company, first called Rimar and then Miteni, eventually changed hands and became a supplier to the pharmaceutical and chemical industries before going bankrupt in 2018 following the water pollution scandal, but the damage to the environment will be permanent, experts say.

Families in the provinces of Vicenza, Verona and Padua are now grappling with the long-term health effects, which include increased risk of cardiovascular problems, caused by water contamination.

Water and air pollution are major concerns confronting the fashion industry. Dyeing and finishing processes, for example, are responsible for 20 per cent of global water pollution. Laundry loads of polyester-based clothes can also discharge hundreds of thousands of microplastic fibres into the water systems, a European parliament study shows.

The global fashion industry is said to be responsible for 10 per cent of global carbon emissions — more than international flights and shipping combined. Global textile fibre production has almost doubled in the two decades between 2000–2020, with a growing number of items being worn between 7 and 10 times before being thrown away, according to the Ellen MacArthur Foundation.

Yet despite this environmental damage, change has been hard to achieve. Some are hopeful that new European legislation will help reduce the industry's environmental footprint, yet others argue that until global fast-fashion groups that produce goods outside the EU are made to abide by the same manufacturing rules and end the supply of cheap items that fuel binge-buying by consumers, reforms will have limited impact.

"We aren't doing enough to fix the problem," says Veneto-based Matteo Ward, co-founder and chief executive of consulting studio WRÅD, and the co-author of documentary series *Junk*, which examines the human and environmental cost of fast fashion. "Social justice, which is a prerequisite for environmental transition, isn't a real priority . . . there are ways to evolve but the fashion industry is yet to find the courage."

According to a 2024 report by private equity firm Ambienta, which focuses on environmentally sustainable businesses, the fashion industry's biggest challenges are the quick wear and tear of low-quality textile items and the limited availability of fibres for reuse or recycling as well as recycling technologies. "Most available recycling processes require 'high purity' textile waste, thus they are not viable for the majority of clothes on the market because these include mixed fibres and colours," according to Ambienta.

Mechanical recycling — the process of sorting, washing, grinding re-granulating and compounding — is economically effective, but it is limited in scope because it only works well with wool items.

The remaining problem is that the scope and accessibility of such recycling techniques is still limited. "[All] these factors together make direct landfill, incineration or shipping abroad more economically appealing than recycling locally," according to the Ambienta report co-authors Federica Mallone and Fabio Ranghino.

Fast fashion, which has made trends accessible to more consumers globally with business models based on high volumes, is considered the main culprit for the rise in consumption and pollution. Data shows that by 2030, 69 per cent of global textile production will be based on polyester, nylon and other synthetic fibres. Only 25 per cent will have a natural origin.

"Today a Shein item costs even less than a sandwich . . . businesses can produce this fast and this cheap only because they use exploited labour and use cheap fossil fuel-based fibres," says Eco-Age co-founder Livia Giuggioli Firth.

Durability should be the first criteria when talking about sustainability in textiles, according to Ambienta, but it is hardly mentioned by any so-called green label. "Likely so because it is in conflict with the overarching high-volume, low-price dynamics underpinning the sector," wrote Mallone and Ranghino.

Last year, the EU introduced an extended producer responsibility mechanism which makes brands responsible for the disposal of each item they introduce to the market. In April, it approved a right to repair directive that would encourage consumers in Europe to fix defective products instead of replacing them. And in May, it passed legislation banning the destruction of unsold textiles and footwear, effective from 2026 (there are exemptions for smaller companies).

But as ever with advances in sustainability, it's complicated. The European Fashion Alliance (EFA), whose members include international fashion chambers and textile organisations, have been broadly supportive of the legislation but have also highlighted problematic aspects of certain proposals.

For example, in a position paper last year, it said the requirement to include recycled fibres in new garments could lead to the production of more blended material which is ultimately harder to recycle with the currently available technology. It also said that when imposing recycling requirements, regulators must take into account the technological barriers and the lack of sorting solutions and disassembling processes.

"We appreciate the European Commission's approach to sustainability in fashion but we ask for certain amendments to the law to safeguard and promote our values and creativity," Carlo Capasa, the chair of the Italian fashion chamber, said at a EFA conference in Brussels this year. "The industry cannot avoid the use of virgin fibres all together and we must incentivise circularity with other industries . . . and we must better define alternatives such as recycle and reuse for unsold products that cannot be destroyed."

Since the European Commission's 2019 Green Deal, EU institutions have been working to pass legislation aimed at minimising the fashion industry's carbon and environmental footprint by making textiles more durable and reusable. Companies have opposed a new requirement to declare the amount of overproduction or unsold goods citing "competition" concerns. The EFA has proposed to make such data available to only the European Commission.

Discussions around the introduction of a Digital Product Passport, or a QR code that contains a garment's textile information, are ongoing but the timeline is unclear. In the US, where this information is already a requirement for most textile products, it has helped ease the recycling process, which currently relies on manual sorting and infrared cameras.

"We have been promoting responsible consumption, then Shein and Temu arrived out of nowhere and made H&M and Zara look like luxury brands . . .

Unless these businesses stop bombarding us with disposable fashion (their business model is based on this vicious cycle) or consumers go on strike, nothing will stop," says Giuggioli Firth. "What makes me hopeful today is legislation. To know that countries such as France or states such as California have started discussing laws to put a tax on waste, for example, is a great step in the right direction."

There is friction, however, in the sector behind the scenes, high fashion labels and industry insiders are growing increasingly frustrated with the way their sector is being targeted by regulation and activists when it comes to sustainability. Consumers also need to do their part, they say, in caring for their clothes and wearing them for longer than just a handful of times, even if their price tag was affordable.

Mallone and Ranghino are hopeful that awareness among younger generations could help bring change. Though consumers in the 18–25 age group are big adopters of fast fashion, the global second-hand market is also growing thanks to "economic convenience and increasing environmental awareness of younger customers", according to Ambienta.

Amazon data included in the Ambienta report shows that 30 per cent of clothes worn by European Gen Z consumers are pre-owned. In the US, 62 per cent of consumers in the same age group consider a second-hand item before buying a new one, says Ambienta citing a Thred Up survey. "This driver is likely to self-reinforce, year after year, as these younger consumers increase their spending power and their share of overall spending grows," said Mallone and Ranghino.

Giuggioli Firth says everyone must do their part. "Change is always bottom up and top down . . . corporates have a duty to change and citizens have a responsibility to start buying less."

Source: Silvia Sciorilli Borrelli (2024) 'Fast fashion: 'We aren't doing enough to fix the problem', Financial Times, 13 Jul. © The Financial Times Limited 2025. All Rights Reserved.

In summary, this chapter has set out multiple mechanisms through which environmental and social systems become commercially relevant. The most obvious of these, of course, is when environmental or social factors are demonstrably of economic benefit. Reducing energy consumption reduces the external costs associated with carbon emissions. This can be claimed as 'going green', though it is really profit maximisation in all but name. Similarly, if a company engages in business practices that its customers, employees or suppliers might react against, it might reasonably worry about the impact on its reputation and, so, on its sales and operating expenses. To avoid losses, a company might change its behaviour. Finally, there is, of course, business opportunity in sustainability. If a company introduces a product or service with game-changing credentials for environmental or social impact, then the possibility arises that they will disrupt the industry and displace currently profitable market leaders.

Note how the channels described here provide ways in which environmental sustainability and social sustainability are financially consequential, and why they might therefore matter for corporate strategy and decision making. They also illustrate how corporate decisions themselves influence the economic opportunities faced by corporations in the future; a decision to make electric cars is not just consequential for carbon emissions, it is also a new way of doing business, generating value and building an entire industry. In this sense, the challenge and the opportunity of sustainability leadership can be stated simply, harkening to Mayer's invitation for companies to produce 'profitable solutions to the problems and people and planet' (Mayer, 2019). In other words, the opportunity is to join the private profit orientation of the corporation with building the strong social and environmental systems on which it depends.

Reflection questions

This chapter has explored the purpose of the corporation, the legal structures that define its obligations and the implications of these elements for corporate sustainability. In the next three chapters, we will explore three key areas of sustainability: climate, nature and social sustainability. As you work through the rest of this book, this chapter provides a grounding to which you can refer as you assess the specific opportunities and constraints your company will face. As you read, refer back to this chapter to critically assess what your corporation aims to achieve, how its goals align with or diverge from the needs and expectations of stakeholders, and assumptions your teams may currently hold about the purpose of the company. These reflections are essential for identifying your company's capacity to act in specific areas of sustainable value creation. As we set out in the section 'How to use this book' in Chapter 1, we encourage you to take the time to discuss the questions below with your teams. This will prepare your company to engage effectively with how climate, nature and social sustainability impact your business' ability to create value as we proceed through Chapters 3, 4 and 5.

1. How would you currently describe the purpose of your corporation?
2. How would stakeholders (employees, customers, investors) describe it? How would your board members describe it?

3. Are there any gaps or areas of divergence within these perspectives?
4. If such gaps and/or divergence exist, why is that important and what, if anything, might it suggest about sustainability leadership for your company?

Recommended reading

Bakan, J. (2005). *The Corporation: The Pathological Pursuit of Profit and Power*. New York, Free Press.

Friedman, M. (1970) The Social Responsibility of Business Is to Increase its Profits, *The New York Times Magazine*, 13 September.

Kraakman, R., Armour, J., Davies, P., Enriques, L., Hansmann, H., Hertig, G., Hopt, K., Kanda, H., Pargendler, M., Ringe, W. and Rock, E. (2017) *The Anatomy of Corporate Law: A Comparative and Functional Approach*. Oxford: Oxford University Press.

Marquis, C. (2020) *Better Business: How the B Corp Movement Is Remaking Capitalism*. New Haven: Yale University Press.

Mayer, C. (2019) *Prosperity*. Oxford: Oxford University Press.

Micklethwait, J. and Wooldridge, A. (2005) *The Company: A Short History of a Revolutionary Idea*. Weidenfeld & Nicolson.

Raworth, K. (2018) *Doughnut Economics: Seven Ways to Think Like a 21st-Century Economist*. Penguin.

Stout, L. (2012) *The Shareholder Value Myth*. Berrett-Koehler Publishers.

United Nations (2015) *Transforming Our World: The 2030 Agenda For Sustainable Development*. New York: UN Publishing. (The 'SDGs'.)

World Commission on Environment and Development (1987) *Our Common Future*. Oxford: Oxford University Press. (The 'Brundtland Report'.)

Notes

[i] Micklethwait and Wooldridge (2005) provide a short, accessible summary.
[ii] This specific list is taken from Kraakman, *et al.* (2017), though, in some variation, can be found in any corporate law text.

iii The classic summary is Honoré, A.M. (1961) 'Ownership', in Guest, A.G. (ed.), *Oxford Essays in Jurisprudence*, Oxford: Oxford University Press, pp. 107–47.
iv Note the contrast with home ownership, where the owner has negative equity if the value of the property falls below that of the mortgage.
v Much of the argument in Mayer (2013) rests upon this observation.
vi The implications of this personal autonomy are explored in Bakan (2005).
vii In some jurisdictions, protecting the company; not so different, actually.
viii Clause 1 of Section 172 *Duty to promote the success of the company*, Companies Act 2006.
ix Strine, L. (2020) Remembering What Comes First Is More Important than Ever. www.ft.com, 27 March. Available at: https://www.ft.com/content/9ee6d82e-6fc2-11ea-89df-41bea055720b.
x Stout, L. (2012) *The Shareholder Value Myth*. Berrett-Koehler Publishers.
xi The argument is presented succinctly in Friedman (1970).

CHAPTER 3
CLIMATE CRISIS: THE LEADERSHIP CHALLENGE OF OUR TIME

This book presents corporate value creation as embedded within environmental and social systems. We explore these systems in the next three chapters. In this chapter, we first ask why climate change matters to corporations, raising a critical distinction between climate change mitigation (reducing the company's impact on global warming) and climate change adaptation (managing the effects of global warming on the company). We then offer practical guidance on how companies can effectively measure their emissions, as a foundation for mitigation and as an input in understanding corporate exposure to climate-related risks and opportunities.

What is the issue?

In Chapter 1, we introduced the concept of the linear economy; a take-make-dispose model of production. This model has generated extraordinary levels of economic growth across the globe. However, this growth has been powered largely through the use of fossil fuels: natural gas, oil and coal. The result of industrial dependence on fossil fuels has been a dramatic, historically unprecedented increase in emissions of carbon dioxide (and other greenhouse gases such as methane), which remain in the atmosphere for many years. These gases (collectively 'GHGs') act as a warming blanket for the planet, trapping heat and creating the greenhouse effect that leads to global warming (see Note 3.1 Carbon equivalents at the end of the chapter). The stabilisation of global temperature requires that GHG emissions reach net zero, in other words, that amounts of GHGs emitted are equal to those captured. The more that emissions remain above net zero, the greater are the risks to environmental and social systems, and thereby to business. The risks are wide-ranging, including damage to physical infrastructure, adverse impact on human health, and geopolitical instability.

It is not least because the risks are so varied and so severe that there is unprecedented intergovernmental commitment to address the problem. The Paris Agreement, which came into force in 2016, is an international treaty on climate change, signed by almost all countries in the world. Its goal is to limit global warming to well below 2 degrees Celsius, preferably to 1.5 degrees, compared to pre-industrial levels. Behind this agreement lies the Intergovernmental Panel on Climate Change (IPCC), which is the primary, global source of scientific consensus. Its advice makes clear the need to act decisively and urgently:

> *Limiting warming to around 1.5°C (2.7°F) requires global greenhouse gas emissions to peak before 2025 at the latest, and be reduced by 43% by 2030 ... For 1.5°C (2.7°F), this means achieving net zero carbon dioxide emissions globally in the early 2050s; for 2°C (3.6°F), it is in the early 2070s. This assessment shows that limiting warming to around 2°C (3.6°F) still requires global greenhouse gas emissions to peak before 2025 at the latest, and be reduced by a quarter by 2030.*[i]

Global emissions have in fact risen each year since the 2016 Paris Agreement and 1.5 degrees looks increasingly implausible. We are therefore mindful that our reference to a target of 1.5 degrees will soon be outdated. Yet we retain it here to make a critical point: targets and commitments are not in themselves sufficient and the evidence of our collective response to the challenge of climate change has so far been one of chronic failure. This does not make the problem go away. Instead, it makes it bigger. The longer it is delayed, the transition to a sustainable economy becomes harder to achieve and the consequences of delay become more significant.

World breaches 1.5C global warming target for first time in 2024

By Attracta Mooney, Jana Tauschinski and Steven Bernard in London

The world breached 1.5C of warming last year for the first time, top international agencies said, as an "extraordinary" spike in the global average temperature sparked fears that climate change is accelerating faster than expected.

Europe's Copernicus observation agency confirmed on Friday that 2024 was the hottest year on record, with average surface temperatures 1.6C above preindustrial levels after greenhouse gas emissions hit a new high.

It was the first calendar year that average temperatures surpassed the 2015 Paris accord target of limiting warming since pre-industrial times to well under 2C and preferably to 1.5C.

"Honestly, I am running out of metaphors to explain the warming we are seeing," said Copernicus director Carlo Buontempo.

He added that a spate of climate disasters last year — ranging from floods to heatwaves — was not a statistical anomaly, but clearly linked to climate change driven by the rise in carbon dioxide and methane.

Copernicus said the years from 2015 to 2024 were the 10 warmest on record.

The co-ordinated release of 2024 data from six climate-monitoring organisations comes just days before president-elect Donald Trump is expected to withdraw the US from the Paris agreement to tackle climate change.

Some businesses around the world have also begun weakening climate targets and rolling back green efforts.

"Hitting 1.5C is like watching the first domino fall in a devastating chain reaction," said Patrick McGuire, a climate researcher at Reading university. "We're playing with fire. Every fraction of a degree unleashes more intense storms, longer droughts and deadlier heatwaves."

The latest data does not represent a definitive breach of the Paris agreement, whose targets refer to temperature averages measured over more than two decades.

But concerns that climate change has gained pace have been fanned by evidence that the world's oceans have been slower to cool than expected after the naturally occurring El Niño warming effect on the Pacific Ocean.

What is "most striking is how much warmer 2024 and much of 2023 have been", said Tim Lenton, chair in climate change and earth system science at Exeter university, noting that the size and persistence of the temperature increases over the period were "extraordinary".

He added: "This is a clear signal of destabilisation in the climate — a less stable system undergoes larger and more persistent fluctuations."

Human-induced climate change was the main driver of the extreme air and sea surface temperatures in 2024, Copernicus said, while other factors such as El Niño, which officially came to an end last June, also contributed.

This year is expected to be cooler than 2024, partly because of the diminished impact of El Niño, which is cyclical. The onset of a weak La Niña cooling cycle was confirmed on Thursday by the US weather agency.

But Samantha Burgess, at the European Centre for Medium-Range Weather Forecasts, said it would still probably rank among the three hottest on record.

"We are now living in a very different climate than our parents and grandparents experienced," she said, adding that it had probably been 125,000 years since temperatures had been as hot as they were today.

> Copernicus said 2024 was the warmest year on the books for all continental regions, except Antarctica and Australasia, as well as for "sizeable parts" of the world's oceans, particularly the north Atlantic, Indian and western Pacific oceans.
>
> Global atmospheric water levels in 2024 reached record levels, at 5 per cent above the 1991-2020 average, fuelling "unprecedented heatwaves and heavy rainfall events, causing misery for millions of people", Burgess said.

 Source: Attracta Mooney, Jana Tauschinski and Steven Bernard (2025) 'World breaches 1.5C global warming target for first time in 2024', Financial Times, 10 Jan. © The Financial Times Limited 2025. All Rights Reserved.

To illustrate the challenge, consider Figure 3.1, which shows the historical growth in annual carbon emissions, coupled with the sharp transition that would have been required (in 2022) for global warming to have remained within 1.5 degrees. The story is a simple one. Historically, large-scale economic growth has been enabled by fossil fuel. To reverse the effects we currently observe in the climate system, this link must be broken. Energy must remain available yet no longer emit GHGs. Herein lies the challenge for companies, which are significant contributors to GHG emissions.

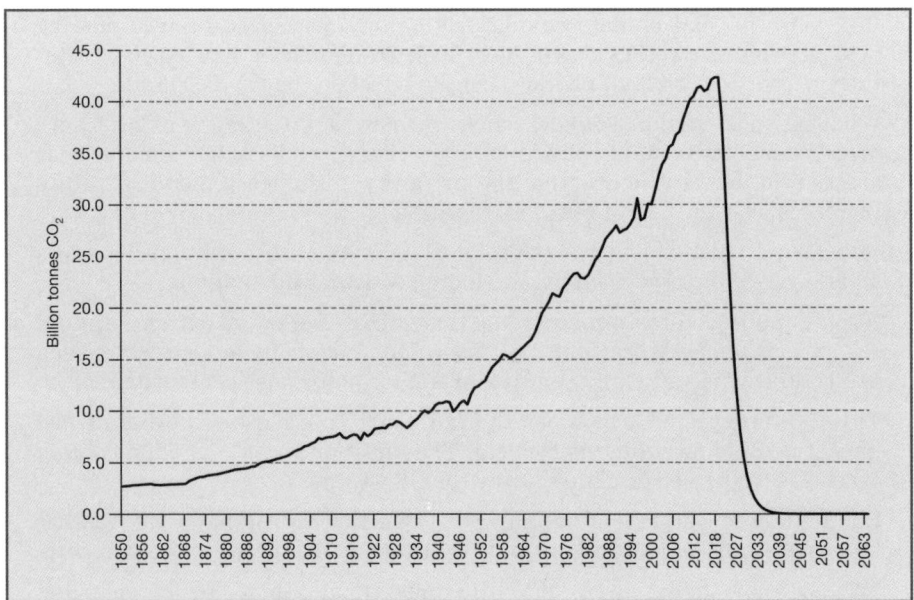

Figure 3.1 Greenhouse gas emissions – historical pathway and transition required to meet 1.5 degree target

Source: Our World in Data.

In many parts of the world, corporate action to address climate change is increasing. It is now common, for example, for companies to set 'net zero' targets and to lay out plans for their realisation. Between 2021–3, the share of the world's 2,000 largest publicly listed companies with net zero targets more than doubled (from 417 to 929 companies) in less than three years, and more than 85 per cent of the world's GDP is currently covered by a net zero commitment.[ii] Typical is Procter & Gamble, which has set an ambition to achieve net zero GHG emissions across its operations and supply chain, from 'raw material to retailer, by 2040 as well as interim 2030 goals to make meaningful progress this decade.'[iii] Our choice of Procter & Gamble is not because it is leading but instead because it is fairly typical of its peers. We could have chosen any company from a long list of household names.

The transition to net zero would bring about dramatic change in how business operates, primarily because all economic activity is fundamentally reliant on energy. The change would affect all industries, not just 'dirty' industries heavily implicated in the extraction and use of fossil fuel but also downstream business that relies on products from those industries. The change would also be systemic, in the sense that the corporate sector has a part to play alongside investors, governments, consumers and civil society; it cannot reach net zero alone. The change is also, to a degree, predictable, in the sense that the science is very clear about the target of net zero and the time horizon over which it should be achieved. This allows leaders and investors to plan.

It is natural, faced with this global transition to a dramatically different way of doing business, to expect it to be expensive. Yet the reality is that the cost of inaction is much greater than the cost of action.[iv] This is therefore not 'cost' but investment. If the corporate sector fails to play its part in containing climate change, it faces ever increasing disruption and failure. This implies that there are opportunities here as well as risks. It is hard to overstate the importance of this economic net benefit from climate change mitigation. Yet this can be hard to see. Consider, for example, that if a company is an incumbent in an industry that contributes heavily to global warming, then transition might well be perceived as a threat. It is natural, therefore, for the incumbent's voice to be negative, to emphasise cost and to lobby against change. Yet there will also be new businesses that emerge and that create value by finding ways to make a positive contribution to addressing climate change.[v] The future leaders of those businesses have, at best, a limited voice currently. It is therefore important to think critically about the nature of the public debate about change.

It is the task of leaders to tune in to and amplify the opportunity that arises from transition. A systems view of embedded corporations enables the framing this moment requires: corporate climate action has to be one of a net benefit to society – and, by extension, net benefit to the corporate sector as a whole. A sustainable economy is more valuable than an unsustainable economy. It has greater opportunities and fewer risks. It is a better place to invest and in which to do business.

Global green subsidy race draws investor attention

By Patrick Temple-West

As the global race for renewable energy accelerates, the billions of dollars of subsidies that the US, Europe and China dole out to vie for market dominance are likely to have implications for investors.

This year, the EU adopted the Net-Zero Industry Act, which aims to make investing in solar, wind and other clean technologies more appealing. The legislation eases bureaucracy, accelerates project approvals, and targets reaching 50mn tonnes of carbon dioxide storage capacity in Europe by 2030.

Investors will have seen that these subsidies have begun to prompt companies to take action. For example, ArcelorMittal, the world's second-largest steelmaker, has started testing a carbon capture project in Ghent, Belgium, according in a Morgan Stanley report in June. This facility will test the feasibility of a full-scale carbon capture at the site as the Act comes into effect, Morgan Stanley said.

Asset manager Invesco said the legislation is "expected to be a game-changer for EU companies transitioning to net zero emissions", in its own report in August. The law will accelerate demand for European-based manufacturers, such as solar cell makers. "The €375bn in grants, tax credits, direct investments and loans from the NZIA will help to spur additional capital and operating expenditures," the report concluded.

The EU's action highlights how the bloc is eager to match renewable energy subsidies adopted by the US and China in recent years. The Biden administration's 2022 Inflation Reduction Act angered many European officials, who worried the $369bn package would lure cleantech businesses and investments away from their region.

It even prompted the EU to accuse Washington of breaching World Trade Organization rules. The head of carmaker Stellantis and other European executives called for Brussels to consider reciprocal measures, or change its rules to respond to the IRA.

The EU should "take action to rebalance the playing field . . . [and] improve our state aid frameworks", European Commission president Ursula von der

Leyen said shortly after the US adopted the IRA. The EU's net zero law was quickly proposed in 2023 to counter the American legislation. "There is a risk that the IRA could lead to unfair competition," von der Leyen warned.

Brussels' net zero law aims to have EU manufacturers meeting 90 per cent of the bloc's domestic demand for electric vehicle batteries by 2030. In addition to responding to the US, the law is an attempt by Brussels to prevent a flood of Chinese EVs in the EU market, says Marco Siddi, a senior researcher at the Finnish Institute of International Affairs.

China's rapid development of electric vehicles, which the government subsidised heavily, has shocked competitors around the world. For example, EV maker Nio received government subsidies as well as grants to build and operate charging stations. Then, in 2020, Nio received a nearly $1bn bailout from state-backed investors. Chinese electric battery makers have been offered subsidies that could account for more than 50 per cent of the cost of the product.

In October, China's biggest electric vehicle maker BYD posted higher quarterly revenues than US rival Tesla for the first time, highlighting how competitive the Asian powerhouse has become.

"In Europe, it is pretty clear that it is not just about subsidies but it is also about industry protection now," Siddi says.

China's top-down central planning for green subsidies cannot easily be replicated by Europe, with its 27 member states. Similarly, the US, which is also nervous about Chinese subsidies, has a complex federal-and-state regulatory apparatus. However, it also enjoys a booming stock market and venture investment ecosystem that can grow cleantech businesses.

Compared with the IRA, Europe's subsidies efforts are "a bit more convoluted", Siddi says. "It is not easy to understand how the industry actually gets the support."

Europe's challenges are about to get tougher as Donald Trump returns to the White House in January. On one hand, the president-elect might roll back some of the 2022 clean energy subsidies. But a full repeal of the IRA is unlikely. In August, 18 Republican members of Congress wrote to Republican House Speaker Mike Johnson, urging him to preserve the law's tax credits and warning that a full repeal would be "a worst-case scenario". The IRA was heavily skewed to fund projects in Republican states.

Additionally, surging electricity consumption in the US is likely to drive demand for all energy sources. Adoption of artificial intelligence and moving manufacturing back into the US are leading to a historic rise in power demand, supporting the case for renewable energy.

> You have the worst of all worlds if you wait, but everyone is afraid to make the wrong move
>
> Janka Oertel, European Council on Foreign Relations

> But the real problem for Europeans is US tariffs. The incoming Trump administration and its tariffs proposals make it hard for businesses to plan now, says Janka Oertel, director of the Asia programme and a senior policy fellow at the European Council on Foreign Relations.
>
> Amid the political uncertainty, "you will have a lot of wait-and-see" — and that is slowing down investment, business expansion, and ultimately decarbonisation, Oertel observes.
>
> "It is a stalemate," she says. "It makes the competitiveness of European companies lower and it slows down decarbonisation."
>
> She adds: "So you have the worst of all worlds if you wait, but everyone is afraid to make the wrong move."
>
> One of the subsidies most at risk when Trump takes office is that for wind power. Trump's election victory immediately hurt shares of European wind companies. The president-elect vowed on the campaign trail to end the offshore wind industry on "day one". Shares of Danish wind manufacturer Vestas, whose biggest market is the US, are now trading at a five-year low.
>
> "The sector I am most concerned about and where I am most interested in how things pan out is wind," Oertel says. "If Chinese producers are able to take advantage of the slumping European wind manufacturers and are able to actually deliver turbines, then it will be very, very hard for the Europeans to maintain an industrial base in the wind energy space," she adds.
>
> For Europe, "that means full energy dependence in the renewable space on China", she says. "That is game over, checkmate."

 Source: Patrick Temple-West (2024) 'Global green subsidy race draws investor attention', Financial Times, 09 Dec. © The Financial Times Limited 2025. All Rights Reserved.

Why does climate change matter to corporations?

As the 'of-on-for' trio of sustainability lenses we introduced in Chapter 1 demonstrates, companies either have an impact upon climate, or else they are affected by it, or – most likely – both. This is a distinction between, on the one hand, 'impact' and, on the other hand, 'dependency'. For you as a leader, both perspectives matter.

The discussion above of GHG emissions is concerned with impact, with business activity leaving a trace on the climate system (the 'of' lens). Raw materials are converted into finished products. Goods are shipped from one location to another. Individual customers ultimately consume products and services. These activities generate GHG emissions, and those emissions contribute to climate change. In contrast, dependency is concerned with how the economics of the company are affected by climate change (the 'on' lens) and with the adaptation that is therefore required. A business that operates in an area that is prone to flooding is probably more at risk now than it was a few years ago. That risk is likely to increase as climate change progresses.[vi] In this case, the financial performance of the company depends upon changes in global temperatures, whether or not its own activities have a significant climate impact.

This difference between impact and dependency is important. From the perspective of the sustainability of your own company's profits, and therefore your share price, what matters first and foremost is dependency. The issues are whether you will continue to be able to rely upon the natural resources that have hitherto supplied your business, whether your customers will continue to buy your product, whether government will start to tax and regulate your emissions-generating activity, and so on. For an oil and gas major, climate change is unlikely to affect your capacity to find and extract fossil fuels, yet it may affect demand and the regulatory environment in which you operate. For an agrifood business, it may be ongoing supply that is the issue, affected by factors ranging from freshwater supply to extreme weather events. On the other hand, if we view corporate activity through the lens of impact, the focus shifts to whether this activity contributes to climate change, thereby imposing external costs on others.

The notion of dependency therefore aligns with accountability to shareholders, while the notion of impact aligns with a broader accountability to stakeholders and society.

Impacts caused by your company's own business activities can also relate directly to the company's dependencies. As we discussed in Chapter 2, the simplest case is when a company has a direct economic incentive to reduce GHG emissions. If it uses less fuel, it saves on energy bills. If it has to pay a carbon tax, then the less it emits, the less it has to pay. Also in this category are cases where the company's impact on the environment has an indirect effect on the company. For example, the less it emits, the more it might be able to attract talented employees, the more likely that its consumers will keep buying its products and services, and the better the terms on which it might be able to raise finance. There might also be an increased ability to tender for future contracts, as customers tighten environmental criteria in their procurement.

It is often not obvious whether an impact caused by a company will ultimately affect the financial performance of that company and, if so, how. Climate risks are inherently non-linear, long-term and systemic. This means they are difficult to accurately assess from historic data. Regulations change in ways that are not always predictable, making it difficult to anticipate the magnitude and timing of change. Yet, as we set out in Chapter 1, the legal and regulatory direction of travel is clear, reinforced by the impact of climate change already being felt in a wide range of industries across the globe. For example, in Europe, where climate losses have increased by 2.9 per cent a year from 2009 to 2023,[vii] countries are responding with legislation. In Italy, for example, it has been proposed that all companies are required to hold insurance to protect their assets from climate-related threats including floods and landslides.[viii]

We invite you to consider these issues of impact and dependency through the lens of Table 3.1 below. Take the example of the airline industry, where the economic mitigation of emissions is extremely difficult to achieve; which of the categories in Table 3.1 do you think applies? The airline has a shared interest with all stakeholders in reducing fuel consumption because to do so is to reduce operating costs. Yet the relationship is more subtle than this. If, for example, reducing costs means reducing prices and so increasing demand, leading to a larger number of flights, then greater fuel efficiency might not result in fewer emissions (this effect is known as the Jevons Paradox, where greater efficiency leads to greater consumption). It might also be the case that the airline's emissions have limited consequences for the economics of the business. After all, they are not direct costs to the business but instead external costs imposed on

Table 3.1 Mitigation (impact) vs adaptation (dependency)

		Impact Do the activities of the company contribute to global warming, and so can the company *mitigate* the causes of climate change?	
		Yes	No
Dependency Is the corporation's own current or future profitability affected by global warming and so does the company need to *adapt* to the effects of climate change?	Yes	**'Endogenous'** The business is affected by its own impacts (and also externally imposed impacts).	**'Exposed'** The business is affected by externally imposed impacts.
	No	**'Exploit'** The business imposes external costs on others.	**'Exogenous'** Impacts are not caused by the business and neither is it affected by them.

environmental systems whenever there is a plane in the air. These only create risks for airlines themselves to the extent that such things as change in government policy (e.g. introducing a carbon tax) and/or change in consumer behaviour (e.g. switching to rail travel) might increase operating costs or reduce demand. The possibility of such change is not guaranteed. Nor is the possibility of technological solutions that reduce impacts and associated business risks. As a result, the financial consequences for the business of its own impacts remain uncertain.

And yet such uncertainties must be understood in the light of the inexorable energy transition we have outlined. The Paris Agreement introduced a clear global imperative to dramatically reduce GHG emissions. Consumers, some of whom have recent personal experience with the impacts of climate change in the form of rising insurance premiums, exposure to smoke or wildfires, or even loss of their homes, are increasingly attuned to the topic. For you as a corporate leader, the prudent assumption is that there is an economic self-interest in planning for transition to a low carbon economy, and therefore in evaluating the business risks and opportunities from both impacts and dependencies related to climate change.

As insurers flee California wildfires the housing market takes a hit, study finds

Nearly 180,000 residents were under evacuation order last night as uncontrolled fires burnt tens of thousands of acres across Los Angeles. The fires, which broke out earlier this week, have ripped through parts of the US's second-most-populous city, and last night the Santa Ana winds were just picking up again.

While wildfires are not new to California, their increasing severity is driving a serious problem for the state's economy: the dwindling availability of homeowners' insurance. Early estimates suggest that insurers could face payouts as high as $20bn from the latest fires — even after they've moved in recent years to reduce exposure to vulnerable properties in the state, with serious implications for California's housing market.

A paper published this week found new evidence that homeowners have been moving away from fire-prone areas when insurance companies reduce coverage. In studying the California market, the researchers found that as more insurers refused to offer coverage for high-risk homes, the number of home loan applications declined.

"Decreased insurance availability alters housing demand by signalling increased risk in a particular location," said the new report, written by researchers from the Federal Home Loan Mortgage Corporation and the Environmental Defense Fund.

California is the US state most affected by wildfires as of 2023, according to the National Interagency Coordination Center. Extreme heat and longer droughts have driven more intense fires, and that has prompted insurance companies to flee.

Last year, State Farm announced it would not renew policies for 72,000 homes and apartments in the state, including 69 per cent of insurance plans in the upscale Pacific Palisades area which was engulfed by the latest wildfires.

The new research paper said that after devastating wildfires in California in 2017 and 2018, insurance companies declined to renew policies on more than 660,000 homes in the following two years.

California is trying to fix the system. At the start of this year, the California Department of Insurance started accepting pre-application petitions from homeowners to more accurately assess their wildfire risks. This move should help insurance companies offer fairer coverage plans.

"This is a pivotal step towards fostering a more resilient community, one that is better prepared to face the escalating threats posed by wildfires," said Firas Saleh, director for North American wildfire models at Moody's.

These tailored petitions will encourage homeowners "to adopt fire-resistant building materials, create defensible spaces and implement other risk reduction measures, thereby potentially lowering their insurance costs while enhancing safety", he said.

The fires are being closely watched by the stock market as well. Edison International, a utility for southern California, saw its shares sink this week. Its shares are down 14 per cent from the start of the year. (US stock markets were closed yesterday for Jimmy Carter's funeral.)

Analysts at Morgan Stanley were cautiously optimistic that Edison equipment did not start the fires. If the company is found to have been negligent in a way that led to the fire, then it would need to reimburse a state wildlife fund up to $3.9bn, Morgan Stanley said on Wednesday.

As climate change continues to foment extreme weather, insurance companies are eager to pull out of vulnerable markets. In 2023, we reported about insurers abandoning Florida as stronger hurricanes hit the state. (Recall, the state's chief financial officer tried to blame the problem on insurance companies' "wokeness").

Now, the devastation of the Los Angeles wildfires has shown how insurance companies — and the housing market — are increasingly reacting to extreme weather.

Source: Patrick Temple-West (2025) 'How California wildfires are hitting the state's housing market', Financial Times, 10 Jan. © The Financial Times Limited 2025. All Rights Reserved.

Corporations and climate change

To understand what transition to a lower carbon economy looks like, and what this demands of business leadership, first we need to know which activities generate GHG emissions. Figure 3.2 presents findings from Our World in Data (2020), which classifies four energy and land-use systems that generate GHG emissions. Of the total carbon emissions across these systems in 2019, 73 per cent arise from the use of energy, of which 17.5 per cent comes from energy in buildings, 16 per cent energy for transport and 24 per cent from energy for industry. Agriculture, forestry and land use make up 18 per cent of global emissions followed by chemicals and cement for industry, which make up 5 per cent and waste, which accounts for 3 per cent via GHG associated with landfill and wastewater.

Technologies, transition durations and trade-offs vary across sectors. Reducing emissions from the production of concrete is a very different challenge from reducing those from transportation, agriculture or the heating and cooling of

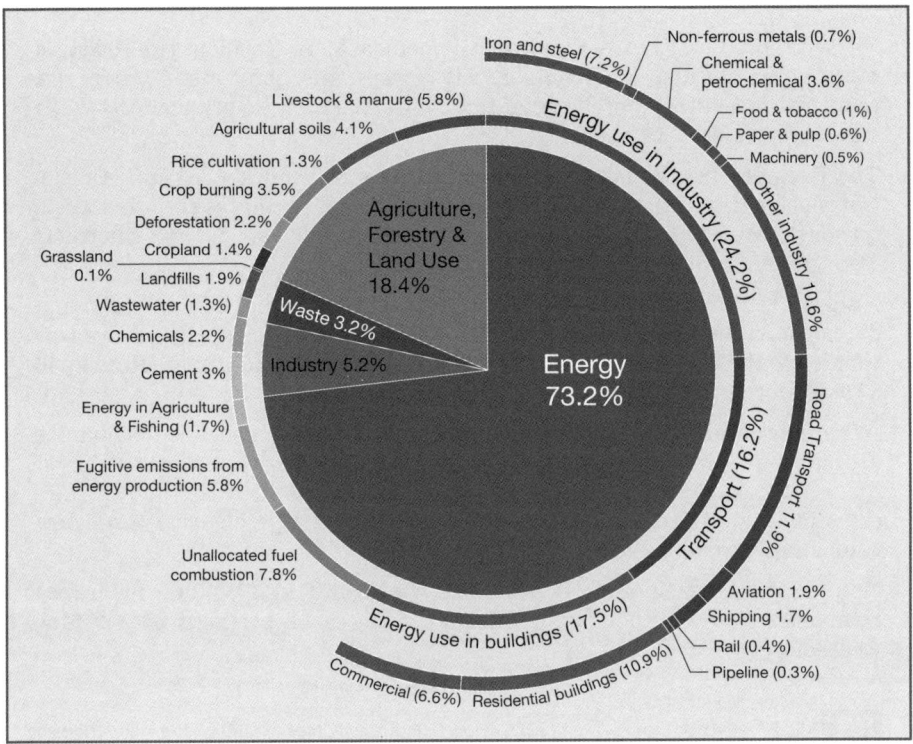

Figure 3.2 Greenhouse gas emissions by sector
Source: Climate Watch, The World Resources Institute, 2020.

buildings. For every company, though, there is the question of what constitutes a realistic transition pathway towards net zero, which includes setting milestones and targets along the way, as well as understanding how other parts of the economy are likely to transition. In addressing these common features of all GHG reductions, we now start with what is needed for your company to understand its own impact on climate change.

What are a corporation's carbon emissions?

Quantification is often a pre-requisite for action. In order to address climate impact, we need to know the scale of the problem and where it occurs. Measurement of a corporation's carbon footprint (its GHG 'inventory') is most commonly guided by the Greenhouse Gas Protocol (GHG Protocol), published by the World Resources Institute (WRI) and the World Business Council for Sustainable Development (WBCSD); WBCSD (2004).

GHG emissions could arise from stationary combustion (e.g. in boilers), mobile combustion (in cars, ships, planes, etc), process emissions (arising from physical or chemical processes) and/or fugitive emissions (from leaks or other releases). Applying the GHG Protocol to measure and categorise these emissions requires determining both an 'organisational boundary' and an 'operational boundary'. The organisational boundary is the entity for which a GHG footprint is to be determined. If, for example, your company has a subsidiary, in which it owns 100 per cent of the shares, then you would calculate the GHG footprint for both companies combined, not just for the parent. The process here is essentially the same as that used in financial reporting; if you look at the financial statements for your company, you will most likely find that they consolidate the accounts of a group of companies, involving, in some cases, business activities conducted through joint ventures or other partially owned companies. The operational boundary concerns the sources of emissions to include in the entity's GHG footprint calculation. These will include those that are within the direct control of the organisation (i.e. within the organisational boundary) and also those arising elsewhere in the entity's value chain as a result of its operations.

The practical application of the GHG Protocol can be illustrated by means of an example. Picture a fairly simple business, by the name of BakeTray. It has a single raw material, aluminium, which is delivered in trucks by its supplier. There is a single manufacturing process, which involves employees transforming aluminium sheets into baking trays. The employees travel to work in their own cars. The company's factory is heated by its own gas boiler. The machinery used for the manufacturing process is powered by externally generated electricity. The trays can only be used once and are recycled[ix] after use.

Suppose that the company wants to determine its carbon emissions for a period of time, say a year. Most straightforward to calculate is emissions from its gas consumption. This is because its use of gas is a directly controllable and measurable aspect of its own operation. CO_2 is emitted as a direct consequence of the company itself turning on the boiler. Next, the company might look to its consumption of electricity. While carbon is emitted by the energy supplier in generating the electricity, it is nevertheless clear that the company's own operations are the source of the energy demand. There is little difference in substance between these two cases of gas and electricity. In both cases, CO_2 is emitted in order that the company can operate its plant. This is true regardless of whether or not the assets producing the heat and electricity are owned by the company.

These two items illustrate what are referred to as 'Scope 1' and 'Scope 2' carbon emissions. The GHG Protocol (Table 3.2) defines Scope 1 emissions as those

Table 3.2 GHG Protocol

Scope 1
Defined as direct emissions from operations, such as the following, whenever these are owned or controlled by the reporting company: • Production of electricity, heat or steam from combustion of fossil fuels. • Certain physical or chemical processes, for example emissions occurring during the production of cement. • Transportation of merchandise, waste and people using fossil fuels. • Emissions from the agricultural sector, including methane from cattle and carbon dioxide from deforestation. • Fugitive emissions, which occur either intentionally or accidentally, for example methane emissions from the processing and transportation of natural gas.
Scope 2
Defined as indirect emissions from the generation of purchased or acquired electricity, steam, heat or cooling consumed by the reporting company.
Scope 3

Defined as all indirect emissions (not included in Scope 2) that occur in the value chain of the reporting company, including both upstream and downstream emissions. These are categorised as follows:
  1 **Upstream (input)** Purchased goods and services
  2 Capital goods
  3 Fuel and energy-related activities
  4 Upstream transportation and distribution
  5 Waste generated in operations
  6 Business travel
  7 Employee commuting
  8 Upstream leased assets
Downstream (output)
  9 Downstream transportation and distribution
10 Processing of sold products
11 Use of sold products
12 End-of-life treatment of sold products
13 Downstream leased asset
14 Franchises
15 Investments

arising directly from sources owned or controlled by the reporting organisation. Scope 2 is also fairly straightforward. It includes emissions associated with external production of the electricity that is purchased by the reporting organisation (i.e. electricity that is consumed within the organisational boundary, yet generated externally).

BakeTray may not measure its GHG emissions directly, but it will know from meter readings how much gas has been consumed by its boiler in any given period of time. These 'activity data' are multiplied by an emission factor, otherwise known as a conversion factor, which translates the activity into CO_2 equivalent. In the case of natural gas, approximately 1kg of CO_2 equivalent is produced for every cubic metre of gas burned. While local estimates may vary for this conversion factor, the calculation itself is straightforward.

In comparison with Scope 1, the distinctive feature of Scope 2 is that the carbon is not emitted by the reporting organisation. The appropriate conversion factor will depend upon the way in which the energy supplier generates the electricity because (for example) electricity sourced from a hydroelectric plant is essentially carbon neutral, while that from a coal-fired plant is carbon-intensive. In the case of Scope 2, a company might rely upon individual suppliers to provide carbon emissions data, in which case those data are said to be 'primary'. Alternatively, the company might employ some sort of industry average, for example the emissions that are typical of energy suppliers in the region. In this case, the data are said to be 'secondary' and they are at best an approximation of the actual level of emissions.

Scope 1 and Scope 2 emissions have in common that, first, they are relatively unambiguously within the scope of corporate responsibility and, second, they are readily measurable. It is important to account for Scope 1 and Scope 2 together because the organisation's emissions from direct fuel consumption would otherwise be misleading; the same amount of CO_2 is emitted, for a given amount of fossil fuel consumption, whether electricity is generated by the entity's own assets or instead by similar assets owned by an external entity.

Scope 3, meanwhile, is the residual category in the GHG Protocol, defined as all indirect emissions (not included in Scope 2) that occur in the value chain of the reporting company, including both upstream and downstream – i.e. within the operating boundary but outside the organisational boundary. This is a broad, eclectic set, allocated into 15 categories (Table 3.2). Without a doubt, Scope 3 is complicated. However, as Figure 3.3 clearly indicates, it is also where the emissions of most companies are concentrated. It is not something your company can credibly ignore.

Scope 3 includes carbon emissions that arise upstream from the entity's own operation, which in our example result from the manufacture of aluminium sheets and from the distribution of those sheets by the supplier's truck. It also includes carbon emissions from employees' cars, in commuting to and from work. Just as the aluminium company provides input in the form of materials, so employees provide input in the form of labour, and this they could not do without commuting. With respect to inputs, the purpose of Scope 3 is to capture all emissions that are incurred outside the reporting entity's organisational boundary, yet that are necessarily incurred in providing products or services and that are therefore inside the entity's operational boundary. The question to ask here is whether the carbon emissions result from activities that contribute to the organisation's output of products or services. Alternatively, did the organisation's activities cause the carbon to be emitted? If yes,

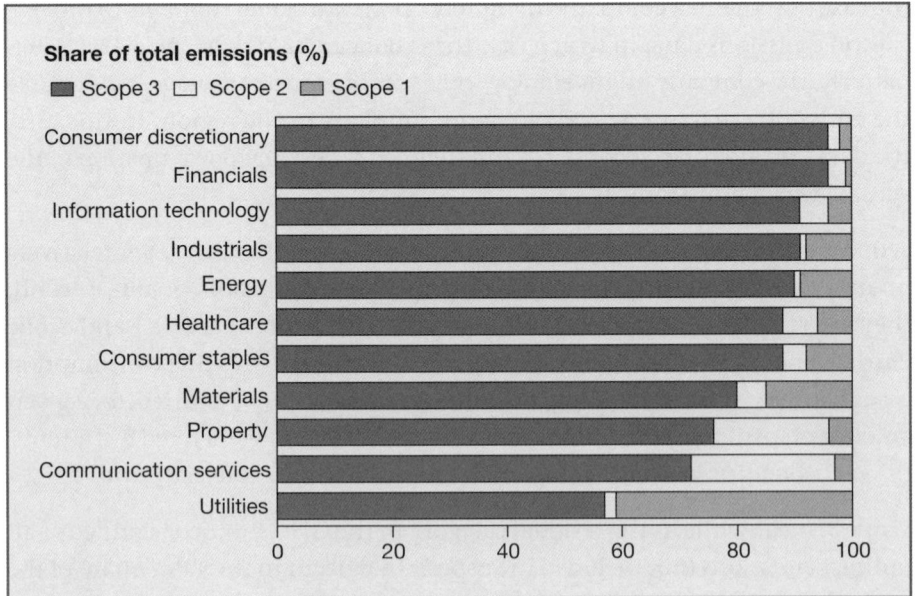

Figure 3.3 Scope 3 emissions dwarf Scopes 1 and 2^x

Source: Hoepner and Schneider research, data from Bloomberg. ©FT

and however far up the supply chain the emissions occur, they are upstream Scope 3. If no, they are not part of the organisation's value chain, and they should not be counted.

In addition, Scope 3 includes carbon emissions from activities that are downstream from the reporting entity, associated with the usage and disposal of the entity's products and services. The relevant items for BakeTray are carbon emissions resulting from the recycling of trays by consumers (see Table 3.3). These are included because they are part of the set of activities that result from the BakeTray business. Again, the purpose of Scope 3 in this regard is to capture all emissions that are incurred outside the reporting entity's organisational boundary, yet that are part of the organisation's value chain.

A common challenge to the reporting of Scope 3 emissions is that it involves double counting. If the aluminium supplier counts its emissions as Scope 1, then are we not double counting if BakeTray also reports them as Scope 3? It might seem so, though actually we are not. To see this, consider how an organisation accounts for its inventory. The underlying principle is that measurement includes whatever costs were incurred for the inventory to be in its present location and condition. BakeTray's inventory of trays therefore includes whatever was paid to its supplier, plus whatever was paid to BakeTray's own employees for converting the raw material into finished product. By analogy, the former

Table 3.3 Value chain emissions

		BakeTray emissions			
		Scope 1	Scope 2	Scope 3	Total
Own operations	Boiler	40			
Upstream emissions	Electric Co.		150		
	Aluminium Co.			400	
	Delivery Co.			5	
	Employee commuting			10	
Downstream emissions	Recycling			15	
		40	150	430	620

Note: The table provides illustrative data for BakeTray's CO_2 emissions, of which 40 are generated within its own operations, 150 through its purchase of electricity and 430 elsewhere in its value chain (mostly upstream in the supply of aluminium).

are Scope 3 and the latter are Scope 1, yet both are part of the cost of producing baking trays and adding them together does not involve double counting; the supplier's labour costs are correctly included in its income statement and are also included within the cost of goods sold in BakeTray's income statement. So, too, upstream carbon emissions can be viewed as an input into the company's operations. In contrast with the supply of materials, there may be no cost associated with emitting carbon, and therefore no expense passed on from the supplier, yet there is still an activity that forms part of BakeTray's supply chain.

For Scope 3, measurement will vary considerably across different types of activity. As of 2025, market practice is nascent and there is considerable subjectivity and uncertainty, both in determining scope (i.e. what to include) and also in measurement. Yet rapid progress is being made and, with the onset of mandatory external reporting (see Chapter 6), the consistency, completeness and reliability of Scope 3 reporting are set to improve dramatically, not least as companies up and down value chains will increasingly be demanding data from one another.

Guidance on Scope 3 is available in the GHG Protocol's corporate value chain standard (WBCSD, 2011). In the BakeTray example, transportation is a relatively straightforward case. For the trucks bringing aluminium to BakeTray's factory, the company can measure activity in terms of distance travelled, which can be multiplied by a measure of fuel efficiency, and then by a factor converting fuel efficiency into carbon emissions. The same process would hold for employee commuting, for which survey data would need to be gathered on distance travelled to work and means of transit. In the case of travel by car, for example, the activity data would be commuting distances and emission factors would be expressed in terms of grams of CO_2 per kilometre travelled. Activity data can again be either primary or secondary. If primary, the data are determined by measuring activities directly, for example by using the fuel gauge of the car. If secondary, measurement is based upon third-party information that is of greatest approximate relevance to the activities in question. If there isn't a meter in place to measure fuel consumption, then published emissions for a comparable asset might be used instead. This could be an expedient way to estimate carbon emissions from trucks owned by suppliers, if direct activity data are not readily available. A further method that could be used is estimation based on cost, whereby monetary spend on different types of goods and services is multiplied by average emissions factors for each.

The difficulty in gathering data – especially primary data – increases as the supply chain gets longer. The questions of scope that we are asking of BakeTray's aluminium supplier would also be asked by that company's suppliers, and of its suppliers, and so on all the way up the supply chain. Practical expedients are allowable in the GHG Protocol's corporate value chain standard (WBCSD, 2011). It is acceptable, for example, to account for only Scope 1 and 2 emissions for business travel, which means measuring the fuel consumed in making the journey but not attempting to measure the emissions associated with manufacturing the plane or car in the first place, nor any other element of the transportation company's value chain.

While it is unavoidably more challenging to measure Scope 3, in comparison with either Scope 1 or Scope 2, there is also a reason to ask whether Scope 3 should be measured at all. BakeTray controls its own operation directly, whereas with Scope 3 it sources inputs from operations controlled by others, and it cannot control such things as whether and how its trays are recycled. This raises a matter of principle, namely whether the company can be held responsible for the actions of others that are ostensibly beyond its control.

Upstream emissions are necessarily incurred in order for the company to be able to do business, in order to be able to supply its customers. Moreover, to the extent that those emissions are incurred because of orders placed by the company, they can be understood to be within the company's control. Downstream is more problematic. It might seem reasonable for a company to accept that it has direct control over its own operation, and to a large degree over its upstream purchasing decisions, yet for it to push back on whether it has control over the use of its products. After all, it is for customers to decide how they will employ the products – whether, for example, they will drive a car in a fuel-efficient manner, or whether instead they value speed, acceleration and braking. In addition, there is also the issue that customers use the products and services from the company in combination with those from other companies, raising the question of which company (or companies) the downstream emissions 'belong' to. Take the BakeTray case. When the trays are in use by customers, there is consumption of gas in ovens, but can that really count as downstream Scope 3 of BakeTray, rather than of the gas company, or of the manufacturer of the oven?

These are difficult questions, most likely to be answered in practice by the development of accepted norms within specific industries. The GHG Protocol makes a distinction here between final and intermediate products. In the case of final products, such as vehicles or washing machines, Scope 3 includes all emissions associated with the use of the product. The point is that selling such products is directly associated with the lifetime emissions from their use. Companies producing less efficient products have a higher carbon footprint from their value chain which, in the context of business transition to a low carbon economy, is an important data point. The situation is arguably different for intermediate products, since these form only part of a final design and manufacture and are therefore less directly implied in emissions from product use and disposal. Yet it has to be acknowledged that the boundary here is not clearly defined. If all parts of a car are made by one company and assembled by another, are the value chain emissions of the two really so different? Unavoidably, there is a need for judgement. The test is whether and how the measurement of GHG emissions provides information that is important for decision making.

Emissions: decision relevance

Our discussion of measurement has focused on emissions themselves, which has obvious relevance to a company's contribution to climate change, and so to the issue of mitigating that contribution. Notice, however, that this does not in itself address the business case for reducing emissions, which is not directly concerned with the impact *of* the company on climate change but instead with managing the effects of climate change *on* risks for the company and *for* business opportunity. Emissions information is decision-relevant in this context, for business leaders and investors' alike, if it influences evaluation of the company's financial risks and opportunities. Such information is likely to vary across different industries, such that the risks and opportunities associated with a company's carbon footprint will also vary. In one industry there might be high exposure to the risk of carbon tax or similar regulation, while in another the challenge might be in financing the capital expenditure required to transition, while in a third industry there might be the opportunity and prospect of a growing market. In each of these cases, while the reduction of emissions is not itself what the business is trying to achieve, it is nevertheless important that the entity understands its carbon footprint because of the business risks and opportunities that arise from it.

This perspective on 'business relevant' Scope 3 cuts through some of the measurement problems that were described in the previous section. For example, it does not call for a high degree of precision in data. Estimation can instead be in 'ballpark' territory because the need is only to understand broadly where in the value chain emissions are concentrated and what order of magnitude they are. This information then feeds the really important questions for you as a business leader, concerned with how much of a challenge you have in meeting your net zero targets, whether this is within your direct control or instead relies upon working with suppliers and other stakeholders, whether you have the technology and financing to transition, whether you or your competitors are likely to achieve transition more quickly and more cost-effectively and (therefore) what the implications might be for revenue growth, profitability and business resilience. Take the example of Jaguar cars, which has taken the radical step of not selling any new cars in 2025 and of effectively re-launching the brand in 2026 with an all-electric range. For the purpose of making this decision, Jaguar did not need precise data for its Scope 3 emissions in 2024. All it really needed to know was that, given the approximate scale of those emissions, its future was not viable without a major change in direction.

Note that emissions do not need to be within your direct control in order to affect your risks and opportunities. And neither does it matter if they are also counted by any other business in your value chain. Instead, what matters is whether information on your value chain carbon footprint provides useful information about the risks and opportunities for your business. If, for example, your company mines iron ore, you are also unavoidably in the (carbon intensive) steelmaking business, which is where most of the emissions take place in the value chain. And if your company sells oil and gas, your revenue is derived directly from providing customers with carbon to release into the atmosphere, with obvious implications for the sustainability of your business model. The banking industry, which creates few emissions of its own, provides the finance that, in turn, enables activities that generate emissions from the 'real economy'. Less directly, downstream Scope 3 might be important as a consequence of the design and marketing of your products. You might sell diesel cars rather than electric cars, appliances that are more or less energy efficient, products from which metals can (or cannot) be recycled at the end of their useful lives, and so on. Such decisions are made by the supplying company. Arguably, they generate an affirmative response to the question we asked of upstream emissions: did my organisation's activity cause the carbon to be emitted? They also speak to opportunity: can my business outperform in the future by meeting increasing consumer demand for low-impact products and services?

Both upstream and downstream Scope 3 are therefore relevant in understanding a company's carbon footprint, yet they are different from one another. Upstream should be understood in much the same way as input costs. They are, in substance, controlled by the company, and they contribute directly to the resources consumed in providing products or services. While measurement is more difficult for Scope 3 than for either Scope 1 or 2, and while control is weaker, upstream carbon emissions are just as relevant as Scope 1 or 2 in determining a company's carbon footprint. In contrast, downstream carbon emissions are more nuanced. However, they are still likely to be important in understanding the impacts, risks, and opportunities associated with a company's business model, particularly in industries (such as oil and gas, iron ore mining, or autos) where the product or service provided has a direct relationship with the downstream emissions that result.

Lifecycle analysis

While the BakeTray example has illustrated the application of Scopes 1, 2 and 3 for an organisation as a whole, a further dimension to consider is that of time. The issue here is the difference between the time period in which carbon is emitted and that in which any given company accounts for it.

In the case of some sectors of the economy, the operating cycle is short. Goods are produced, sold and consumed, and packaging recycled or disposed of, all within a short period of time. In contrast, the lifecycle can be considerably longer in other industries. The extended lifecycle might be upstream as, for example, in the pharmaceutical industry, where product development can take years. More likely, the product has a long life in use. In the construction industry, for example, there are considerable carbon emissions associated with the construction itself, yet considerably more associated with operating the asset over the following decades, and with its ultimate decommissioning. Energy-efficient design is therefore critical in evaluating the carbon footprint of the constructor. The same is true in the auto industry and, even more so, in the case of aviation. If a company manufactures jet engines, for example, the lifecycle emissions will be significant in both Scope 1 and 2, yet overwhelmingly they will be in Scope 3, as a result of fuel consumption during the life of the engine.

In determining your company's footprint during a given period of time, the convention is to evaluate the emissions generated as a result of activities during the period, regardless of when the emissions themselves take place (WBCSD, 2011).

This requires determining the lifecycle emissions of products (see Note 3.2 at the end of the chapter). If you purchase an item of capital equipment, your emissions in the period include all of those associated with producing that equipment in the first place. If you sell an item of capital equipment, your emissions in the period include all of those associated with using that equipment over its useful life, as well as any end-of-life disposal or recycling emissions.

Net zero: the role of carbon offsets

We have focused so far on carbon emissions. Yet the stabilisation of global temperature does not require that we achieve zero carbon emissions, but instead that we achieve *net* zero, whereby any GHG emissions released into the atmosphere are negated by an equal amount taken out, by means of carbon capture and storage.

The case for offsets runs as follows: the individual corporation does not itself have to undertake carbon reductions. Instead, it can purchase 'carbon credits' – in other words, it can make a net zero claim by acquiring the right to carbon reductions that take place elsewhere. These could either be in the form of carbon capture or instead the result of greater energy efficiency that reduces currently expected emissions. Either way, the effect is to reduce the carbon that would otherwise be in the atmosphere. This mechanism of carbon credits is attractive because, for most corporations, and given current technology, the complete elimination of carbon emissions is either infeasible or uneconomic.

In principle, there is much to like about offsetting. The problem of climate change is caused by the emission of greenhouse gases. It does not matter where those gases are emitted, or by whom, but only that those emissions take place somewhere. Likewise, it does not matter – for climate change – where and how emissions are reduced and/or where and how greenhouse gases are captured and stored, just so long as additions to GHGs are always matched by withdrawals. So, suppose you have an industry that is very expensive to decarbonise, while there are also relatively inexpensive projects available elsewhere that would either reduce or capture carbon. There is a net gain to the economy if the industry does not reduce its own emissions but instead pays to reduce emissions elsewhere, by funding the projects through offsets. The payment takes place by means of a carbon offset credit, whereby the purchasing company acquires the unique, certified right to be associated with the carbon reduction, thereby transferring that right from the entity in which the reduction takes place. The purchaser is then able to use ('retire') the credit in order to have a credible claim to have reduced net emissions in that period of time.

So far, so good. When applied in practice, however, a range of difficulties apply. Different carbon offset schemes vary in quality, in the sense of having stronger or weaker claims to being genuine reductions in emissions, a fact that has led to much contestation and even derision within the industry.[xi] One issue is 'additionality'. The purchase of offset credits must be a necessary condition for the associated carbon reduction to take place. If, in the absence of that source of funding, the project would anyway have been economic to undertake, then it cannot sell offset credits. The point here is that the purchase of the credits would not have led to any mitigation of global warming. In contrast, if a project is economically infeasible in the absence of payment for credits, then the payment enables the carbon reduction to take place, thereby making the effect 'additional'.

A second issue is 'permanence'. Carbon removal means taking carbon out of the atmosphere and storing it permanently. If a tree grows, capturing carbon along the way, but it is then felled and burned as firewood – or if there is a forest fire – the carbon is released. The overall effect of growing and burning is net zero, but there is no permanent carbon capture, and no benefit in mitigating global warming. In general, any form of biological carbon capture runs this risk. Geological carbon capture is very much more effective because it involves underground storage in rock form, yet currently it is technologically underdeveloped, small-scale and very expensive.

Finally, carbon offsets can put social systems at risk, for example as competition for land with housing or agriculture raises tensions with communities in geographies where offset projects are undertaken.[xii] In this way, offsets demonstrate the need to understand not just environmental systems, but also social systems, and how the two systems interact.

There is also the issue of availability. There is a time dimension in thinking about offsetting, and with it a challenge that increases. We have not yet reached a level of atmospheric GHGs that scientific consensus regards as unsafe, and we therefore technically have a carbon budget 'left' to spend. This allows a window of time for transition. As we get closer to 2050, however, and if we are on target, then we will have exhausted the sources of carbon reduction that are least expensive, and we will also have fewer options to acquire credits based upon reducing emissions.[xiii] It will be increasingly difficult for any organisation to continue to consume fossil fuels and to assume that this consumption can be offset. What works now – such as helping to fund a transition in power generation from coal to renewable – will be increasingly hard to make work in the future because such opportunities will be increasingly hard to find. In this regard, the mindset that 'we can always offset' is dangerous, and what might seem like a credible net zero transition plan may actually be based upon an unrealistic imagination of the future. The priority must be to reduce emissions directly, as close to zero as possible and as quickly as possible. We discuss the issue further in Chapter 4, where we introduce the 'mitigation hierarchy'.

Climate transition

It is one thing to understand where and why GHG emissions arise in a company's value chain. It is another thing to act upon such information and to take carbon out of economic activity. Moreover, and building on the discussion in Chapter 2, your scope for action as a business leader is governed by fiduciary duty and the reality of operating in competitive markets. Eliminating GHG emissions cannot be an end in itself; after all, the surest and simplest way to achieve such a target would be to shut down operations altogether. Instead, you are tasked with building a business case for decarbonising.[xiv]

Our view of corporations as embedded in systems upon which they depend offers you the foundation required to build this business case. The effects of climate change might manifest as physical risks (e.g. extreme weather events), as transition risks (e.g. changes in consumer demand or in government regulation) or as opportunities (e.g. new markets for 'green' products or services). These might go hand-in-hand with a business case for a corporate commitment to net zero, as opposed to be being a concern with reducing GHG emissions as an end in itself. It is, of course, difficult to separate these factors from the core business. The issues concern how your business will source the energy on which its activities depend, whether and how it can adapt its products and services to meet changing consumer demand, whether and how its activities are resilient and its risk management processes effective, and so on.

For you as a leader, a test of how deeply climate transition has been embraced by your organisation at a strategic, not just cosmetic, level is whether it has integrated impact and dependency into core governance, strategy, management and finance, for example whether you have articulated a transition plan that connects a net zero target with governance structures, investment decisions and interim milestones.[xv] These hold for other dimensions of sustainability as well.

Reflection questions

In the next two chapters, we build on our discussion of climate to present impacts and dependencies related to sustainability in natural and social systems. Working from the conceptual foundation of the purpose of the corporation we outlined in Chapter 2, you can view this chapter as well as Chapters 4 and 5 as building blocks that deepen your sustainability subject expertise. While climate, nature and social aspects of sustainability have distinctive attributes that warrant focused consideration, they are also interdependent. As you progress through the book, therefore, continue the practice we introduced in Chapter 1 of engaging on the questions at the end of each chapter with teams who enable you to translate your learning into action. The questions we raise will be relevant for the content for each of the chapters on climate (this chapter), nature (Chapter 4), and social systems (Chapter 5). As you reflect, watch for how these systems interact with each other, and with the business in which you are a leader.

1. To what extent do your company's GHG emissions disclosures include Scope 3? Evaluate the decisions made by the company on what is included and what is excluded. Where do you see the line being drawn, and why do you think it is drawn in this way?
2. Does your company's disclosure of GHG emissions align with your understanding of where there are risks and opportunities for the business? Are the disclosures presented only in terms of impacts *of* the company, or also as impacts *on* the company and opportunities *for* the company?
3. Consider also the reliability of your data and where (and why) you see greatest weakness in this regard. How could you address this? What would you prioritise and what resource would this work require?

Recommended reading

Axelsson, K., *et al.* (2024) Oxford Principles for Net Zero Aligned Carbon Offsetting (revised 2024). Oxford: Smith School of Enterprise and the Environment, University of Oxford. Available at: https://www.smithschool.ox.ac.uk/sites/default/files/2024-02/Oxford-Principles-for-Net-Zero-Aligned-Carbon-Offsetting-revised-2024.pdf.

Bansal, P., Durand, R., Kreutzer, M., Kunisch, S. and McGahan, A.M. (2024) Strategy Can No Longer Ignore Planetary Boundaries: A Call for Tackling

Strategy's Ecological Fallacy. *Journal of Management Studies*, 17 May. Available at: https://doi.org/10.1111/joms.13088.

Fankhauser, S., Smith, S.M., Allen, M., Axelsson, K., Hale, T., Hepburn, C., Kendall, J.M., *et al.* (2021) The Meaning of Net Zero and How to Get It Right. *Nature Climate Change* 12, no. 1, 20 December: 1–7. Available at: https://doi.org/10.1038/s41558-021-01245-w.

Figueres, C. and Rivett-Carnac, T. (2020) *The Future We Choose: Surviving the Climate Crisis*. New York: Alfred A. Knopf.

Helm, D. (2020) *Net Zero: How We Stop Causing Climate Change*. Williams Collins.

IPCC (2022) Climate Change 2022: Mitigation of Climate Change. www.ipcc.ch. Available at: https://www.ipcc.ch/report/ar6/wg3/.

Our World in Data (2020). Available at: https://ourworldindata.org/ghg-emissions-by-sector.

Sharpe, S. (2023) *Five Times Faster*. Cambridge University Press.

TCFD (2020) *Guidance on Scenario Analysis for Non-Financial Companies*. Task Force on Climate-related Financial Disclosures.

TPT (2023) *Disclosure Framework*. Transition Plan Taskforce (TPT).

WBCSD (2004) The GHG Protocol: A corporate reporting and accounting standard (revised edition).

WBCSD (2011) The GHG Protocol: Corporate Value Chain (Scope 3) Accounting and Reporting Standard.

Note 3.1 CO_2 equivalents

Carbon dioxide gets most of the attention in discussion of climate change but other gases are also contributors to the greenhouse effect that generates global warming. They are methane, nitrous oxide, refrigerant gases, sulphur hexafluoride, water vapour and ozone. The reason for the focus on CO_2 is twofold. First, CO_2 is by far the most important greenhouse gas. Second, the global warming potential of other greenhouse gases is conventionally expressed in terms of its CO_2 equivalent. CO_2 is therefore a common currency, allowing a target expressed as a reduction in CO_2 emissions to be interpreted as a target to reduce greenhouse gas emissions in general.

The atmospheric impact of greenhouse gases varies in two ways. The first is that these gases vary enormously in the extent to which they radiate heat back towards the earth. Most are significantly more potent than CO_2 in this regard. The second variable is duration, which refers to the length of time that the gas remains in the atmosphere. The concept of a CO_2 equivalent takes into account both of these variables, and it typically expresses the global warming effect of any given gas in relation to that of 100 years' worth of a ton of CO_2. Hence, one ton of CO_2 emissions has a CO_2 equivalent of one, while one ton of methane and nitrous oxide are estimated to have, respectively, CO_2 equivalents of 25 tons and 310 tons. In other words, a given amount of nitrous oxide has global warming potential 310 times the same unit of carbon dioxide. To give some practical shape to these concepts, each of the greenhouse gases and their CO_2 equivalents is listed below, including, for the past year, 10 years and 100 years, the contribution to global warming from each. It can be seen that, while the potency of CO_2 is relatively low, this is overwhelmed by its volume, making it the dominant greenhouse gas. This is not to ignore the very significant contribution of methane (see Chapter 4) and nitrous oxide.

Note 3.2 Lifecyle analysis

Commonly used standards for lifecycle analysis are ISO 14040 (which provides a conceptual framework) and ISO 14044 (which provides complementary technical guidance). A GHG footprint for products is determined in a four-stage process. In stage I, goal and scope definition is achieved by specifying the target audience and the reasons for the study. For example, the purpose might be to compare the impact of one product design over another, to determine which to bring into production. In order to do this, it is essential to define the function that the product serves over its lifetime in order that similar levels of functionality can be compared in terms of their respective footprints. In stage II, the analysis of lifecycle inventory, the company determines the flows during the product's life, which are those to and from the biosphere, including the use of raw materials, the return of waste and the generation of emissions. These flows occur in a series of identified processes, for example the extraction of raw materials,

Table 3.4 GHG emissions by sector

	% of total carbon dioxide emissions	% of total methane emissions	% of total nitrous dioxide emissions
Power	30	-	3
Electricity	29		
Heat	1		
Industry	30	33	8
Steel	8		
Cement	6		
Oil & gas extraction	5		
Chemicals	4		
Coal mining	2		
Other	6		
Mobility	19	-	2
Road	15		
Aviation	2		
Maritime	2		
Buildings	6	-	-
Residential	4		
Commercial	2		
Agriculture	1	38	79
Forestry	14	5	5
Waste	-	23	3
	100%	100%	100%

factory conversion into finished product, distribution to the consumer, and the subsequent use by the consumer. In stage III, the lifecycle impact assessment, the inventory of flows is converted into specific impacts, which can be either primary, such as CO_2 emissions, or (much more subjectively) secondary, such as the social and economic effects of the global warming resulting from those CO_2 emissions. In stage IV, interpretation, impacts are often monetised in order to allow alternatives to be compared using a cost–benefit analysis. Since this involves an evaluation of externalities, it is rarely able to draw directly upon market prices and so, inevitably, it is a subjective process.

Related is ISO 14025, a standard on environmental labels and declarations. While designed for business-to-business transactions, it is possible (though unusual) for this standard to be used also in consumer markets.

Notes

i   IPCC (2022) Climate Change 2022: Mitigation of Climate Change. www.ipcc.ch. Available at: https://www.ipcc.ch/report/ar6/wg3/.

ii   Net Zero Stocktake 2023, Net Zero Tracker, n.d., https://zerotracker.net/analysis/net-zero-stocktake-2023.

iii   P&G (2021) P&G Accelerates Action on Climate Change toward Net Zero GHG Emissions by 2040. us.pg.com, 15 September. Available at: https://us.pg.com/blogs/net-zero-by-2040/.

iv   Alex Cooper, *et al.* (2021) What the Shell Judgment Means for US Directors. The Harvard Law School Forum on Corporate Governance, 22 July. Available at: https://corpgov.law.harvard.edu/2021/07/22/what-the-shell-judgment-means-for-us-directors/.

v   Yoon, J. (2023) Chipmakers Race to Curb Emissions as Demand Surges. *Financial Times*, 15 June, sec. Semiconductors. Available at: https://www.ft.com/content/5880d4aa-a88a-4514-afcd-798e8f29e9ff.

vi   *Financial Times* (2023) US Insurers/Climate Change: Less Reliable Models Augur Poorly for Policyholders. www.ft.com, 23 June. https://www.ft.com/content/1934a781-1842-42ac-97e0-f1113ce323af.

vii   European Environment Agency (2023) Economic Losses from Weather- and Climate-Related Extremes in Europe – 8th EAP. www.eea.europa.eu, 6 October 6. Available at: https://www.eea.europa.eu/en/analysis/indicators/economic-losses-from-climate-related.

viii   Naik, G. (2024) Italy to Require Companies Buy Insurance for Climate Risks. *Insurance Journal*, 3 December. Available at: https://www.insurancejournal.com/news/international/2024/12/03/803300.htm.

ix   The assumption of effective recycling after use is in fact a significant leap. In the United States, which has relatively sophisticated recycling infrastructure compared to a global baseline, the Environmental Protection Agency estimated rates of aluminium recycling to be around 35 per cent in 2018, the last available data as of May 2025. For detailed analysis, see US EPA (2017) Aluminum: Material-Specific Data, www.epa.gov, 7 September. Available at: https://www.epa.gov/facts-and-figures-about-materials-waste-and-recycling/aluminum-material-specific-data#:~:text=In%202018%2C%20the%20total%20 recycling.

[x] Schneider, F. (2023) Why Carbon Emissions Reports Need Handling with Care ... *Financial Times*, 30 May. Carbon footprint. Available at: https://www.ft.com/content/37ac4900-a0d8-4e82-9850-ba4a5ad3ac6d.

[xi] Blake, H. (2023) The Great Cash-For-Carbon Hustle. *The New Yorker*, 16 October. Available at: https://www.newyorker.com/magazine/2023/10/23/the-great-cash-for-carbon-hustle.

[xii] Hodgson, C. (2022) Surge of Investment into Carbon Credits Creates Boom Time for Brokers. *Financial Times*, 2 May. Available at: https://www.ft.com/content/739a5517-4de6-43f7-ae47-1ce8d4774d50.

[xiii] Murray, S. (2023) Can Carbon Markets Accelerate Progress towards Net Zero? *Financial Times*, 15 June, sec. Moral Money. Available at: https://www.ft.com/content/5349cb46-4c33-4a2e-840a-b8fc94de7254.

[xiv] Paterson, M. (2023) Climate Change, Insecurity, and Economic Transformation in *Climate Change, Conflict and Insecurity: Hot War*. Routledge.

[xv] Averchenkova, A. and Chan, T. (2023) Governance Pathways to Credible Implementation of Net Zero Targets about the Authors. Available at: https://www.lse.ac.uk/granthaminstitute/wp-content/uploads/2023/10/Governance-pathways-to-credible-implementation-of-net-zero-targets.pdf.

CHAPTER 4
WHY NATURE MATTERS TO BUSINESS, AND WHAT TO DO ABOUT IT

In Chapter 3, we emphasised the significance of climate change for business. Climate change often dominates headlines – and deservedly so. However, there is another vital element of environmental systems for you as a leader to consider: across the globe, nature and biodiversity are at a watershed moment. Nature and climate are deeply interconnected and share a common concern: economic activity produces externalities, leading to unsustainable environmental depletion. The effects are on specific natural resources such as freshwater, soil, minerals, forests and species on land and in the water, each crucial natural systems on which the economy depends.

Like climate change, environmental degradation has been the byproduct of economic activity. WWF Living Index (2024) reports a staggering 73 per cent average decline in the relative abundance of monitored wildlife populations around the world between 1970 and 2020, caused mostly by change in land use. Deforestation has been running at an annual average rate of an area roughly equivalent to the size of Portugal. Overall, change in land use accounts for approximately one quarter of global GHG emissions, as carbon sinks become sources of emissions. In turn, global warming accelerates biodiversity loss.[1] Meanwhile, the result of growth in demand for freshwater is such that only 37 per cent of rivers longer than 1,000 m remain free flowing over their entire length. The Colorado River in the United States is a salient example; a once mighty river that carved the Grand Canyon, it now runs dry before reaching the sea. At the same time, extreme flooding has become a threat to lives and

---

1   The terms 'nature' and 'biodiversity' are often used interchangeably in practice, even though the former refers to all natural resources and the latter to species variation. One reason for this practice is that biodiversity is a measure of a healthy ecosystem, and therefore of the capacity of natural resources to generate (valuable) ecosystem services.

livelihoods from the Americas to Asia, with catastrophic consequences.[i] Climate change will accelerate this trend. The Global Footprint Network estimates that we are currently consuming at a rate that is 75 per cent in excess of the carrying capacity of the planet.[ii] All of this speaks to natural systems in crisis, and an attendant need for leadership and innovation at speed and scale.

As summarised below (Figure 4.1) by WWF (2022), the expansion of economic activity in its various forms in recent decades (since 1970) has had a rapid and dramatic effect on reducing global biodiversity and forest cover. Similar patterns can be observed in data relating to other aspects of environmental impact, such as ocean warming, soil degradation, plastic pollution and toxic waste. The scale and rate of change is similar to that of GHG emissions and global warming, as illustrated in Chapter 3. This is not surprising given that growth in economic activity is the common driver.

The degradation of natural systems is not just a concern for environmentalists and nature lovers. It is also a looming economic threat, albeit one that remains underacknowledged and poorly understood. Natural systems have no substitute. They are the source of literally everything – energy, water, air, genetic materials and minerals. They also absorb waste and have the capacity to recycle. And because they are systems, comprising interacting and interdependent parts

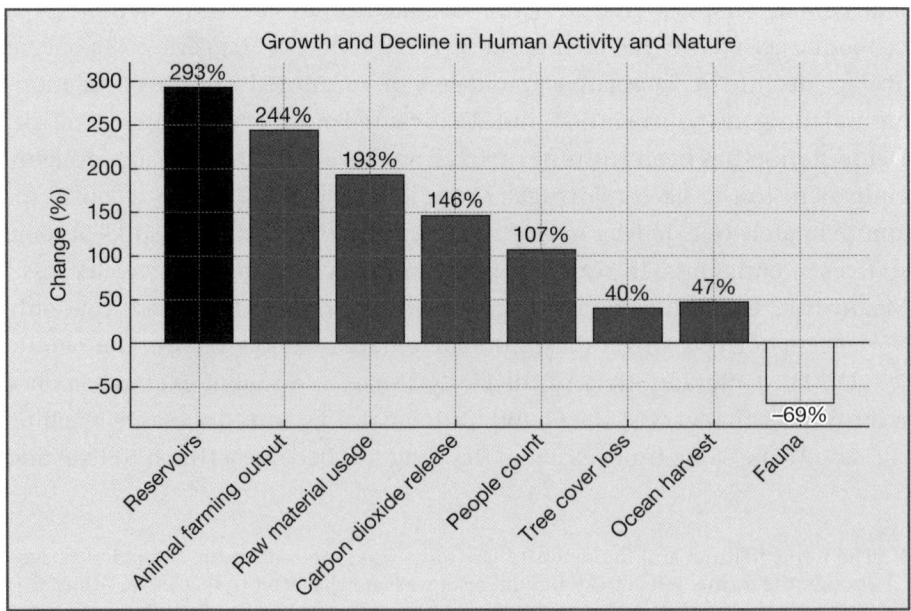

Figure 4.1 Economic expansion and environmental degradation

that form a whole, there are (often unexpected) properties that can emerge from them. In short, they are to be handled with care, if we wish to minimise potentially devastating global threats as a result of their degradation.

As we know from social history, effects of degradation of natural systems include disease outbreaks, drought food insecurity, mass migration and social unrest, all of which can have significant effects on economic systems and so on business prospects.[iii] A recent example is COVID-19, which can be understood as a specific realisation of an increasing likelihood of pandemic outbreaks. The mechanism for such outbreaks is that, as land use for economic activity expands, there are increased animal-human encounters and thereby greater transmission risk.[iv]

It is not an overstatement to say, in the words of a *Financial Times* piece, 'nature's future underpins the future of business'.[v] Significant financial costs incurred by companies as a result of nature risks include credit downgrades, legal action, reputational damage, impairment of assets, supply chain disruption and stock price decline.[vi] Corporate impacts and dependencies on natural systems expose companies to physical risk, transition risk and systemic risk, and can do so in ways that are sudden and severe.

Investment sector seeks to put a value on biodiversity

By Jessica Rawnsley

The world is in the throes of one of the biggest extinction episodes in its history. Of the 8.7mn species of animals and plants on the planet, more than 1mn are in danger of being wiped out, according to the UN.

By some scientific estimates, we are losing species at up to 1,000 times the natural rate of between one and five a year. Pummelled by overfishing, deforestation, rising temperatures and extractive agriculture, much of the natural world is on the brink.

Yet the financial services industry has long neglected biodiversity, even as the topic of carbon emissions climbed the agenda and sustainability funds proliferated. That is partly because biodiversity — the range of animals, plants and insects that form an ecosystem — is more difficult to price than a tonne of carbon, or the returns from a solar plant.

A poacher knows how much a dead elephant costs; a logger the price of an acre of felled forest. But what is the value of an elephant that is allowed to thrive in an intact forest? And how can that forest be valued for more than its carbon?

In recent years, however, an increase in engagement and awareness has been driven "both by investors waking up and seeing the fragility of nature, and the realisation that there is an inflation and GDP impact", says Martin Frandsen, a global equities portfolio manager at Principal Asset Management who invests in biodiversity.

More than half the world's economic output — about $58tn of global GDP — is moderately or highly dependent on nature, according to an analysis from PwC. Investors are also increasingly interested in addressing biodiversity risks in their portfolios, and companies in future-proofing their supply chains.

At this year's COP16 biodiversity summit in Colombia, a significant financial sector presence turned up to the negotiations. "You could tell by the number of discussions being had, but also the level of discussions, how much awareness and understanding of this topic has moved forward since the last COP," says Gayaneh Shahbazian, biodiversity engagement manager at Morningstar Sustainalytics, a research and analytics company.

Some of the push came from COP15's Global Biodiversity Framework Fund, set up to support investment in biodiversity and scale financing before 2030, in order to stem nature loss.

Regulation is a driver, too — notably, the EU's Corporate Sustainability Reporting Directive, which demands that thousands of companies report on environmental topics such as biodiversity, and The Taskforce for Nature-related Financial Disclosures, set up to improve reporting of nature-based risks and dependencies.

In line with shift, a growing number of asset management groups now offer funds that promise to protect the planet's natural ecosystems. Greensphere Capital launched a £150mn nature-based VC fund at the end of last year to invest in UK spinouts that help mitigate climate change and biodiversity loss. A string of other funds are focusing on ocean biodiversity, including the €50mn Katapult Ocean and €200mn Ocean 14 Capital.

The sector remains "innovative and experimental", says Shahbazian. The number of funds on offer has grown rapidly, with global assets held in biodiversity funds and ETFs more than doubling to $3.7bn in the past three years.

Broadly, the funds fall into three categories: solutions-focused; risk-orientated; or a combination of the two.

Solutions-focused funds direct investments to companies working to stem biodiversity loss: for example, through regenerative agriculture, or alternatives to petroleum-based plastics. Riskoriented funds invest in companies that aim to reduce their negative impact on biodiversity, by increasing resource efficiency or shifting supply lines.

"It's very difficult, if not impossible, to invest in companies that restore biodiversity," says Fotis Chatzimichalakis, a portfolio manager at Impax Environmental Markets plc. "But we are definitely investing in companies that stop the loss of biodiversity, which is a massive move in the right direction."

The UK's 2021 Environment Act illustrates how government policy can drive financial innovation. Peter Bachmann, managing director of sustainable infrastructure at Gresham House, set up the Environment Bank to help developers meet a requirement of the law stipulating that they must improve a new construction site's biodiversity by at least 10 per cent.

Developers can buy units of "habitat banks" to meet their obligations off-site. A few thousand acres are under development across England; the aim is to scale to tens of thousands.

"We've created a new infrastructure asset class where we are taking unproductive, non-food grade land and turning it into woodlands, wetlands and grassland where you can see a demonstrable uplift in biodiversity," Bachmann explains. "It's a unique product that taps into the obligations of the act but, ultimately, can still make money. As far as we're aware, we're the only ones that have created an investable product around creating habitat banks at scale to date."

Bachmann, Shahbazian and Chatzimichalakis are unanimous that, for biodiversity funding to grow, government policy is critical — both in reducing negative impacts, such as reforming harmful agricultural subsidies, and in de-risking and encouraging private sector investment.

"Financial sectors are at the stage where they know about it, they want to integrate it, but how to take action is less clear," says Shahbazian. "The recurring message I heard at COP16 was there isn't enough clarity from governments in terms of regulatory signals for the financial community to act at scale."

"There's a bit of a regulation vacuum at the moment when it comes to biodiversity," adds Chatzimichalakis. "We need a clear framework in place so we can all understand what we mean when we say biodiversity-related funding. Now it can mean 10 different things to 10 different people."

Biodiversity finance has risen to $208bn a year from $166bn three years ago, according to research group BloombergNEF. But this still falls far short of the so-called "biodiversity financing gap": an annual $700bn shortfall in funding needed to reverse biodiversity decline by 2030. And it is eclipsed by the $7tn a year still invested in "nature-negative" activities that cause biodiversity loss, according to the UN Environment Programme.

Nevertheless, the opportunity for investors — and for planetary health — is large. As the naturalist and broadcaster David Attenborough argued in a review of the economics of biodiversity: "Bringing economics and ecology together, we can help save the natural world at what may be the last minute."

Source: Jessica Rawnsley (2024) 'Investment sector seeks to put a value on biodiversity', Financial Times, 09 Dec. © The Financial Times Limited 2025. All Rights Reserved.

Like the World Economic Forum research we referenced in Chapter 1, research conducted by S&P Global finds that 85 per cent of the world's largest corporations (the S&P Global 1200) have 'significant' dependency on nature in their direct operations.[vii] While methodologies to arrive at such estimates vary, the numbers are striking and the story they tell is consistent. The European Central Bank has started to report on the way in which nature risks affect the financial sector, emphasising the need for companies to manage these impacts and dependencies.[viii]

In our modern economy, it is all too easy to forget that, without nature, there can be no economic activity. While there are several sectors of the economy directly implicated in biodiversity impact (notably agriculture, construction, extractives, tourism and water), there are many others that are either major customers of those industries (such as fashion, food and beverages, household products, personal products and transportation) or else suppliers of services to them or to their customers (such as banking, insurance and other professional services). Consider the construction industry, which affects biodiversity directly through change in land use, and which draws heavily upon raw materials such as timber, sand, gravel, iron ore and water, and on processed materials such as concrete, steel, glass and plastic. Next, consider how much your company's activities rely upon the use of buildings, bridges and roads provided by the construction sector, or on construction companies as customers or clients. No sector is divorced from nature, however remote it might seem from daily operations.

The potential effects of the degradation of natural systems, especially in interaction with climate change, are many and varied. A central concern is that – especially on a global scale – natural systems are subject to human influence, yet not entirely subject to human control. This is similar to climate change, where we are capable of warming the planet, yet we are currently not capable of either reversing that warming or of understanding the full effects that warming might have. There is therefore obvious merit in an approach that prioritises the conservation of nature, rather than allowing its depletion and then learning from bitter experience where the system's breaking points lie. This is especially important because 'tipping point' effects are common in natural systems. We are already experiencing the gradual melting of the polar ice caps and, by 2040, it is expected that there will be no summer ice at the North Pole.[ix] As the ice cover recedes, and its white surface is replaced by dark ocean, less heat is reflected back into the atmosphere, more heat is therefore absorbed, more greenhouse gases are released from previously permanent capture in tundra regions, there is greater exposure to forest fires in Arctic regions, which releases yet more heat, and so the process continues. Related, a gradual effect of melting ice is to disrupt the flow of ocean currents, with the risk that the Gulf Stream could 'switch off' and thereby dramatically change global weather patterns.[2]

An important concept here is that of 'planetary boundaries', which can be understood as the carrying capacity of the Earth, being the limit of its ongoing ability to provide for human consumption. There are generally understood to be nine planetary boundaries, relating to things like climate change, freshwater use, land conversion, biodiversity loss, and so on. Currently, most of these boundaries are being exceeded, and the excess is getting larger. These are critical, human-induced pressures on the very systems upon which we critically depend. Moreover, if we exceed a planetary boundary, its systemic character means there is a risk that we will accelerate the extent to which we continue to exceed it, and that excess might ultimately cause irreversible collapse. The notion of the 'precautionary principle' is that we should not go close to planetary boundaries because it is too risky to learn what lies beyond, especially in the presence of positive feedback loops. And so planetary boundaries are best understood as bright lines, not to be crossed.

Let's take a look at the nine planetary boundaries:

1 **Stratospheric ozone depletion**. The stratospheric ozone layer in the atmosphere filters out harmful ultraviolet (UV) radiation from the sun. We are within this boundary, following the Montreal Protocol.

2 **Loss of biosphere integrity (biodiversity loss and extinctions)**. The main drivers of change are the demand for food, water and natural resources, causing severe biodiversity loss and leading to changes in ecosystem services. These drivers are either steady, showing no evidence of declining over time, or are increasing in intensity.

3 **Chemical pollution and the release of novel entities**. Emissions of toxic and long-lived substances such as synthetic organic pollutants, heavy metal compounds and radioactive materials have potentially irreversible effects on living organisms and on the physical environment. These are poorly understood scientifically.

---

2 Formally, the Gulf Stream is the Atlantic Meridional Overturning Circulation (APOC).

4 **Climate change.** Concentrations of carbon dioxide in the atmosphere have already exceeded the planetary boundary, triggering several Earth system thresholds and positive feedback effects.

5 **Ocean acidification.** Around a quarter of the CO_2 that humanity emits into the atmosphere is ultimately dissolved in the oceans, increasing acidity and compromising marine species' capacity for shell and skeleton formation. Losses of these species would change the structure and dynamics of ocean ecosystems and could potentially lead to drastic reductions in fish stocks.

6 **Freshwater consumption and the global hydrological cycle.** The freshwater cycle is strongly affected by climate change, yet human pressure is now the dominant driving force determining the functioning and distribution of global freshwater systems. Water is becoming increasingly scarce – by 2050, about half a billion people are likely to be subject to water-stress, increasing the pressure to intervene in water systems.

7 **Land system change.** Forests, grasslands, wetlands and other vegetation types have primarily been converted to agricultural land. This land-use change is one driving force behind the serious reductions in biodiversity, and it has impacts on water flows and on biogeochemical cycling of carbon, nitrogen and phosphorus and other important elements.

8 **Nitrogen and phosphorus flows to the biosphere and oceans.** Biogeochemical cycles of nitrogen and phosphorus have been radically changed by industrial and agricultural processes. A significant fraction of applied nitrogen and phosphorus enters the sea, threatening marine and aquatic systems.

9 **Atmospheric aerosol loading.** Aerosols influence the Earth's climate system, affecting cloud formation, patterns of atmospheric circulation and the rate of absorption of solar radiation. Aerosols also have adverse effects on many living organisms, though these are not well understood.

Natural capital

For our purposes, one way of understanding the resources represented by natural systems is by analogy to financial resources. Just as 'financial capital' can be defined as shareholders' claim on the resources of a company, with shareholders earning a profit (net income) when that capital increases and incurring a loss when it decreases, the current state of nature can also be understood as a stock of capital, which can be either enhanced or depleted. Specifically, we can define 'natural capital' as 'the stock of natural ecosystems on Earth including air, land, soil, biodiversity and geological resources ... (which) underpins our economy and society by producing value for people, both directly and indirectly' (NCC, 2016). A forest forms part of the stock of natural capital and the various ecosystem services it provides comprise its income. These services include carbon capture, species habitat, flood protection, as well as recreational and other benefits, and so on. These ecosystem services can be understood as the flow of benefits from nature for human activity.

Notice the link here to our framing of sustainable business as strong business in strong systems. If the stock of natural capital is maintained, then so too is the recurring stream of benefits that the capital provides. In other words, if the current generation maintains natural capital, then future generations are bequeathed the same capacity to consume. If, on the other hand, natural capital is depleted, the system is weakened or even destroyed. Economic activity is ultimately unsustainable if capital is consumed. We can enjoy the yield from natural resources and ecosystems but, if we deplete the resources themselves, future yields will be lower.

Taking care of a system means not exploiting it beyond its limits. A current example of global significance is the Amazon rainforest, which is currently under threat from corporate activity, primarily from the beef industry. A 2024 analysis[x] in leading science journal *Nature* estimated that between 10 and 47 per cent of Amazon forests will be exposed to tipping points, resulting in what is known as 'Amazon dieback'. Amazon dieback refers to the large-scale degradation and potential collapse of the Amazon rainforest into a more savanna-like ecosystem. Large-scale clearing for agriculture, logging and infrastructure reduce the forest's ability to generate its own rainfall. As a result, trees become weaker, tree cover decreases, and less moisture returns to the atmosphere, leading to drier conditions and accelerating forest loss.

The consequences of Amazon dieback are far-reaching. One major concern is biodiversity loss, as the Amazon is home to an unparalleled number of plant and animal species, many of which are found nowhere else. The Amazon also plays a crucial role in regulating global climate by acting as an enormous carbon sink, absorbing CO_2 from the atmosphere. As dieback occurs, the forest shifts from being a carbon absorber to a carbon emitter, accelerating climate change even further. Because the Amazon influences rainfall patterns in the hemisphere and beyond, Amazon dieback could lead to droughts and agricultural losses affecting millions of people.

As Amazon dieback illustrates, ecosystems often carry with them the risk of reaching a critical, irreversible threshold, beyond which the system collapses – with far-reaching effects. This risk applies to natural capital that is 'renewable' in these sense that it has the capacity to continually supply ecosystem services. Natural capital associated with agriculture is renewable. If we take care of our natural systems, they can feed us indefinitely, as well as providing other essential materials in perpetuity, such as timber for construction or fabric for clothing. In contrast, 'non-renewable' resources include fossil fuels and other minerals. These comprise a finite stock, which can be depleted but not enhanced. In the case of minerals such as aluminium, there is the possibility of recovery and reuse, though, as we mentioned in Chapter 3, recycling rates for even this highly recyclable material are far from 100 per cent. In the case of fossil fuel, however, usage equates to depletion. Once fossil fuels are extracted and burnt, they are gone and cannot be replaced. Even in the absence of concern about global warming, this raises the issue of substitution, being the need to find alternative sources of renewable energy.

Why are natural systems being degraded?

As is the case with global warming, environmental degradation results largely from externalities, in other words, from the unpriced, adverse consequences of economic activity. To see this, consider that many natural resources – the atmosphere, oceans, rivers, forests, wildlife – are either not privately owned or else they are owned in common. They are therefore readily treated as 'freely' available. In the absence of effective quotas, the limit to fishing is as many fish as you can catch. In the absence of regulation (or the absence of enforcement of regulation), rivers and oceans are costless resources; they are public wastebins, for everything from the toxic agrochemicals that seep from farmers' fields to the plastics that we routinely discard.[xi] Privately, these decisions make economic sense because the actor does not bear the cost. Collectively, however, it is critical that there remains abundance in the resources on which economic activity depends. If instead those resources are inexorably depleted, then economic activity is not sustainable.

The new corporate green goal: being 'nature positive'

By Susannah Savage in London

Marco Lambertini holds up his hands and splays his fingers: that is how many companies turned up to previous UN conferences on biodiversity, says the veteran conservationist, with only a flicker of exaggeration.

While big business has flocked to the UN's recent climate summits to talk about decarbonisation, protecting nature has remained the domain of conservationists, philanthropists and other ethically minded types.

This has started to change. About 1,000 businesses and financial institutions went to the last biodiversity summit, COP15, held in Montreal, Canada at the end of 2022, according to Business for Nature, a coalition of businesses and conservation groups. This week record numbers are expected to be at COP16 in Cali, Colombia.

Their expanding presence points to nature's rise up the corporate agenda. From agribusinesses to asset managers, companies around the world are increasingly touting their ambitions to be "nature positive" alongside their net zero targets.

At its core, nature positive means halting and reversing biodiversity loss, targeting an overall increase in nature — trees, species, ecosystems — by 2030, relative to a 2020 baseline.

"Recognising the value of peatlands, forest, ocean, their capacity to regulate the climate, and not only to store carbon, is really important," says Laurence Tubiana, chief executive of the European Climate Foundation and an architect of the 2015 Paris climate accord.

Global wildlife populations have shrunk by an average of nearly 75 per cent over the past 50 years, according to a report published this month by the World Wildlife Fund. The UN estimates that nearly 1mn animal and plant species are in danger of extinction.

While the Earth's rising temperature is one of the biggest drivers of biodiversity loss, the destruction of the natural world is in turn catastrophic for climate change. In 2023 — the hottest year on record — forests, plants and soil absorbed almost no carbon dioxide in net terms as drought and wildfires depleted these natural carbon sinks, according to the preliminary findings of a study led by French research organisation, the Laboratory for Climate and Environmental Sciences.

"Until now, nature has buffered climate change massively," explains Lambertini, a former directorgeneral of the WWF who today heads the Nature Positive Initiative. "More than 50 per cent of the CO_2 emissions of anthropogenic nature have been neutralised by forests, wetlands and the ocean. Now, as all that is weakening . . . it's failing, and that is exacerbating climate change with it." Nature positive is "a goal", he adds, "not a slogan".

For some, however, the distinction may not be clear. Scientists and environmental groups worry that companies and governments are starting to brandish the term as a buzzword, before the definitions and metrics needed to ensure accountability have been put in place and without having grasped the scale of the work required. For example, you can now make 'nature positive' investments, book a 'nature positive' holiday, and buy a 'nature positive' coffee.

Biodiversity-linked claims are more challenging to substantiate than those around climate, warns Michael Wironen of global non-profit the Nature Conservancy. While greenhouse gases are fungible and emissions can be tallied in neat units, nature is far messier, he explains. "I think when it comes to really establishing credible definitions and metrics around nature positive, there's still a lot of work to be done," he says.

Previous biodiversity targets for businesses fell flat and nature positive is an even "more ambitious goal", says Professor Martine Maron from Australia's University of Queensland. Yet "everybody is jumping on the new bandwagon," she adds. "There is a risk that they're going to discover that delivering that is a lot harder than they realise."

Nature positive's advocates respond that metrics and governance are on the way. A global biodiversity framework adopted by 196 countries at COP_{15} provides the means to achieve nature positive, they say. For the first time, it included specific targets that made it clear that businesses must play a role in reversing nature loss, says Eva Zabey of Business for Nature.

But two years on, many of the details around how governments and companies should go about implementing the targets set out in Montreal still need to be thrashed out.

On a global scale, it is clear what the nature positive goal means, says Jenn-Hui Tan, chief sustainability officer at Fidelity International. "The challenge is, when you take that big aspiration, what does that mean, operationally, at either an individual or organisational level? That's where the complexity comes in."

The impact of the decline of carbon sinks has served as a wake-up call about the "synergies between nature and climate", says Lambertini.

Climate scientists have acknowledged that the failure to factor this in to their models is why the scale of climate change has been worse than many predicted.

The message is increasingly sinking in for the corporate world too, says Wironen of the Nature Conservancy, as the financial risks tied to biodiversity loss are becoming clearer. The World Economic Forum estimated in a 2020 report that more than half of global GDP at the time, or about $44tn, was "moderately" or "highly" dependent on nature.

"We rely on nature ecosystems to provide us with the things that run our society, whether that's food, fuel or fibre," says Wironen. "It's fisheries, it's medicines, it's a whole slew of things that we depend on nature for."

Companies in agriculture, forestry and other land-based sectors are already feeling the impact of degraded ecosystems, from declining crop yields to supply chain disruptions, says Paul McMahon of SLM Partners, a global asset manager that buys farmland and implements regenerative practices to improve soil quality. "Businesses are realising that protecting nature is not just a moral obligation, it's a strategic necessity."

For Olam Food Ingredients, one of the world's biggest suppliers of food and drink ingredients, the alarm rang with the bees.

As one of the world's largest almond growers, OFI says it spends between $8mn and $11mn a year on honeybees needed to pollinate almond trees. Despite this, productivity on the farms started to decline "because the bees were stressed by their industrialised environment", says Rishi Kalra, executive director and group chief financial officer. "So, we worked with partners to create natural habitats for bees on our farms and reduce their exposure to agrichemicals. What we saw was that productivity steadily increased."

Now OFI — whose parent company Olam had previously come under criticism for clearing rainforest in Gabon for palm oil production — has plans to convert 2mn hectares of land within its supply chains to regenerative agriculture by 2030.

"We know the importance of building a nature-positive economy," says Kalra. "If we don't focus on nature, the business that we operate may not even exist in years to come."

As the capital value of the natural world rises, investors are taking note. From pension funds to insurance firms, many are recognising the financial risks posed by nature loss and seeking ways to align their portfolios with nature-positive outcomes.

Environmental, social and governance investing has evolved, according to Fidelity's Tan, as the systemic risks related to nature become more apparent.

"These are longer-term system risks that affect everybody, not just any individual sector or company," he says. "You have to think about how could nature impacts or dependencies affect a company's business, and what, if anything, is a company doing?"

In January, members of investor network Fairr representing a combined assets under management of $51tn said that biodiversity was the second most important theme after climate, in the network's annual survey. "Biodiversity and nature" was also the top response to the question: "Are you focusing on any new ESG theme this year?"

There are even emerging investment vehicles specifically targeting biodiversity. ASN Bank in the Netherlands launched a biodiversity fund, which aims to deliver financial returns while directly investing in nature-positive projects.

Such funds are still rare but represent a growing trend as investors come to believe that aligning portfolios with environmental outcomes can generate value — not just risk mitigation but tangible financial returns.

Nature positive may be infiltrating corporate sustainability strategy documents around the world, but Queensland University's Maron argues there is an "urgent need" for safeguards and guidance around some of the claims being made.

Part of the problem is the term itself. While Lambertini and the Nature Positive Initiative have come up with a strict definition, in practice there is nothing to enforce it, leaving companies and other institutions free to use their own.

"There is this concern that people just assume that, 'I do my net zero and I do it in a way that's sort of nice for nature, might use nature-based solutions, but I'm not actually really monitoring the absolute change in biodiversity'," says Professor EJ Milner-Gulland from the University of Oxford. "That's not nature positive. That's just, using some nature-based solutions."

Maron gives the Australian government's planned reforms of national conservation — which she welcomes — as an example. "They developed this pathway of reforms called the nature positive plan and they're introducing nature positive bills . . . The problem is what sits underneath this so far does not look nature positive at all."

The frameworks aim to ensure that any loss in biodiversity from development is offset by conservation efforts elsewhere, often using a dynamic counterfactual of what would have happened in the absence of the business's activity. So, if the koala population, for example, was declining anyway, additional decline caused by the company's or government's activity would be offset, but the overall decline could continue.

The plans would be better characterised, she says, as "biodiversity no net loss" or "net gain". "Just because they're using the term doesn't make it nature positive."

"Having a target is very different from having a credible plan with sufficient investment to actually achieve it," echoes Wironen. "We see companies set ambitious goals that might depend on technological breakthroughs or external factors, but without robust infrastructure and realistic investment, these commitments risk being superficial."

It is also intrinsically harder to define and measure progress on nature and biodiversity than on climate, adds Wironen. "Mitigating a tonne [of greenhouse gases] in Pakistan has the same effect as mitigating a tonne in London as it does in Argentina. With nature and biodiversity, it's inherently non-fungible. The species you have in Argentina are different from the ones you have in Pakistan, as are the ones you have in London, and the ways in which an organisation impacts them, or a corporate impacts them, are much more complicated than really a simple question of emissions."

This lack of a global standard for measuring biodiversity means that companies could, intentionally or otherwise, manipulate data to present themselves as nature positive without making substantial changes.

"There is no one global metric [for] diversity so you need to have this trade off between usability and accuracy, and that trade off is really difficult because there's a lot of data limitation," says Milner-Gulland.

"Whenever we measure biodiversity, what we're doing is measuring a proxy or component or something we're particularly interested in, or something that's easy to measure, or we're using some kind of metric that doesn't really reflect the underlying biodiversity that's there."

This creates "room for greenwashing", she says. "There's lots and lots of loopholes that you can exploit by choosing your metric appropriately or inappropriately."

For many advocates of nature positive, though, the worries around greenwashing miss the broader potential of the initiative.

"What's bigger, the risk of greenwashing or the risk of a failed transition?" asks Fidelity's Tan. He and others argue that clearer frameworks and better governance will soon help bridge the gap between ambition and action.

"Right now, the corporate says, 'I do a certain thing. Well, that's very great. We're very happy with that.' But how does that contribute to a broader objective of nature positive? No corporate can answer that question by themselves," says Tan.

He hopes COP16 will provide a greater level of policy certainty, with governments due to put forward their national biodiversity strategy and action plans in Colombia. These will "provide the baseline against which you can measure corporate progress", he says.

Rather than companies seeking to take advantage of vagueness, "there's a yearning for clarity and specificity", says Joshua Katz from McKinsey.

Some 130 businesses called on governments to enact tougher policies to reverse and halt nature loss in a letter organised by Business for Nature in July.

More than 300 companies, from food retail giant Carrefour to pharmaceutical powerhouse GSK, have also signed up as early adopters of the Taskforce on Nature-related Financial Disclosures, which aims to create a standardised system for companies to assess and report their biodiversity risks, much like existing frameworks do for carbon emissions.

This involves four main steps: assessing how their activities rely on and affect natural ecosystems, setting standardised metrics to track these impacts, transparently disclosing risks and strategies, and integrating this information into broader business decisions. For example, a beverage company might need to report how its water use affects local supplies, which would help investors understand potential environmental risks.

The Taskforce on Nature-related Financial Disclosures is a voluntary initiative, but Wironen from the Nature Conservancy sees the approach as a step in the right direction.

"If TNFD follows the same path as the climate-focused [disclosures], which moved from voluntary guidelines to becoming part of various regulatory frameworks, we could see a major shift in how companies address and disclose their environmental impacts. That would be a real sea change."

"Nature targets are more complex . . . but they're not unachievable," says Tan. The Science Based Target Network is proving exactly this, he adds, referring to the 17 companies, including GSK, Nestlé as well as LVMH and H&M, which signed up for the first scientific targets for nature last year.

The problem may not be a lack of metrics but a surfeit of them, says Lambertini. "The climate community did a super important thing: straight after Paris, they developed a net zero pathway, and then they attached a global standardised way to measure emissions," he says.

"Now, we need to do the same for nature. One won't work because nature is more complex, but the 600 different methods that we have today are too many and confuse everybody. So we're going to try to condense those into a small set of good enough — scientifically and practically speaking — proxies called the state of nature."

With this, Lambertini hopes to eliminate or reduce the risk of greenwashing. "We need to put some order in this area of claims and contributions," he says. "Companies say they are contributing to conservation, but it's not enough. What we need is for contributions to match the scale of the problem."

Source: Susannah Savage (2024) 'The new corporate green goal: being 'nature positive'', Financial Times, 21 Oct. © The Financial Times Limited 2025. All Rights Reserved.

A critical reason for this natural capital depletion is known as the 'tragedy of the commons'. To illustrate, suppose that there is no restriction on the harvesting of trees in tropical rainforests. If someone (perhaps for a fee) takes the time and trouble to access the trees, fell them and transport them to market, they benefit privately from the income that tropical hardwoods can bring. Yet such trees grow slowly. They can be harvested but, if the depletion exceeds the natural rate of growth, the harvest is taken out of capital, not just out of income. There are fewer trees left. And, as the natural capital diminishes, so too does its capacity to provide a flow of benefits. If everyone could agree to restrict the felling of trees to within a sustainable yield, then all is well.[3] But that might be a difficult line

---

3   The classic analysis of whether such agreement is feasible is Ostrom, E. (1990) *Governing the Commons*. Cambridge: Cambridge University Press.

to hold because the private gain to any individual who fells a tree will be high, while the effect of the loss of natural capital will be shared across the community as a whole, making the private incentive to realise the gain stronger than that to remedy the loss. The problem is made worse because each person knows that every other person benefits privately from over-felling, and also that the quickest to over-fell will gain the most.

A tragedy of the commons arises in cases of what economists describe as common pool resources, where the resources are available to be used by anyone (i.e. their use is 'non-excludable') but where use reduces the availability of resources for everyone else (i.e. the consumption of resources is 'rival'). The over-consumption, and hence depletion, of common pool resources is a tragedy because the 'rational' pursuit of individual self-interest leads to collective ruin.[4] The problem is actually worse still. A forest is not just a source of timber. As the discussion of Amazon dieback demonstrates, it also provides other ecosystem services, not least carbon capture, the benefits from which are shared globally. Nobody can be excluded from those benefits and neither does the benefit to one person diminish that to another; such services are therefore what is known as a 'public good'. When the trees are felled, the value of the timber is captured in the market price of exchange. Yet the value of ecosystem services simultaneously disappears. This loss of a public good is a cost to society that the market price does not capture, making the private cost-benefit calculation different from that at the system level.[5] Moreover, there is no private economic incentive to plant the forest anew and make good the depletion. This is because nobody can be excluded from consuming public goods, meaning that there is no market-based method of securing payment for their provision; if individuals cannot be prevented from enjoying the services provided, why would they pay for them? The public good is simply lost.

Unfortunately, examples of tragedies of the commons are, well, common in practice. The Ogallala Aquifer supplies water to nearly 50 per cent of irrigated farmland in the Great Plains of the United States. For decades, it has been systematically drained at a rate faster than it is replenished. The Proceedings of the National Academy of Sciences estimate that the aquifer will be

---

4 The classic analysis of the tragedy of the commons is Hardin (1968).
5 Carbon emissions can also be interpreted as the supply of a 'public bad', as a cost from which nobody can be excluded and where the detriment to one person does not preclude detriment to any other.

70 per cent depleted within 50 years. Air quality in many major global cities, and water quality in many rivers, are further examples. In short, there is 'market failure' arising from the consumption of common pool resources, meaning that the optimal allocation of economic resource is not achieved by market mechanisms alone. The underlying problem is that current, private incentives and capacities to consume are such that natural capital is relentlessly depleted, leaving reduced resources available to future generations. A troubling reality is that more and more of the natural world is falling into this category and, so, becoming vulnerable to this problem, primarily as a consequence of increasing rivalry.

Figure 4.2 illustrates the extent to which global growth in 'produced capital' has come at the expense of depletion of natural capital. The chart is striking because of the rate of annual depletion, amounting to an overall loss of around 25 per cent over a period of just 20 years (barely a blink in the eye of geological time). Moreover, the trend is clear and – however disturbing in itself – the trend understates the problem because it implies a linear capacity of the system to absorb further decline, as opposed to the more likely scenario that further decline triggers tipping points of accelerating collapse in natural systems.

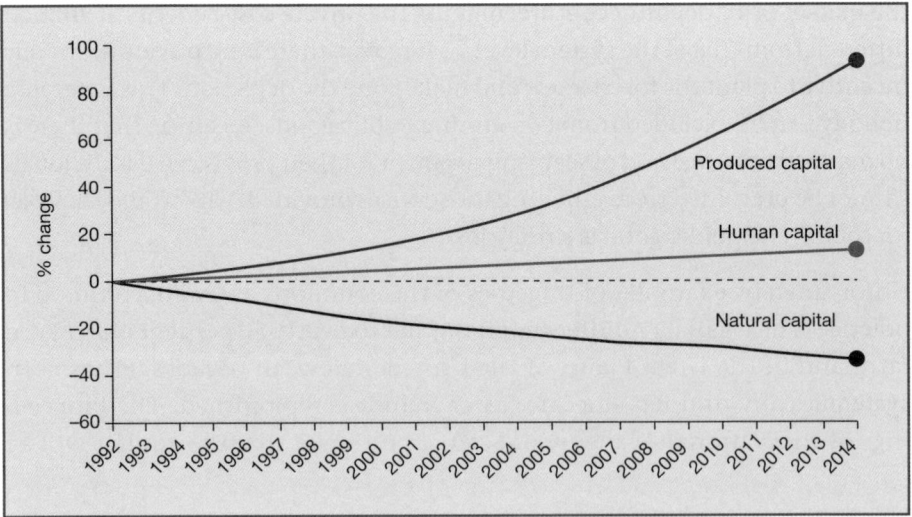

Figure 4.2 Global changes in produced, human and natural capital per capita, 1992–2014.

Source: Dasgupta 2021.

To put this into context, we will build on the historical experience of GHG emissions to illustrate the challenge faced by natural systems. In the relatively early stages of the Industrial Revolution, around the year 1800, the global population was 1 billion. By 1960, that had increased three times to 3 billion. By 2000, that had doubled, to 6 billion. We are now at 8 billion, heading towards 10 billion. Earth's human population is now 1,000 per cent the level of 200 years ago. Meanwhile, the standard of living, and therefore the amount of consumption, has been rising at about the same rate. To illustrate the effect, picture the earliest factories, which burned through coal and polluted horribly, but on a scale that had no appreciable impact on global warming. And now picture how much our capacity to pollute has accelerated. To the earliest industrialists, a temperate climate was a public good; nobody could be excluded from releasing carbon into the atmosphere and also nobody was materially affected by what anybody else did. The latter is no longer the case and, as the reality of rivalry has broadened, so too the scope of pollution has changed. While non-excludability remains prevalent, the atmosphere is nearing its carrying capacity and so it is playing out its own tragedy of the commons. The current generation is still flying in fossil-fuel powered planes, constructing with steel and concrete, eating a carbon intensive diet, and using energy generated by burning fossil fuels; private incentives are being realised in the present at a cost to be carried in the future.[xii]

The key here is that what has happened with GHG emissions is paralleled by what is happening with natural resource use. Just as we have outgrown the capacity of the atmosphere to absorb carbon dioxide, our use of natural resources has outstripped the capacity of natural systems to sustain corporate activity in its current form. This story of natural capital depletion applies across oceans, river systems, forests and biodiversity, as Figure 4.2 illustrate. A specific example, of increasing importance, is the degradation of soil quality, caused by factors including monoculture, chemical fertiliser and climate change. While easily taken for granted, soil is immensely important, being the source of 95 per cent of global food supplies, while also acting as a major carbon sink. While soil forms very slowly, the WWF estimates that (for example in the UK) it is being destroyed ten times faster than it is being created.[xiii] At first sight, this is a private matter, because the economic effect of the declining yield will be felt by the private landowner directly. Yet that land will, in due course, be owned by future generations and, while land has always been understood as an infinite source of renewable crops, its degradation gives it the character of rivalry; its overconsumption now comes at the expense of future generations.

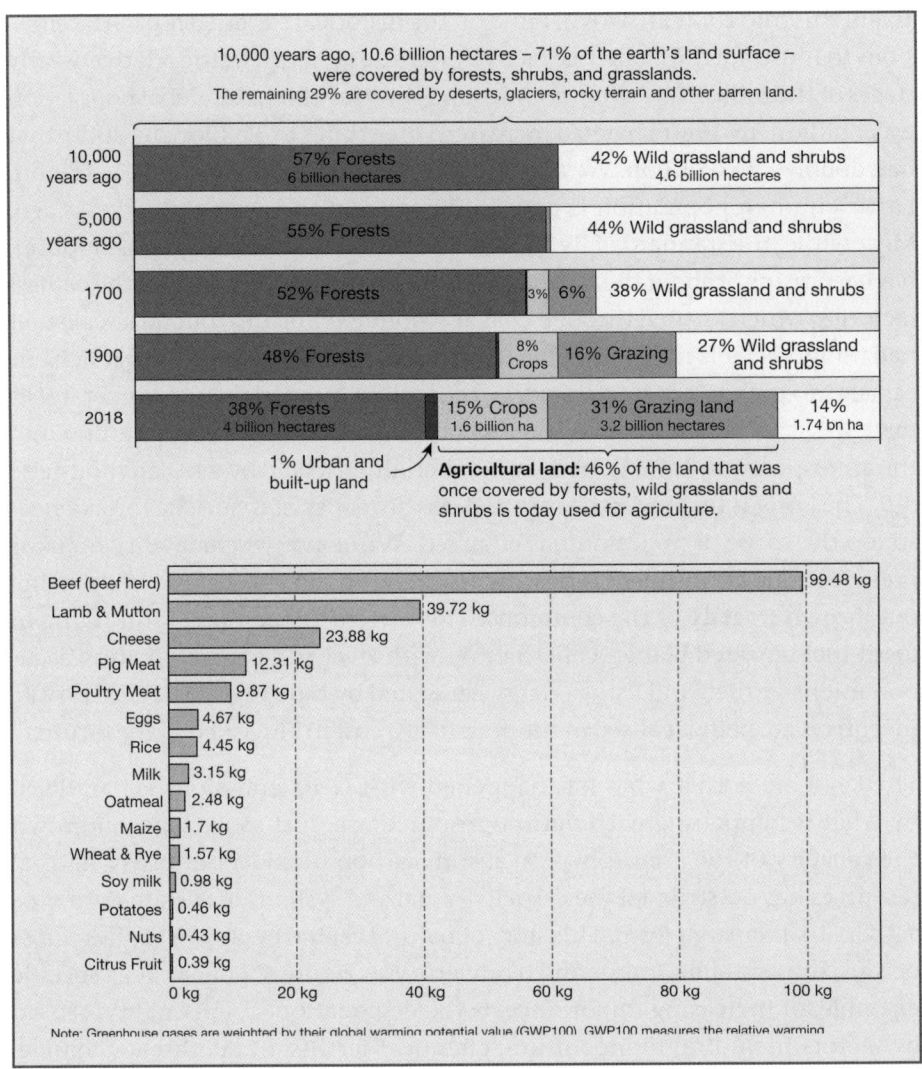

Figures 4.3 and 4.4 Environmental impact of different food sources

Source: All data from OurWorldinData.org.

A particularly important transition has therefore been taking place, from ecosystem services that were once public goods but that increasingly should be understood as common pool resources. In other words, rivalry in consumption is a much more profound concern than ever it was. We are discovering the finite capacity of what could previously be considered, in effect, unlimited. And while the tragedy of the commons is often illustrated with local examples the reality now is global. This is why the term 'anthropocene' is used to described our current age as one of unprecedented human-caused change in our atmosphere, land use and biodiversity. Natural capital depletion has become global in scale and thereby increasingly consequential for human society in its entirety. In this regard, it is very similar to climate change.

The scale of loss of our impact on the natural world – historical and prospective – is staggering. With his characteristic eloquence and poignancy, natural historian and broadcaster David Attenborough summarises the problem as follows.[xiv]

> *Today, we ourselves, together with the livestock we rear for food, constitute 96% of the mass of all mammals on the planet. Only 4% is everything else – from elephants to badgers, moose to monkeys. And 70% of all birds alive at this moment are poultry – mostly chickens for us to eat. We are destroying biodiversity, the very characteristic that until recently enabled the natural world to flourish so abundantly. If we continue this damage, whole ecosystems will collapse. That is now a real risk.*

Half of the world's habitable land is used for agriculture.[xv] Particularly striking is that more than three-quarters of this land is used (directly or via animal feed) for livestock production, a staggering inefficiency, given that meat and dairy contribute a relatively small percentage of the world's protein and calorie supply, while, in some cases, having as much as two hundred times the greenhouse gas emissions of plant-based alternatives (see Figure 4.4).[xvi] Freshwater is increasingly scarce globally and yet dairy milk continues to be consumed, even though its production requires 600 litres more freshwater per litre of milk than a soy-based alternative (see Figure 4.5). Human-induced climate change is acting in tandem with changes in land use to create risk to environmental systems and the social systems – and businesses – that rely on them.[xvii]

The role of business

Business has been both an enabler and a beneficiary of economic growth and so too, therefore, of attendant depletion of natural systems. Moreover, corporations are not just passive suppliers of human needs but also active agents in creating 'need' in the first place. This aspect of corporate contributions to emissions has received increasing attention due to rising awareness of the concept of 'advertised emissions', which is the increase in GHG emissions resulting from consumption attributable to advertising and marketing activities.[xix] While its reception by

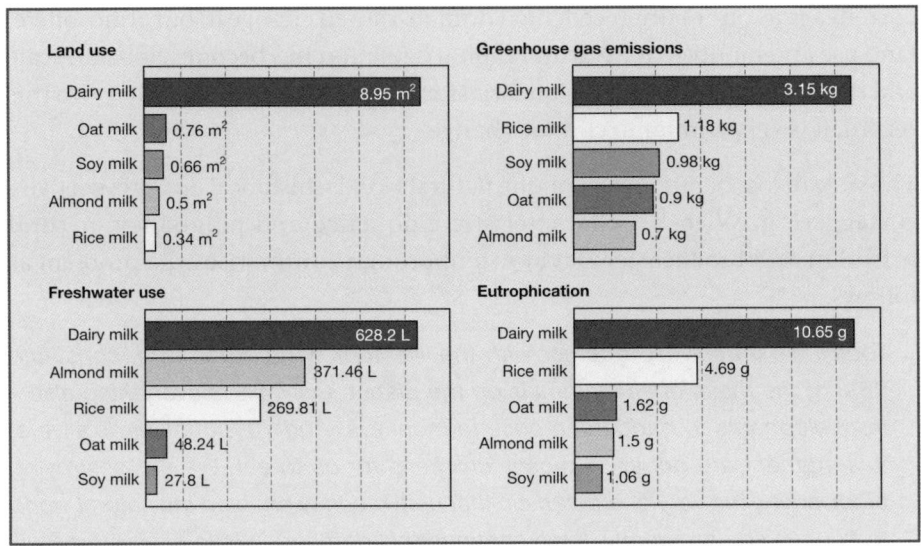

Figures 4.5 Environmental footprints of dairy and plant-based milks[xviii]
Source: All data from OurWorldinData.org.

advertising industry bodies has been far from enthusiastic,[xx] and the problem of precise attribution of specific emissions to particular activities is indeed a knotty one, the concept raises important questions for sustainability leaders to consider. Writ large, it is difficult to make the case that the rate of growth of consumption has not been fuelled by corporate incentive. Recalling Chapter 2, the point here is not that corporations are, in some sense, behaving badly; they are not, and neither are their leaders. They are instead doing what they are designed and incentivised to do. The need is to change those incentives.

To take a simple example, consider that, in many countries, thirst can be quenched by drinking water from a tap. Yet in those same nations – ours, the UK, as an example – take a look at the supermarket shelf. The choice and variety of drinks is remarkable. Each has its own niche, its own brand, its own premium price, each appealing to a particular consumer segment. Next, consider how much space is taken up by bottled water and multiply this by all of the points of purchase on the planet; corner shops, hypermarkets, market stalls and traffic-light vendors to name but a few. Imagine how much fossil fuel is burned in heating, cooling or lighting all of this space, in transporting all of that water from its source and in creating the packaging in which it sits. Imagine what happens to all of that plastic once the water has been consumed. (In fact, we do not need to imagine: the OECD has calculated that about 9 per cent of plastic is currently recycled, the rest incinerated, placed in landfill or disposed of in an 'uncontrolled' manner', including being burned in open pits or dumped directly onto land or water. Should current trends hold, the same research estimates the recycling rate will rise to just 17 per cent by 2060).[xxi]

Now ask whether the cost of any of these externalities is clearly available to you at the point of purchase. Several innovative retailers including the Dutch supermarket Albert Heijn[xxii] and the athletic brand Allbirds[xxiii] have trialled efforts at such an approach. However, for the vast majority of purchases, the answer is, 'highly unlikely'. If a multibuy pricing mechanism is applied to any of those bottles of water (such as 'buy 2 get 3') then you are being encouraged not just to buy more but also to waste more. To the extent that waste is not a cost that the company has to bear, its profits are higher than they would otherwise be. If it failed to exploit this opportunity, then its competitors would take its place. Current incentive regimes mean markets can fail on a globally consequential scale.

Why should companies care?

When markets 'fail', in the ways described above, the economist's classic solution is government intervention. In the case of the tropical rainforest, this might be done by means of payment for the ecosystem services that the forest provides. Governments around the world could make payments to the host country, in exchange for conserving the forest. This would be beneficial to the global economy, yet it would also be very challenging to implement, both politically and practically. In such a situation, the economist's 'solution' to market failure is therefore often itself a failure, as we discussed in Chapter 2.

In addition, even for current stakeholders, governments cannot always provide adequate protection of private property rights, either because these are not established in law, or else because there is no practical way to make use of any laws that do exist. For example, the general 'polluter pays' principle can be hard to enforce. Suppose that your company has private property rights over a plantation. But then suppose that some form of atmospheric pollution causes damage to that plantation, affecting growth, quality and thereby also value. What if your company doesn't know where the pollution is coming from? Or that you do know, but that the origin is a major industrial zone or (worse) an entire geographic region, against which you have no realistic hope of enforcing legal action? Either way, the polluter is not made to pay.

In general, the costs of defining, policing and enforcing property rights might be such that, in effect, those rights have little economic substance.[6] These practical limitations of government are part of the context in which corporations must operate, with respect to both impact and dependency. They create challenges for corporate decision making that would not exist in the economist's 'ideal' world but that do exist in the reality with which business leaders must contend.

While corporate impact on nature has not yet captured the public imagination at the same level as corporate contribution to climate change, this is changing quickly.[xxiv] Though separated by several years, there are parallels between the 2015 Paris Agreement on climate and the later agreement reached in Montreal in 2022 at the UN Convention on Biological Diversity; both agreements signal tighter social expectations on corporate impact.[xxv] This will manifest in several ways, including: increasing investor and lender demand for higher standards of environmental performance; changing consumer behaviour; court cases against directors, for example because of failure in the duty to act in the best interests of the company by not embedding nature-related risks in decision making; greater supply-chain transparency, along with increased due diligence legislation (for example on sustainable product sourcing); and even legal recognition of the rights of nature, making court cases easier to bring.[7]

For corporations embedded in, impacting and dependent upon natural systems, these asks are too big to be addressed by a 'business as usual' approach. The need is for a fundamental rethink. It is hard to overstate the scale of the change that is needed. As a business leader, you have the extraordinary opportunity and the challenge to redefine the relationship between the corporation and natural resources. A reflection to drive home this point: consider, for a moment, the staggering levels of innovation corporations have generated since the Industrial Revolution. In this context, is it not striking that our conception of economic activity and consumption has changed little since the eighteenth and nineteenth centuries, when we first realised how to harness at scale the resources of nature? Astonishingly,

---

6   The role of transactions costs in this context is the critical insight of the Nobel Prize-winning economist Ronald Coase (1960). He identified that the problem of externalities would 'solve itself' if all parties concerned could negotiate, at zero cost, with one another.

7   For an expanded discussion, see CCLI (2023).

the linear economic model persists. Braungart and McDonough (2009) offer an evocative illustration of this point:

> *Imagine what you would come upon today at a typical landfill: old furniture, upholstery, carpets, televisions, clothing, shoes, telephones, computers, complex products, and plastic packaging, as well as organic materials like diapers, paper, wood, and food wastes. Most of these products were made from valuable materials that required effort and expense to extract and make, billions of dollars' worth of material assets. The biodegradable materials such as food matter and paper actually have value too – they could decompose and return biological nutrients to the soil. Unfortunately, all of these things are heaped in a landfill, where their value is wasted. They are the ultimate products of an industrial system that is designed on a linear, one-way 'cradle-to-grave' model.*

As we have already emphasised, the linear economy can be understood in terms of a traditional industrial manufacturing model, based upon the four stages of take, make, use and lose.[xxvi] The level of waste in a linear economy is itself unsustainable. A 'circular economy' is instead one in which there is zero waste, and where economic growth does not breach planetary boundaries. A 'regenerative economy' goes further still, extending beyond 'do no harm' and seeking instead environmental gain (alongside financial gain). This is aligned with processes found in nature itself, which has an inherently circular economy. There is no waste in nature, no landfill. Nature takes its organic material and decomposes it. Nutrients that are a part of that material are recycled in substance and continuously reused. In this way, nature offers a powerful frame for innovation, a mechanism to develop corporate value propositions that are robust, holistic, and elegant.[xxvii] Leaders who create the culture, structure and resource for this kind of innovation are poised to create value for their companies and industries as they build strong businesses in strong natural and social systems.

The challenge for you as a business leader is significant but can be stated simply. How do we move from a linear economy to a more circular or regenerative economy? In the next sections, we consider how you can lead your company in this journey.

Re-framing business and nature

Think of the problem as identifying waste. Companies either create waste by having an impact upon natural systems or else they depend upon resources that are being wasted, or both. With respect to impact, the question is whether the company is creating waste, in the sense of converting something useful into something useless. Whether or not such impacts have immediate economic consequences for corporations will depend in part upon whether the costs become internalised in some way, for example as a result of environmental legislation, consumer demand or investor pressure. If there is even just a risk that this might happen, then the company has an incentive to pay attention to its impacts, because a resilient business, in which risks are managed effectively, is more valuable than one that is inherently more vulnerable to external change. Yet the economic consequence need not result from potentially internalised cost. It could also arise from economic opportunity; it is here that new thinking can generate the greatest payoff.

The economic rationale for there being opportunity is simple. It is that no system benefits from waste and, in principle, there must therefore be benefit in seeking its elimination. We have seen already that market failure is, by definition, synonymous with economic inefficiency. The corollary is that correcting that failure is synonymous with economic gain.

Consider your own consumption decisions. Would you prefer to live in an energy-efficient home or, instead, one that (at your expense) allows heat to escape when it is cold outside or that cannot be cooled efficiently when it is warm? When you replace an item of electrical equipment, an old bike, or maybe a carpet or a mattress, would you prefer to have to dispose of such things yourself, expecting them to end up in landfill, or would you prefer that someone can find value in them, not just collecting them from your house but perhaps also paying for them? When you buy detergent, do you need or want plastic packaging that is so durable that it will last many years longer than its contents? The central theme here is that, as a consumer, you do not benefit from waste and you would prefer a system in which, ultimately, you are not paying for it.

Regenerative agriculture sparks venture capital interest

By Freya Pratty

Regenerative agriculture is based on the idea that, as well as producing food, farming should also benefit the land's biodiversity, and its water and soil quality.

Definitions differ, but practices typically involve minimising ploughing to reduce disturbance to the soil, and annually rotating the types of crops planted on the same site to increase the diversity of nutrients and minimise pests. However, unlike organic farming, regenerative agriculture permits the limited use of artificial fertilisers and pesticides.

"It's a different way of thinking about the land," says Mark Durno, agri-food managing partner at venture capital group Rockstart — and a former farmer. "It's about thinking of it as something that's alive, rather than as a blank canvas."

Now, the phrase "regenerative agriculture" is firmly cemented in corporate parlance, too — cropping up in the sustainability plans of big food companies such as Nestlé, Unilever and Danone.

Off the back of this rising interest, there are also a growing number of tech start-ups building regenerative agriculture tools — and investors are increasingly willing to channel money to them. Between 2021 and 2023, VC funds poured $1.4bn into regenerative agriculture start-ups, according to data provider Dealroom — a 46 per cent increase on the three years prior.

But does tech have a role to play in a movement that is, at its heart, low-tech — or at least sceptical about high-tech intensive agriculture?

One of the main areas where tech companies are active is the development of digital tools to issue carbon credits to farmers. Regenerative agriculture can, in theory, increase the amount of carbon sequestered in the soil, enabling farmers to then earn carbon credits.

The voluntary carbon credit market — where companies aim to offset their emissions by funding schemes that draw down carbon — is currently worth about $2bn but could exceed $250bn by 2050, according to research by Morgan Stanley.

Danish company Agreena is one of the start-ups now working on tools to monitor the amount of carbon sequestered and issues carbon credits. Its chief executive, Simon Haldrup, says that technology's role is to provide the infrastructure that makes regenerative agriculture financially viable.

"The whole foundation of regenerative agriculture is super low-tech," he says. "Then, there are the layers downstream, the monitoring and verification. That is all about technology and data because it's a financial infrastructure that's being built."

Although Agreena has received VC funding, Haldrup says that companies such as his "don't play well with the general playbooks of most VCs". Regenerative agriculture businesses have longer time horizons than the software companies that VCs typically invest in, Haldrup says — making it hard for exit-focused investors to back the businesses.

But, beyond carbon credits, investors also cite opportunities in the tools that help farmers work out which techniques will work best on their land.

"If you're a farmer and you're going to transition to regenerative agriculture, the biggest barrier is knowledge and understanding best practices," explains Durno. "We look towards things like generative AI [artificial intelligence] as an interface for farmers to get simpler agronomy advice."

Leslie Kapin, director of impact for VC company Astanor Ventures, says start-ups working on biobased alternatives to conventional synthetic fertilisers, pesticides and herbicides can also fall within the regenerative agriculture bucket.

Fertiliser is a multi-billion-dollar industry, and finding alternatives could make for a lucrative opportunity. New technologies can also allow farmers to spray existing fertilisers and pesticides more precisely, thereby reducing the amount used.

Ken Giller, emeritus professor of plant production systems at the University of Wageningen in the Netherlands, says that, while scientists are divided on the legitimacy of soil-based carbon credits — in part because of difficulties in quantifying the amount of additional carbon sequestered — he is most convinced by technologies such as green ammonia.

A key fertiliser ingredient, ammonia is often derived from fossil fuels through a carbon-intensive process. However, so-called green ammonia has a much smaller carbon footprint.

For Giller, a central problem with investors piling into regenerative agriculture is that, at its heart, the practices do not deliver increased profit margins — a dynamic that no amount of technology can solve. "You can design a perfect crop rotation system which would help to build more soil organic matter," he says, "but that might actually mean leaving out some of the more lucrative crops."

He also cautions that the surge in popularity of regenerative agriculture may be for the wrong reasons. "Regenerative agriculture is a branding that people find very attractive," he says, warning that companies' interest in the term needs to be "verifiable and measurable," rather than a marketing exercise.

Yet investors are bullish about both the ecological impact and financial returns that regenerative agriculture tools can bring. Kapin argues that incoming regulation and sustainability targets will make the sector still more appealing, with the EU's Green Deal, in particular, targeting greater biodiversity and healthier soils. "That's the reason why we invest: because of the sizeable market we're seeing," she says.

Source: Freya Pratty (2024) 'Regenerative agriculture sparks venture capital interest', Financial Times, 25 Jan. © The Financial Times Limited 2025. All Rights Reserved.

And now view these issues from a corporate perspective. The point is that, if consumer preference is not being met, profitable opportunity is being left unrealised. That opportunity might not be immediately obvious. If it were, it would likely be standard market practice already. What matters here is to recognise the potential value from disruptive innovation. Existing market behaviours, norms and institutions become accepted, locked in, unchallenged. They survive because they are 'the way things are done'.

This can calcify momentous inefficiencies: a report by economic consultancy Dalberg found that, across the lifecycle, plastic is responsible for generating an annual 1.8 billion tonnes of greenhouse gas emissions (GHG) a year – more than aviation and shipping combined – at an annual cost to society, the environment and the economy of US $3.7 trillion.[xxviii] Competitive advantage comes from thinking differently, from disrupting the norm. Suppose that a business seeks to implement a 'sustainability agenda' such that it uses fewer natural resources per unit of output in its operations, increasing margins while also reducing environmental impacts. While laudable, what actually is the efficiency gain? Natural resources are still being depleted. The company is now creating waste more slowly, but it is still creating waste, still operating under an extractive, linear model. Worse, if volume increases offset the per-unit efficiencies, then absolute waste might actually be increasing, even while eco-efficiency claims are being made. For you as a leader, the invitation is to enter a space that is more innovative, engaging and inspiring – the adaptive, creative, leadership we put forth in this book.[xxix] For natural systems, the first step is framing. Ask yourself and your team: where is my business creating waste?

Take the example of the car industry, which has long created waste in the form of carbon and other emissions, for which it does not have to pay. The industry has achieved considerable eco-efficiency gains over time, with cars of a given size burning ever less fuel per mile. Yet these gains are readily lost. The average size of a car has grown, increasing fuel consumption. Greater production efficiencies have lowered costs and so too (in a competitive market) prices, leading to more cars being sold, and more fuel being burned. What the established industry did not do was change its fundamentally linear model, which relied upon converting fossil fuel into waste. In contrast, electric vehicles (EVs) represent a market opportunity by means of reducing that waste. Gradually, and albeit at different rates in different places and points in time, EVs are becoming the new norm, the new 'the way things are done'. The market is being disrupted accordingly. By 2024, China was firmly established as the world's largest producer of EVs, while Volkswagen – for the first time in its long and distinguished history – announced plans to close factories in Germany, with the potential loss of thousands of jobs. However, the story doesn't end here, because manufacturing processes for electric cars remains essentially linear and, so, wasteful of natural resources such as iron ore and lithium; it is far from being a sustainable business. But that, too, will change, because there is value to be created from the elimination of waste. Seeing opportunity for leadership in this space, another German manufacturer – Porsche – is transitioning to 'zero impact factories' with the design principle of eliminating waste by relying on renewable energy, using materials that are either biodegradable or recovered and reused, avoiding hazardous chemicals, and so on. The rates of progress across these dimensions inevitably will vary and in 2024, Porsche and BMW lowered their expectations with respect to the decline of the market for internal combustion engines, with both increasing investment in this inherently unsustainable business. Yet the direction of travel is clear, and so too the reason for it. An industry that is inherently destructive of the planet's limited natural resources ultimately cannot survive. Innovators in the industry will find ways to create value while eliminating waste, while others will either develop their operations in a similar way or risk becoming uncompetitive.

Such innovation can take several forms. In their book on the circular economy, Binder and Braun (2024) offer five business model archetypes, each of which offers ways to think about innovation in your own business. These are the optimisation of resource use, capitalisation of regeneration and restoration, valorisation of waste, monetisation of extended product life and servitisation of products. Each of these can be understood as different ways of tackling the challenge of waste, potentially comprehensively so, if all options are explored. Optimising resource use and capitalising regeneration and restoration are both ways to make better use of inputs, while monetising extended product life and servitising products are both ways to utilise products more efficiently and capturing value from waste reduces loss at the end of the value chain.

An illustrative example of optimising resource use is the disruption of the dairy industry by brands such as Alpro and Oatly. The economic and physical reality is that dairy milk is staggeringly inefficient in relation to its non-dairy counterpart. Consider the data in Figure 4.7, that one litre of dairy milk requires approximately 630 litres of water and $9m^2$ of land, in contrast with 50 litres and $1m^2$ for oat milk. Keeping such data in mind, picture that a carton of non-dairy milk might sit alongside its dairy alternative on the supermarket shelf, packaged in a similar way, offering essentially the same product, priced in much the same way and yet with nowhere near the same level of waste. The business proposition seems fairly clear.

An example that combines several archetypes of circular economy business models is IKEA, which is applying design principles around both repairability and adaptability (extended product life) and recycling and recovery of materials (optimisation of resource use and valorisation of waste). CreditNature is building a consulting business by means of capitalising regeneration and resoration, creating markets to connect landowners with private sector investors. Rent the Runway and Vinted are both disruptive presences in the fashion industry, with the former offering fashion as a service rather than a product (servitisation of products, allowing a much higher rate of product utilisation) and the latter creating a market for clothes that would otherwise languish in a wardrobe or end up in landfill (monetisation of extended product life).

In addressing the issue of waste in your own company, you should be guided by the 'mitigation hierarchy', which sets out the priorities of avoid, minimise, restore and (in some cases) offset on the pathway to (net) zero waste. The most effective (and often most innovative) approach is to avoid. Returning to the example of deforestation: the simplest and most effective way to mitigate loss is to avoid deforestation in the first place. The greatest contributor to declining biodiversity is changing land use, being deforestation for agricultural land, and so an avoidance strategy could be one of innovating to grow a profitable market for environmentally sustainable alternatives, while empowering consumers with information about the environmental impact of their consumption decisions.

Multiple fast-food chains have started to take this approach, introducing plant-based items to their menus alongside their standard offerings. Next best is minimising impact, a diluted form of avoidance. For fast-food chains, this might involve increasing sales of food items whose production is not associated with deforestation, for example shifting the meat-based product offer from beef to chicken. Next is restoration, which might apply to mineral extraction, where a company has an obligation to 'make good' the site after the closure of operations, notwithstanding that there might be many years of depleted forest during operations, and many more to reach some degree of maturity in a restored ecosystem. For the fast-food chains, and others implicated in deforestation, this invites creative engagement with the consumer, for example selling premium products where the higher price directly funds restoration, capturing a market segment that combines relative affluence (hence corporate revenue) with ecological awareness and conscience (hence willingness to contribute to

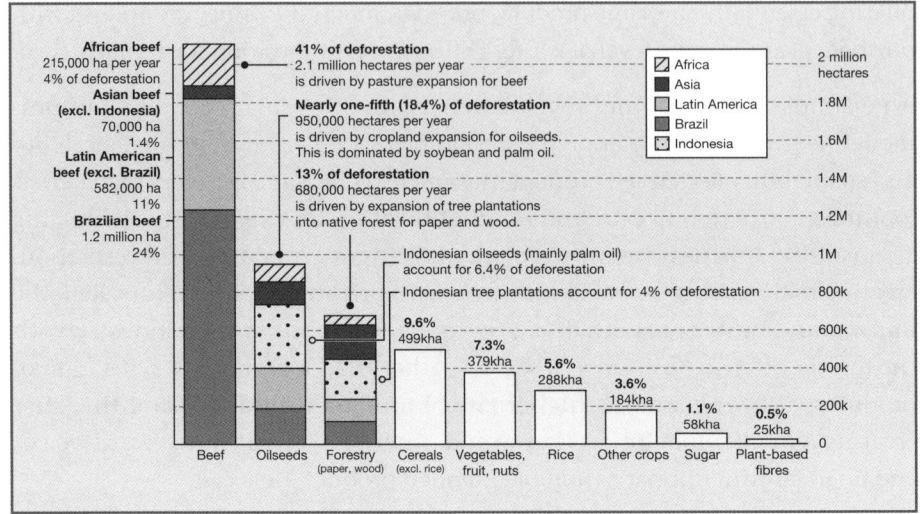

Figure 4.6 What are the drivers of tropical deforestation?

restoration). Each of these approaches is currently visible in industry, though it is important to emphasise that as long as a business's core value proposition rests on product offerings that contribute to deforestation, the business's diversification of market offerings is only a partial pursuit of a sustainable strategy.

The final option is offset, where damage done in one location is compensated by means of gain somewhere else. This might be attractive at first sight to any business that is dependent upon resources that are at risk, for reasons such as security of supply, volatility or upward pressure in pricing, and transition factors such as tighter regulation or shifting consumer preferences. Yet there are several reasons to avoid offsetting if at all possible. Offsets might appear inexpensive currently because they are also largely ineffective; they are likely to become significantly more expensive as regulation tightens and quality increases, and especially so if many companies have a mitigation strategy that depends upon them.[8] This is particularly true when it comes to natural resources: loss of biodiversity, clean water or clean air is not something that can be truly 'offset'. Finally, it is quite possible that the numbers just do not add up – the aggregate need means that offsetting is not viable as a complete solution.[xxx]

---

8 Ineffectiveness arises in a variety of ways, similar to those for carbon offsets. For example, replanted forests are often vulnerable to fire or disease and cannot be considered permanent.

The re-framing of the relationship between your business and nature is concerned not just with impact but also with dependency. The question for the latter is whether the resources upon which the company depends are being wasted, regardless of whether the activities of the company itself are drivers of that depletion. Recall that sustainability concerns not just the impacts of a company but also the capacity of the company to sustain its own profitability. It might, for example, be the wasteful business models of other entities that threaten the natural resources on which the business depends. The economic effects will vary, ranging from issues of supply chain resilience to exposure to volatility in commodity prices. Here the need is to identify where your business activity is at risk, and to increase business model resilience by reducing reliance upon threatened sources of natural capital.

Evaluating nature and your business

Having re-framed the issue of business and nature, your next stage is evaluation. It is one thing to know that certain types of impact and dependency arise throughout your value chain but another to quantify them reliably or to otherwise determine their significance.

Some structure is needed here. In categorising information, you can apply the same lenses that were introduced in Chapter 3, in particular the distinction between Scope 1 and Scope 3. While these terms were developed for purpose of measuring GHG emissions, they work by analogy for other corporate impacts. On that basis, Scope 1 includes the direct use of natural resources in the company's own operations, while Scope 3 includes indirect use by suppliers, consumers and others, throughout the company's value chain. And while GHG emissions can be understood in relation to net zero targets and related international agreements, so too metrics for other environmental impacts can be set according to science-based targets, commitments to net positive biodiversity impact and similar benchmarks.

Critical here is for you and your teams not to feel that the management of sustainability requires a full range of metrics to be identified and monitored. On the contrary, most important is to identify those that really matter, and to focus measurement efforts accordingly. If your value chain includes sectors that are primary drivers of nature loss – such as agriculture, fishing, forestry, infrastructure or extractives – then this is one place to find impacts that are material to your stakeholders.[xxxi] In practice, estimation is both inevitable and essential when assessing impact and dependency on systems. Inevitable because – to a greater or lesser degree – your current reality is that you might simply not know the provenance of your inputs, nor the consequences of your outputs. Each of your inputs has come from a direct supplier but, prior to that, there might be a long supply chain, with all manner of processes undertaken by a geographically disperse range of actors. And each of your outputs might be used in a variety of ways and disposed of with greater or lesser recovery and reuse of materials. Yet estimation is essential because 'we have no idea' is not an adequate response to understanding and managing important business risks and opportunities.

Moreover, estimation need only be ballpark accurate in order to do the job of focusing the attention of your board and teams and, in this regard, data are not that difficult to obtain. For example, while the provenance of purchased timber might not be known, what can be done is to measure how much of it came with certification from the Forest Stewardship Council, or similar. While such approaches inevitably rely upon the efficacy of the certifier, when methodologies are transparent, they are likely to be a step in the right direction. Similarly, even if direct information from a supplier is not currently attainable, there are likely to be industry averages that can be used as a proxy, and that are likely to be applicable across different geographical locations. An example might be the quantity of water used per kg of cotton cloth produced in India, or average agrochemical runoff per hectare of arable land in the United States. Remember that you are looking for estimates on activities that are an important part of your business. If this is not something already fairly well understood by your management team, or by those of your suppliers or customers, then either your business is overlooking activities that create business risks or opportunities or else there is a capability deficit that needs to be addressed.

Measurement enables you to set targets and monitor performance. As with climate, targets can be aligned with science-based transition pathways and – by making use of (biodiversity) offsets – they can be net as well as gross. Authoritative guidance in this area is developing rapidly – see, for example, the Task Force on Nature-related Financial Disclosure (TNFD, 2023) and the SBTi FLAG methodology (SBTi, 2023).[9] While metrics and targets remain more robust for climate than they are for nature, progress on the latter is gathering significant pace.

One caveat to the above: there are limits to the extent to which nature lends itself to the solutions being progressed for climate. The relative lack of progress is not only because climate has received much greater attention but also because nature is inherently more challenging from a measurement perspective.

Three measurement challenges stand out. First is that nature varies by location; while a tonne of GHG emissions has the same effect on global warming regardless of where it takes place, the sustainability importance of water, soil or forest depends upon where it is located, and on which economic activities are dependent upon it. Second is that natural resources interact with one another, meaning that they typically cannot be understood in isolation but instead only as part of an ecosystem. In turn, for corporate activity, this makes the relationship between impact and dependency more remote and difficult to pin down. Third is the property of non-linearity we have already mentioned, whereby an ecosystem can survive depletion for an extended period but is vulnerable to collapse; a veritable death by a thousand cuts.

None of these challenges presents a reason not to get started. On the contrary, they describe precisely the space in which you can lead. Impact on natural resources can be identified whether or not serious degradation of the associated ecosystem can be anticipated with precision. Reputational and other licence-to-operate risks can be factored into decision making. Dependency upon at-risk natural resources can similarly be identified, with adaptation strategies developed and enacted. If your business has a material impact on natural resources, then you ought to be able to identify what it is, and your rebuttable presumption should be that your target is to eliminate the impact. If your business has a material dependency on natural resources, then you should also be able to

---

9   See also, for example, the Science Based Targets Network (SBTN – https://sciencebasedtargetsnetwork.org/) and the following online tools: ENCORE (Exploring Natural Capital Opportunities, Risks and Exposure – https://www.encorenature.org/) which is designed to help organisations explore their exposure to nature-related risk and take the first steps to understand their dependencies and impacts on nature; Trase (https://trase.earth/), which provides data and insight that empowers business, government and civil society to eliminate deforestation and transition towards more sustainable and equitable agricultural supply chains; and ForestIQ (https://forestiq.com/), which is a platform for financial institutions to help enable their transition to deforestation-free financial portfolios.

identify what it is, and your rebuttable presumption should be that your target is the minimisation of any associated risks. Either way, action is what leadership invites and requires.

Action on nature as a business

When it comes to action, we should not underestimate the scale of the problem. Business is tasked with meeting society's needs and demands, while not depleting natural systems. That is a big ask. Economic activity implies consumption, and consumption implies the use of resources. Societal demand for consumption has increased enormously in recent decades and continues to do so. It is an even bigger ask because you as a business have a clear economic self-interest in fuelling that increase in demand.

In addressing this challenge, an important step is to recognise that there are two cycles, two circular flows, associated with corporate activity. One is biological and the other is technical.[xxxii] The biological cycle is the process of nature, which repeatedly cycles and recycles its major nutrients – carbon, hydrogen, oxygen and nitrogen. As we have already underscored, there is no waste in nature. From a corporate perspective, the focus of the biological cycle is regeneration after use. Take coffee as a simple example and picture a linear process in which we grow, roast and grind but then discard the coffee grinds after use, even though they are full of nutrients that could be restored to nature. If, rather than discarding, it is possible to reintroduce the grinds back into the natural cycle, then this simple example has a circular design.

The technical cycle, meanwhile, is of our own invention. We have learned to extract minerals and to process and employ them in a variety of ways. The circularity challenge is to recover those minerals after use, rather than further mining a finite supply. Take as an example here the construction of buildings. If you construct a building out of reinforced concrete, then the first part of the linear process is not only very consuming of CO_2 and natural resources but also not designed for output that can be reused. It is often very difficult to repurpose a concrete structure, and too often the 'solution' is to tear it down and build something else. A more modular and more flexible design would instead enable a building to have a life beyond its initial intended use.

The relevance of each of these two cycles will vary across industries. In general, if there are separate processes associated with the decomposition and/or recovery of materials, then the respective cycles must not contaminate one another.

For example, the use of wood might reduce the carbon footprint of building construction, yet there might not be the ultimate possibility of disposing of the wood in a biodegradable way, because it has been strengthened, treated or coated by means of a chemical process. Similarly, if cars are painted in such a way that the paint cannot readily be removed from the steel, then the steel cannot be recycled without loss of quality; it is instead 'downcycled'.

A useful way to think about redesigning products and services is to focus on what the consumer is paying for but not consuming. For example, a customer does not consume a bottle and contents; instead, they can be understood as borrowing the former and consuming only the latter. The idea is not new, of course, but the days of returning glass Coca-Cola bottles are mostly long gone, with the company now being the world's largest purchaser of single-use plastic. In effect, Coca-Cola's old model is being rediscovered by Patagonia, where the drive to eliminate waste is leading inexorably to a model where the company takes back, repairs and re-sells clothing, rather than always making anew. In effect, the new Patagonia consumer is borrowing the item of clothing for as long as it is needed, and the incentive to throw it away is being lost.

Changes such as those described above might be unimaginable or infeasible in the absence of higher-level systems changes. For example, a charging network is needed in order to persuade would-be customers to switch to an electric car. In some sense, such thinking is incompatible with a conventional understanding of business, which sets individual companies in direct competition with other individual companies. In this chapter, we have described the conflict between a modern capitalist system, which has unleashed unprecedented growth in consumption, and natural systems, which have been depleted as economic activity has grown. In this regard, there is a limit to how much any individual corporation can do on its own. Recall that the tragedy of the commons is a problem of collective action. Rational individual action leads to collective ruin. It is possible, of course, that greater efficiency in the use of natural resources could prevent a tragedy of the commons from arising because the collective rate of consumption might be maintained within the natural boundary of the system.

In other cases, however, the maintenance of natural capital calls for change at a system-wide level. The implication is that business leaders must work with other stakeholders in their industries and value chains. The need is to understand that 'how do I take care of my own company and my own shareholders?' is a question that extends beyond the boundary of direct control because your agency is contingent upon the actions of others. The risk, otherwise, is that you do your best but that, several years down the road, you find yourself acknowledging that you could not succeed. When you lead from the view that your ability to create value is fundamentally impacted by the health of the systems on which your company impacts and depends, you are better able to identify not only risks but also points of collaboration to ensure these systems endure.

Reflection questions

This chapter has explored the critical importance of nature to business, emphasising corporate impact and dependency on natural systems. We also point out that nature and climate are intrinsically linked. Both play a vital role in shaping risk and opportunity for your company. A key insight from this chapter is therefore the interconnectedness of climate and natural systems. When businesses address them in a siloed manner, the result is partial insight and missed opportunity.

As you move through this book, you will find that this integrated perspective is vital as you navigate sustainability for your business. Moreover, the ability to view these relationships holistically sets the stage for deeper integration of sustainability into business strategies. Chapter 5 builds on this integrated approach by presenting the social aspects of sustainability. As you transition to this topic, it is important to pause and reflect on the key questions at the end of this chapter, both individually and as a team. These reflections will deepen your understanding of the connections between nature, climate and your business, preparing you to engage with the social aspects of sustainability in a similarly holistic manner.

By learning to incorporate the insights you have gained so far on climate and nature with social sustainability in the following chapter, you will be better equipped to address sustainability in its entirety. Recognising how climate, nature and social systems collectively impact your business will enhance your ability to create value that is resilient and sustainable over the long term. This is a strategic advantage worth striving for.

1 Consider what your customers are paying for but not consuming as, for example, with packaging that is thrown away after use, or clothing that is given away or tossed away before reaching the end of its useful life, or capital equipment that your customer acquires but rarely uses. How can your company benefit from eliminating this waste?

2   In cases where the process of consumption itself causes externalities, for example because it requires the burning of fossil fuel, consider what systems-level changes would be required to change the economics of the industry, making it relatively more profitable to provide products or services that do not generate externalities.

3   Finally, consider how to reduce the dependency of your business on inputs that generate externalities. In food retail, restaurant, entertainment and hotel businesses, for example, how can product placement, product information and messaging around consumption shift demand?

Recommended reading

Binder, J. and Braun, M. (2024) *The Circular Business Revolution*. FT Publishing International.

Braungart, M. and McDonough, W. (2009) *Cradle to Cradle: Remaking the Way We Make Things*. London: Vintage.

CCLI (2023) *Biodiversity Risk: Legal Implications for Companies and their Directors*. London: Commonwealth Climate and Law Initiative.

Hardin, G. (1968) The Tragedy of the Commons. *Science*, 162, 1243–8.

Heal, G. (2016) *Endangered Economies: How the Neglect of Nature Threatens our Prosperity*. New York, NY: Columbia University Press.

Hoffmann, A. and Vanham, P. (2024) *The New Nature of Business: The Path to Prosperity and Sustainability*. Wiley.

IUCN (2021) *Guidelines for Planning and Monitoring Corporate Biodiversity Performance*. International Union for Conservation of Nature.

Kolbert, E. (2014) *The Sixth Extinction: An Unnatural History*. New York: Henry Holt and Company.

NCC (2016) *Natural Capital Protocol*. London: Natural Capital Coalition.

Rockström, J., Steffen, W., Noone, K., Persson, Å., Chapin III, F.S., Lambin, E.F., Lenton, T.M., Scheffer, M., Folke, C., Schellnhuber, H.J. and Nykvist, B. (2009) A Safe Operating Space for Humanity. *Nature*, 461: 472–5.

SBTi (2023) FLAG Science Based Target-Setting Guidance.

Seddon, N., Smith, A., Smith, P., Key, I., Chausson, A., Girardin, C., House, J., Srivastava, S. and Turner, B. (2021) Getting the Message Right on Nature-Based Solutions to Climate Change. *Global Change Biology* 27, no. 8, February: 1518–46. Available at: https://onlinelibrary.wiley.com/doi/full/10.1111/gcb.15513.

TNFD (2023) *The TNFD Framework*. Task Force on Nature-related Financial Disclosure.

WWF (2024) Living Planet Report 2024 – Building a naturepositive society. Almond, R.E.A., Grooten, M., Juffe Bignoli, D. and Petersen, T. (eds). WWF, Gland, Switzerland.

WWF (2023) Nature in transition plans: why and how? WWF-UK.

Notes

[i] Reed, J. and Bokhari, F. (2022) 'It's the Fault of Climate Change': Pakistan Seeks 'Justice' after Floods. *Financial Times*, 26 October. Available at: https://www.ft.com/content/e69ece7d-11fb-4a8f-91ea-35b98d4b54db.

[ii] WWF International (2022) Living Planet Report 2022. livingplanet.panda.org. Available at: https://livingplanet.panda.org/en-gb/.

[iii] Craig, D. and Mrema, E. (2024) Businesses Must Address Nature-Related Financial Risks. Here's Why. World Economic Forum, 8 January. Available at: https://www.weforum.org/agenda/2024/01/businesses-address-nature-related-financial-risks/.

[iv] Hoffmann, A. (2020) The Planet after the Pandemic. *Project Syndicate*, 2 June. Available at: https://www.project-syndicate.org/commentary/green-covid19-recovery-strategies-by-andre-hoffmann-2020-06.

[v] Murray, S. (2023) Why Nature's Future Underpins the Future of Business. *Financial Times*, 30 November, sec. Moral Money. Available at: https://www.ft.com/content/ca666c93-65f4-4070-9ca8-0f3a44d19319.

[vi] BloombergNEF (2023) When the Bee Stings: Counting the Cost of Nature-Related Risks. Available at: https://tnfd.global/wp-content/uploads/2023/12/BNEF_Nature-Risk_v1.11f_MASTER_COMPLETED.pdf.

[vii] S&P Global (2023) How the World's Largest Companies Depend on Nature and Biodiversity. www.spglobal.com, 10 May. Available at: https://www.spglobal.com/sustainable1/en/insights/special-editorial/how-the-world-s-largest-companies-depend-on-nature-and-biodiversity.

viii Boldrini, S., *et al.* (2023) Living in a World of Disappearing Nature: Physical Risk and the Implications for Financial Stability. *Social Science Research Network*, 1 January. Available at: https://doi.org/10.2139/ssrn.4630721.

ix Hancock, L. Six Ways Loss of Arctic Ice Impacts Everyone. World Wildlife Fund, n.d. Available at: https://www.worldwildlife.org/pages/six-ways-loss-of-arctic-ice-impacts-everyone#:~:text=We%20lose%20Arctic%20sea%20ice.

x Flores, B.M., *et al.* (2024) Critical Transitions in the Amazon Forest System. *Nature* 626, no. 7999, 14 February: 555–64. Available at: https://doi.org/10.1038/s41586-023-06970-0.

xi OECD (2022) The Current Plastics Lifecycle Is far from Circular – OECD. www.oecd.org. Available at: https://www.oecd.org/en/publications/2022/02/global-plastics-outlook_a653d1c9.html.

xii Marquis, C. (2024) *The Profiteers*. Hachette UK.

xiii WWF, Saving the Earth: A Sustainable Future for Soils and Water. WWF, n.d. Available at: https://www.wwf.org.uk/our-reports/saving-earth-sustainable-future-soils-and-water.

xiv See Preface to Dasgupta (2021) *The Economics of Biodiversity*. London: HM Treasury.

xv Ritchie, H. (2019) Half of the World's Habitable Land Is Used for Agriculture. *Our World in Data*, 11 November. Available at: https://ourworldindata.org/global-land-for-agriculture.

xvi *The Economist* (2021) Treating Beef like Coal Would Make a Big Dent in Greenhouse-Gas Emissions. *The Economist*, 2 October. Available at: https://www.economist.com/graphic-detail/2021/10/02/treating-beef-like-coal-would-make-a-big-dent-in-greenhouse-gas-emissions.

xvii See the analysis in WWF (2023).

xviii All data from OurWorldinData.org.

xix Purpose Disruptors, 'Advertised Emissions', Purpose Disruptors, n.d. Available at: https://www.purposedisruptors.org/advertised-emissions.

xx IPA, IPA, AA and ISBA Release Joint Statement about Advertised Emissions. Ipa.co.uk. Available at: https://ipa.co.uk/news/advertised-emissions.

xxi OECD (2022) The Current Plastics Lifecycle Is far from Circular – OECD. www.oecd.org. Available at: https://www.oecd.org/en/publications/2022/02/global-plastics-outlook_a653d1c9.html.

xxii Lapatza, B. (2023) Dutch Retailer Albert Heijn Trials 'True Price' Scheme. *Food Matters Live*, 19 April. Available at: https://foodmatterslive.com/article/dutch-albert-heijn-introduces-true-price-social-environmental-costs/.

xxiii Allbirds M0.0NSHOT – the World's First Carbon Zero Shoes. (2023) Allbirds UK. Available at: https://www.allbirds.co.uk/pages/moonshot-zero-carbon-shoes.

xxiv Murray, S. (2023) Why Nature's Future Underpins the Future of Business. *Financial Times*, 30 November, sec. Moral Money. Available at: https://www.ft.com/content/ca666c93-65f4-4070-9ca8-0f3a44d19319.

xxv Drejer, C. (2023) Avoiding Carbon 'Tunnel Vision'. Why Protecting Biodiversity and Nature Are Core to Being a Sustainable Business. Accessed 7 November 2023. Available at: https://impact.economist.com/sustainability/project/sustainable-technology/avoiding-carbon-tunnel-vision.html.

xxvi See the discussion in Raworth (2018).

xxvii Braungart, M. and McDonough, W. (2009) *Cradle to Cradle: Remaking the Way We Make Things*. London: Vintage.

xxviii Dalberg (2021) Plastics: The Costs to Society, the Environment, and the Economy. A report for WWF. Available at: https://wwflac.awsassets.panda.org/downloads/wwf_pctsee_report_english.pdf.

xxix Botsman, R. and Rogers, R. (2010) *What's Mine Is Yours: The Rise of Collaborative Consumption*. New York: Harper Business.

xxx Smith School University of Oxford (2024) The Oxford Offsetting Principles. www.smithschool.ox.ac.uk, March. Available at: https://www.smithschool.ox.ac.uk/research/oxford-offsetting-principles.

xxxi WWF International (2024) Living Planet Report 2024. livingplanet.panda.org. Available at: https://livingplanet.panda.org/en-gb/.

xxxii See Braungart, M. and McDonough, W. (2009) *Cradle to Cradle: Remaking the Way We Make Things*. London: Vintage.

CHAPTER 5
WHAT IS SOCIAL SUSTAINABILITY AND WHY DOES IT MATTER TO BUSINESS?

Located in a country ranked as one of the most business-friendly jurisdictions in the Americas, the Cobre Panama mine provided 1.5 per cent of the world's copper and 5 per cent of Panama's GDP in 2023.[i] Mine sites receive regular critique due to their impact on nature and biodiversity, and Cobre Panama was no different. In addition, however, it had become the focus of highly public criticism for its allegedly poor delivery of benefits to the host community. Widespread street protests and press claims of neo-colonial expropriation of national resources combined with a searing social media campaign supported by a cadre of Hollywood actors and high-profile activists to create a firestorm Panama's political leadership decided it could not endure. Just weeks after First Quantum Minerals, a Canadian company, was granted a 20-year renewal of its concession to operate the mine, public backlash had turned the project into a political football. The contract was cancelled and the government offered reassurances that similar projects would be prohibited in future.

The Cobre Panama case typifies the impact and dependency of companies on social systems. Significantly, it also highlights the interdependence between social and environmental systems: copper is one of the raw materials critical to the transition away from fossil fuels. So far in this book, we have concentrated on the relationship between corporations and the natural systems. In this chapter, we turn our attention to the relationship between business and social systems.

Businesses are embedded entities operating within natural and social systems. Our approach in this chapter rests on the proposition that business is part of, and not separate from, society. Corporate activities directly affect the quality of life of employees, suppliers, customers and others, while also significantly shaping the opportunities available to people and communities, the safety and security of their surroundings and their community norms. In turn, and because companies depend on social systems, these same factors affect a company's value proposition.

The United Nations Global Compact (UNGC) describes 'social sustainability' as 'identifying and managing business impacts, both positive and negative, on people'. To this, we add our lens of a sustainable corporation as one that creates profitable products and services as it strengthens natural and social systems. The economic rationale for such efforts is clear: as with framing of corporate impact and dependencies on natural systems we discussed in Chapter 4, market failure is synonymous with economic inefficiency; correcting that failure is correspondingly synonymous with economic gain. Most importantly, for corporations embedded in social systems, the strategic stewardship of these systems is fundamental.

With all this said, what does 'good' look like for corporate impact and dependency on social systems? Social systems inevitably touch on issues that are open to subjective judgement.[ii] Neither what constitutes a 'problem' in society nor what represents an acceptable 'solution' is universally agreed between cultures, governments, generations or individuals. At the same time, people and communities universally possess personal experience with issues related to social systems. Whether through socioeconomic (in)equality, gender or ethnic identity, or freedom of personal belief or expression, one's experience with social systems may generate viewpoints that are deeply held or powerfully felt. Individuals or groups may even, consciously or unconsciously, extrapolate their particular experience to universal demands or claims that are difficult to falsify. The predictably contested nature of evaluating social systems means corporate leaders require a framework through which to focus their efforts and evaluate progress.

To develop this, we suggest leaders begin with two core concepts: social licence to operate and human rights. These provide a foundation to assess and improve a company's ongoing impacts and dependencies on social systems and their connection to value creation.

Business and social licence to operate

Corporate 'social licence to operate' refers to the acceptance of a business' activities by its stakeholders. The legitimate foundation for corporate social licence to operate is built on protection, defence and delivery of human rights, which we describe in detail later in this section. Yet, social licence is as influenced by public perception of the company as it is by 'objective' corporate behaviour. Crucially, this means that social licence is dynamic: it is granted by communities and can be lost with startling speed. Similar to a brand, a company's social licence to operate is a classic example of a 'strategic asset' and it must be built and maintained, even at significant financial cost. Growth in access to social media, increased regulatory scrutiny and political uncertainties are but a few factors that heighten risk to social licence to operate for companies across the world today. Public sentiment against corporations that are seen to be pernicious or predatory may turn negative quickly, invite attention from regulators and policy makers and harm the financial prospects of the company.[iii]

Even though stakeholders might grant a social licence to operate, a company may not have its impact and dependencies on social systems fully in hand. For example, affected stakeholders may not yet have full information about the impact of a company's operations (e.g. long-term health effects of industrial pollution) or they may lack the efficacy (political or otherwise) to organise around a given issue at a given moment.[iv] Such circumstances can change quickly.[v] In a world where social media allows the experience of individuals and communities to be shared easily, the local can become global in an instant. For this reason, the ultimate duty to proactively address risks to human rights resulting from corporate activities is an important issue for your a company's executives and board.

A strong social licence to operate benefits all aspects of your business. It can be an enormous source of pride and motivation for employees, enhancing recruitment and retention. It creates confidence among external stakeholders, lowering the cost of capital for investors, reducing the risk of regulatory intervention and enhancing terms of business with suppliers. Combined with a clear understanding of human rights, insight into social licence enables you to identify where your company's impact and dependencies on social systems might exist.

Crucially, social licence is about trust: corporations, like NGOs, governments and any other organisation, will make mistakes, missteps and misjudgements. The key is in how your company responds in this inevitable scenario. Your ability to listen and co-create solutions with stakeholders is crucial to building and maintaining the trust upon which social licence depends. One powerful definition of trust is 'a confident relationship with the unknown':[vi] through your actions, you provide stakeholders with the assurance that you are committed to working in a manner that protects, respects and defends human rights. Indeed, to secure and maintain social licence to operate is simply a starting point. Leadership requires that your company moves beyond this towards proactively protecting human rights and linking the company's relationship with social systems to ongoing value creation.[vii] To deliver this, we will describe the United Nations Sustainable Development Goals as an articulation of human rights that business can use to safeguard and strengthen social licence and identify potential corporate impacts and dependencies on social systems.

While, when managed well, your company's relationship with social systems can be a boon for the business, the opposite is also true. Employee engagement[viii] and well-being at work brings companies benefits in terms of reputation, recruitment, retention,[ix] and higher productivity.[x] Conversely, employee dissatisfaction is a catalyst for costly turnover[xi] and low performance[xii] as well as reputational damage and, in more extreme cases, a range of risks including high-profile whistle-blowing and legal action. In 2023, investment bank Goldman Sachs was ordered to pay US $215 million to settle a class action lawsuit from 2,800 female staff on the grounds of gender discrimination resulting in lower pay and fewer promotions for women. Multiple well-known fast-food franchises, including McDonald's and Taco Bell, have faced class-action lawsuits from as many as 10,000 staff at once, charged with mishandling wages. A BBC investigation into sexual abuse on tea plantations supplying well-known British brands including Lipton and PG Tips gained widespread media attention.[xiii] Such risks extend beyond employees to company suppliers: global brands including H&M, Zara, Apple[xiv] and Amazon have faced ongoing criticism from journalists, social media and regulators regarding working conditions in supplier factories.[xv]

Such reputational and operational risks become particularly acute in a context of highly disaggregated, globalised supply chains. The 2013 collapse of Rana Plaza, a building in Bangladesh housing garment factories used by numerous global fashion brands, resulted in the death of more than 1,100 workers and numerous life-altering injuries. The incident also put a spotlight on the exposure of major global retailers including Benetton, Walmart and Zara to subcontractors that were typified by unsafe working conditions. The resulting industry-wide scrutiny continues to this day.[xvi]

And yet business impact and dependencies on social systems are not all about risk. Good business practices in this area are about opportunity and building strong businesses. In the face of significant recruitment challenges following the COVID-19 pandemic, Hilton Hotels, one of the largest players in the global hospitality industry, developed a staffing strategy based around onboarding refugees, formerly incarcerated individuals, and survivors of human trafficking into the organisation.[xvii] The company, which consistently leads in global rankings of best places to work,[xviii] found this strategy enabled them to solve critical staffing shortages. It is worth noting that 40 per cent of Hilton employees have been at the company for more than a decade, and internal candidates fill almost 60 per cent of positions at the corporate director level and above. In tandem with meeting a business need, Hilton's recruitment strategy increased opportunity for advancement and for the benefits that come from a diverse workforce. This pattern has been repeated with refugees in particular by more than 350 companies including Starbucks, Cofra, Google, Airbnb and SAP through TENT,[xix] a programme that enables refugees to fill vacancies not only in hospitality but also in retail, professional services, manufacturing and a range of other industries across more than 10 countries.

Amazon, Hilton and Starbucks to hire thousands of refugees across Europe

By Tim Bradshaw

Amazon has pledged to hire at least 5,000 refugees across Europe over the next three years as part of a new drive by dozens of companies to help recruit people fleeing war in Ukraine and other crisis-stricken regions.

The tech giant's commitment is the largest among more than 40 companies including Hilton, Marriott, ISS and Starbucks, which together said they would hire more than 13,000 refugees.

The announcements were made at an event in Paris on Monday organised by the Tent Partnership for Refugees, a non-profit group founded by Hamdi Ulukaya, chief executive of US food company Chobani.

The move, ahead of World Refugee Day on Tuesday, forms part of the growing movement towards corporate social responsibility initiatives, as activist shareholders demand companies take measures that can support wider societal goals.

"One thing we believe at Amazon is diversity of employment makes us a stronger company," said Ofori Agboka, Amazon's vice-president of people experience and technology.

Alongside Amazon, staffing agencies Adecco, ManpowerGroup and Randstad said they would help 152,000 refugees find work, while Accenture, Generali and Indeed will help to train another 86,000 displaced people.

Welcoming the effort, Margaritis Schinas, vice-president of the European Commission, said: "The opening of the EU's borders to Ukrainians over a year ago showed Europe at its best. However, one year on [from Russia's invasion], far too many refugees remain unemployed, despite our endemic skills shortages, their high levels of education, desire to earn a living and legal right to work."

Millions of Ukrainians are now living across Europe, forming part of a global refugee crisis that the UN estimates has displaced more than 110mn people from conflicts and persecution in regions including Sudan, Syria, Ethiopia and Afghanistan.

Amazon, which employs more than 200,000 people across Europe, is partnering with Tent to offer support with immigration and legal fees, mentoring and training. It will help new employees to learn local languages through a combination of automated translation technology and local liaisons, to overcome what Agboka described as one of the biggest challenges in integrating displaced people.

The "vast majority" of roles would be in its retail operations, including fulfilment and distribution, with "eligibility to move into jobs that are in different levels of the organisation that are commensurate with their skills and abilities", Agboka said.

The company will also provide IT-related training for 10,000 Ukrainians globally through its Amazon Web Services arm.

Amazon's European initiative follows a previous commitment launched in September in the US to hire 5,000 refugees by the end of next year. Agboka said the company was receiving applications from refugees from Ukraine, Venezuela, Syria and Turkey.

"We're hoping that number grows," he added.

Source: Tim Bradshaw (2023) 'Amazon, Hilton and Starbucks to hire thousands of refugees across Europe', Financial Times, 19 Jun. © The Financial Times Limited 2025. All Rights Reserved.

In the United Kingdom, a country with comparatively low and slowing rates of social mobility,[xx] accountancy firm PwC has combined co-creation workshops and UK Social Mobility Commission data to design recruitment programmes for individuals from a wide range of socio-economic backgrounds.[xxi] One objective of the programme is to ensure that a lack of diversity among those reaching leadership within the firm does not create reputational and recruitment risk for the company. To identify barriers to recruitment and retention, senior partners worked closely with apprentices, recruits and employees through journaling exercises, collaborative design sessions and analysis of personal finances. The company has put actions to support social mobility in place throughout the organisation, introducing targets for workforce socio-economic diversity at all levels of the firm. One such action is a cash advance provided to school leavers as part of their first month's salary. These funds ensure that all recruits can join social events with new colleagues and purchase work-appropriate attire, two issues flagged during programme design as barriers for recruits from diverse socio-economic backgrounds to full participation in corporate life. Importantly, the advance is provided by default to remove any stigma associated with requesting funds. Similarly, the company publishes salaries on all apprentice programmes to ensure that remuneration expectations are clear to all applicants from the outset. These concrete, achievable steps enable the company to diversify its talent pipeline as well as strengthen employee engagement and its licence to operate.

Negative social externalities have in common the deprivation of one or more human right(s). The effect of these deprivations may persist within social systems across generations. This often results in social patterns that are readily visible through statistics, which can be a valuable source of insight for you and your teams. A ready example comes from the historical, legal deprivation of human rights for Black people in the United States. While legal deprivations no longer persist in their precise historical forms, ongoing social and economic exclusion is evident. Today, 3 per cent of all US firms are majority-owned by Black people, with just over 1 per cent of US firms owned by Black women.[xxii] It is in this context of latent opportunity that corporate leaders may take an interest in start-ups such as BLK + GRN,[xxiii] a company that has grown in less than five years to a platform representing products from more than 135 US businesses owned by Black women. BLK + GRN has built a value proposition focused on removing toxic chemicals from products frequently marketed to Black women and on supporting entrepreneurship by Black women in the United States. Their 'challenge the marketplace' ethos has resulted in growth in an industry currently worth US $7 billion annually in the US alone.[xxiv] One business in the same sector, Sundial Brands, was purchased by Unilever in for an estimated $1.6 billion. Berkshire Partners, which typically makes equity investments of $100 million to $1 billion, invested in Mielle Organics, another brand in the sector, which was subsequently purchased by Procter & Gamble for an undisclosed amount.

Such potential for gains is not uncommon: Boston Consulting Group has estimated that, if venture capital investment in female-founded companies matched that of companies founded by men, the global economy would stand to grow by up to US $5 trillion.[xxv] While such extrapolations are admittedly imperfect, the message is clear that there is a business case to be built for addressing social exclusion – what is market expansion, after all, if not satisfying previously unmet demand? Statistics on business ownership are just one example of the kind of data that can help signal where such opportunities exist. In the case of women's – and Black women's – entrepreneurship in the United States, the story the numbers tell is stark. For you as a business leader, statistics like these are an invitation to be curious: could these outcomes signal the presence of current or historical deprivations of human rights? What value is lost or inefficiency is introduced as a result of current or past exclusions, and might there be a business case for you to consider unlocking value as a result?

The ongoing existence of slavery and forced labour in corporate supply chains offers a salient example of the signals data can send about social systems. Despite decades of widespread awareness, the International Labour Organisation estimates that the number of people subjected to forced labour across the globe *increased* by 10 million individuals between 2016 and 2022.[xxvi] For business leaders, such statistics are cause for attention. There are significant risks associated with reliance on a social system in which human rights are not upheld, as well as on extraction from a social system to earn profit. Loss of social licence represents real financial risk. In addition, burgeoning regulation in some jurisdictions makes companies' obligations to social systems increasingly explicit. Recent years have seen European governments as well as the United States, Canada, and Norway[xxvii] enforce mechanisms through which importers are expected to demonstrate that their goods are produced without forced labour.[xxviii]

Such legal developments are enhanced and enabled by advances in technology. Digital tagging and tracking systems have leapfrogged previous technology to provide buyers, consumers and investors with previously unimagined levels of insight into supply chains. Global Fishing Watch, a partnership between Google and conservation organisations, can now effectively identify 'ghost ships', notorious for egregious forced labour and human trafficking throughout the seafood and maritime sectors.[xxix] Altana AI, a start-up, is working with Global 500 companies and the US Customs and Border Protection department to develop what the founder has called 'Google Maps for the supply chain'.[xxx]

Kenzen, another USA-based company, has created digital wearable devices for workers to monitor a range of health signals in high-risk industrial environments.[xxxi] Such improved insight into supply chain, sourcing and working conditions combines with increased attention from investors[xxxii] to companies' impacts and dependencies on social systems. Technology and regulation are moving in such a way that companies' ignorance of their supply chain, in the words of *Financial Times'* Sarah Murray, 'will no longer be bliss'.[xxxiii] Human rights and social licence combine to provide you with a basis on which to assess your current impact and dependency on social systems, and identify not only how to minimise risk but to identify opportunity.

Business and human rights

The concept of human rights is a powerful analytical tool. It makes the difference between a miscellany of ad-hoc norms adopted by corporations based on their own judgements and the ability to speak meaningfully about social systems across companies. Human rights are, unsurprisingly, themselves contested and – inevitably – imperfect in substance and form. And yet they represent the grounding on which business can build strategy and assess impact through its relationship with social systems. While implementation of human rights varies widely, they offer the closest thing you have to an internationally established basis for assessing progress in this area. Because of this, fluency with the 'language' of human rights is essential for leaders. Without this, your ability to formulate, evaluate and communicate corporate impact and dependencies on social systems will be fundamentally constrained. It is all too easy for companies to miss, misread or misunderstand their impact and dependencies on social systems. Conversely, human rights enable you and your team to work from a transparent framework to build strategy in this area, simultaneously strengthening your social licence to operate.

Human rights in their contemporary form were articulated in the 1948 Universal Declaration of Human Rights (UDHR) by the United Nations General Assembly. The Declaration enumerates a range of cultural, political, social and civil rights and contends that all people are entitled to these rights regardless of identity markers (i.e. citizenship, ethnic origin, religious belief or gender). Classic human rights charters maintain that the obligation to protect and defend rights sits with nation states. However, as early as the 1970s, the claim that businesses have human rights obligations received serious attention. An early catalyst for this was the blurring of lines between corporate and state activity during the Cold War era. In this context, the United Nations was asked to examine the 'role and effects of multinational companies in the development process, particularly in developing countries, and their implications for international relations'.[xxxiv] Through this effort, the difficulty of fully disentangling corporate activity from its national and even geopolitical context became increasingly evident. Corporations became implicated in the delivery of – or failure to deliver – human rights.

Since these early years, the field of business and human rights has developed substantially. Today, business is acknowledged as a fundamental actor in the global human rights ecosystem. In 2008, Professor John Ruggie, then Special Representative of the UN Secretary General, responded to a request from the UN Human Rights Council to develop a policy framework for human rights related to corporate activities. The resulting report, 'Protect, Respect and Remedy: a Framework for Business and Human Rights' – often referred to as the 'Ruggie Report' – clearly set out that companies, not only nation states, have the responsibility to 'protect and respect' human rights, as well as to 'remedy' harms resulting from human rights violations.[xxxv] The report received wide support from governments and corporations and is today considered foundational in the area of business and human rights.

In particular, Ruggie's framework states that it is incumbent upon companies to undertake due diligence on human rights risks within their 'sphere of influence'. For you as a corporate leader, the concept of 'sphere of influence' is important here: akin to the concept of Scope 3 we have already discussed, a company's sphere of influence is not limited to the direct impacts of its activities. Rather, it refers to 'the potential and actual human rights impacts resulting from a company's business activities and the relationships connected to those activities', a potentially far-reaching scope.

To facilitate implementation of the Ruggie report principles, the UN developed the Guiding Principles on Human Rights.[xxxvi] These set out the steps companies are expected to take to commit to human rights, ensure that their efforts to protect these rights are effective, and report on progress. States as well as citizens have the power to prosecute violations. While litigation is (unsurprisingly) complex, it is far from unheard of.[xxxvii] One landmark 2024 decision by the European Court of Human Rights found the Swiss Government's failure to meet its own targets to reduce GHG emissions to be a violation of human rights.[xxxviii] While the Swiss Government subsequently rejected the ruling, it nevertheless highlights a new potential for legal risk and garnered significant media attention. As with the protections for environmental systems we discussed in Chapter 4, delivering on the UN Guiding Principles typically requires successful strategic collaboration with civil society and governments, i.e. organisations with expertise on human rights protection and the mechanisms to redress when violations occur.

Climate lawsuits harness human rights to press for more action

By Amy Bell

When a group of Swiss women were vindicated in a legal claim that their government had failed to protect them from the impact of heatwaves, the move was hailed as a breakthrough for climate litigation.

Other litigants were watching on the sidelines, waiting to see what they could learn from the ruling by the European Court of Human Rights in April. Its decision in favour of the KlimaSeniorinnen — senior women for climate protection Switzerland — made it the first international court to give a ruling on the legal obligations of governments in fighting climate change, demanding fuller measures from the Swiss government.

The ruling found the government had "critical gaps" in its domestic regulations, including "a failure to quantify, through a carbon budget or otherwise, national greenhouse gas limitations". But the ECHR declined to be "detailed or prescriptive" on what measures the Swiss government should take to comply with its obligations, instead calling for action "compatible with the conclusions and spirit of the court's judgment".

Although the Swiss parliament's lower house voted to disregard the decision, the government has until October to come up with a plan for how it will implement the ruling. "The main thing in the KlimaSeniorinnen case is that Switzerland has to legislate," argues Joana Setzer, research fellow at the Grantham Institute on Climate Change and the Environment, at the London School of Economics. "The court is not saying exactly what to do — it's not saying how to brush your teeth, it's just saying 'brush your teeth'."

For now, the exact consequences of the Swiss case remain to be seen, but it highlights how human rights law is being used to hold governments and companies to account for their impact on climate change. The 2,400-strong group of women, mostly in their seventies, had argued that the Swiss government had failed to protect them from "serious adverse effects of climate change on lives, health, wellbeing and quality of life" by not meeting targets to help tackle carbon emissions and warming.

"It's the first time an international court has said that governments have a clear obligation to quantify a carbon budget," says Louise Fournier, legal counsel at campaign group Greenpeace International, which supported the Swiss women.

Despite the ECHR's general reluctance to take on so-called *actio popularis* claims — which are pursued in the public interest but without clear links to injured parties — the finding has created a precedent. It has also vindicated the group's arguments that its legal right to demand action on climate change had been improperly denied under the court's charter.

Adam Weiss, programme director at climate litigation group ClientEarth, which also backed the case, says the Swiss women were able to link individual impact to the broader cause: "They said, we're not just any old people, we're older people who belong to a group who are particularly vulnerable."

Similar arguments about curbing fossil fuel use are now being applied by Greenpeace Norway. In 2021, it submitted a challenge at the ECHR to the Norwegian government's decision to expand oil and gas drilling in Arctic waters. The campaign group argues that this would overshoot what it considers the country's fair share of global carbon emissions.

Weiss expects to see human rights arguments being applied to more climate change and environmental litigation. Because many countries have human rights protection in their constitutions, judges are already familiar with how it works.

ClientEarth has pending cases in Belgium and Germany, for example, which assert a human right to breathe clean air as part of a right to a healthy environment. Like the Swiss case, the goal is to focus on individual litigants as part of a broader argument.

Fournier points to lessons from the KlimaSeniorinnen case that other litigants could draw on. First, there was a clear protagonist that pressed for, and eventually established, its legal standing to take action. It was the Swiss women who organised themselves through campaigning and through the lawsuit — deciding at every stage whether to appeal and what the next steps should be.

Second, detailed groundwork was done to establish a comprehensive range of evidence and arguments over what might constitute a country's "fair share" of carbon use, based on its own historic contribution to global emissions and its ability to respond to climate change. In this case, Greenpeace International contacted other climate litigants across Europe to make sure everyone agreed with the arguments used to build its case, as the outcome could be beneficial for their cases too. "It was the KlimaSeniorinnen name on paper, but actually an effort by climate litigants around the world," says Fournier.

Most of the climate litigation cases filed so far are against governments, but those against companies are receiving more attention.

> Challenges made through courts or other regulatory bodies, such as advertising standards agencies, over alleged corporate "greenwashing", have been the most successful, Setzer says. She cites the withdrawal of BP adverts in a campaign lauding the oil group's low carbon credentials in 2020, after ClientEarth complained they misled.
>
> While early greenwashing cases mostly targeted oil companies, she says there has been a shift towards targeting a wider range of companies that appear to be good but whose claims are misleading: "The fear of litigation is very powerful, especially corporate litigation."
>
> Yet claims against states and companies can take years to resolve, says Setzer. The Swiss case was first filed in 2016.
>
> "I think we have to be creative about finding legal pathways that are faster," says Weiss. "Maybe we should be targeting the courts where justice moves more quickly."

Source: Amy Bell (2024) 'Climate lawsuits harness human rights to press for more action, Financial Times, 13 Sep. © The Financial Times Limited 2025. All Rights Reserved.

As the Cobre Panama example illustrates, human rights are linked to simply maintaining licence to operate and delivering a successful business. A robust strategy for corporate impact and dependencies on social systems is characterised, at minimum, by corporate acknowledgement of the comprehensive suite of potential impacts on human rights related to their business model and the need to work across stakeholders to ensure these rights are protected. In the words of the UN Human Rights Commission, 'even if States do not fulfil their obligations, all business enterprises are expected to respect human rights, meaning they should avoid infringing on the human rights of others, and should address adverse human rights impacts with which they are involved'.[xxxix] Importantly for leaders, however, human rights frameworks do not stop at the imperative to 'do no harm'. Rather, the human rights framework contains an inherent aspect of aspiration. To manage corporate impacts and dependencies grounded in human rights requires you and your teams to assess performance on an ongoing basis. As with so much in business, this work is never done.

Human rights provide a powerful framework for companies to build competitive advantage rooted in a pragmatic, comprehensive view of their impact and dependencies on social systems. They also offer companies a strong foundation for identifying trade-offs and prioritising resource allocation within the business. Companies cannot do everything: a human rights lens enables you to identify which social concerns are most significant to your business and therefore where you should focus. By setting out 'what good looks like' in the complex area of social systems, a strategy grounded in human rights empowers leaders to participate actively in conversations that shape evolving norms, expectations and regulations, and to do so with consistency and credibility.

Business, human rights and the United Nations Sustainable Development Goals

In Chapter 1, we set out the 17 Sustainable Development Goals (SDGs) as a guide to the areas where corporate leadership on social systems is required. In addition, we introduced the UN Global Compact as a set of core commitments for business to ensure it is acting in a manner that is aligned with minimum standards of good practice. In the face of the inevitably complex characteristics of social systems, the SDGs and Global Compact together provide a basic roadmap for business seeking to identify priorities on sustainability leadership.

Human rights form the conceptual foundation of both the SDGs and the Global Compact. The SDGs serve as a framework for you to understand your company's impacts and dependencies on social systems, highlighting areas of risk and opportunities for value creation. They accomplish this in at least three key ways.

First, they offer the ability to map areas where corporate impacts and dependencies on social and environmental systems overlap or mutually reinforce. Second, their specificity enables you to identify shared challenges within your industry, such as human rights violations in supply chains, and thus set the stage for you to catalyse action more widely than your own firm. Third, the SDGs are aspirational – they do not start from the corporate status quo. In this way, they draw attention to vulnerabilities in social systems that your teams might otherwise overlook or assume are 'too big', 'too complicated' or outside their remit. Some of these, of course, fall into the remit of government. However, corporate impacts and dependencies on social systems mean that the line between business and government responsibility is not always straightforward and therefore worthy of your attention.

Let us now walk through an example of how the SDGs can help a company identify ways in which progress on one SDG is related to progress on another, and build around these potential synergies. In this example, as is frequently the case, there is a connection between the health of environmental and social systems. Arla Foods, a dairy cooperative of more than 11,000 farmers based across seven

European countries, owes its incumbent social licence to operate in large part to its treatment of farmers, farm workers and the animals on which it depends. Yet rising awareness of the deleterious environmental impact of the dairy industry has complicated this picture significantly. Dairy accounts for between a quarter and a third of GHG emissions from a 'typical' European diet[xl] and is highly intensive in terms of use of land and freshwater. Demand for non-dairy milks has surged in recent years, with up to one third of the UK population consuming plant milks on a regular basis.[xli] Starting in 2005, Arla Foods understood the need to take serious measures to reduce and eventually eliminate GHG emissions. Since that time, the company has managed to decrease its emissions by 22 per cent while increasing milk production by 40 per cent. Progress to date has come from the use of renewable energies and waste reduction, as well as improvements in farming practices. The crucial question is whether the rate of progress will be enough to maintain corporate licence to operate considering increasing consumer and regulatory scrutiny of the dairy industry, and how this will be balanced with the needs of thousands of farm operators.

To deliver this change, dairy industry operators will need to work effectively with farmers, their families and the many communities and social systems on which they impact and depend to deliver substantial – potentially existential – changes to incumbent agricultural practice. Getting this right without loss of social licence to operate involves a delicate balancing act and clear-eyed view of trade-offs, as mounting political action by farmers disenfranchised by 'green' measures in Europe has made clear.[xlii] In an attempt to overcome this dilemma, Arla Foods is pioneering a strategy that links two SDGs: SDG 8 (decent work and economic growth) with SDG 15 (life on land). In this case, a global producer of dairy products has chosen to link their pay to dairy farmers not only to milk quality but on land use and GHG emissions from farms. Farmers who demonstrate strong environmental performance receive an income premium.[xliii] This approach allows the company to incentivise farmers in their supply chain to pursue practices that diminish stress on environmental systems, crucial for the resilience of the company's supply chain and the company's ongoing ability to exist. By extension, it incentivises innovation to improve and scale such practices and to develop new solutions.

The industry represents a clear example of the pain and predicament of finding the balance between business, social and environmental value in incumbent industries. The environmental impact of dairy is significant. Will their approach to balancing the needs of their farmers, customers and the environment prove sufficient to secure the future of their industry? Will Arla's primary product be dairy in the future, or will other forms of farming enable them to deliver value for investors as well as environmental and social systems? These questions are endemic to today's dairy industry as a whole. Arla's experience illuminates how the SDGs can enable companies to spot synergies between their impacts and dependencies on environmental and social systems and create competitive distance between themselves and others in an industry ripe for disruption.

Next, we turn to an instance in which a focus on the SDGs has enabled collaboration to address corporate impacts and dependencies shared across companies within an industry. Since the 1990s, work in garment factories has been one of the most frequent entry points for women across the globe to enter the formal labour force. The industry currently employs over 90 million workers, 75 per cent of whom are in Asia, and between 60 and 80 per cent of whom are female.[xliv] These individuals make up the workforce on which global fashion brands are entirely dependent under their current business model. And yet challenges of factory workers in global supply chains are numerous, as we set out at the start of this chapter.[xlv] In the context of the fashion industry, relative to males, female garment workers tend to disproportionally lack access to basic financial services and career advancement, as well as facing discrimination, harassment or gender-based violence associated with their work.[xlvi] SDG 5 – gender equality – draws corporate attention to the fact that that, while income from formal work is essential for female garment workers, this income may be associated with persistent human rights violations.

We have already noted the myriad challenges presented by incumbent business models in the fashion industry.[xlvii] Among these, the risks presented by gender inequality are substantial. Reputational risk resulting from significant risk of exploitation is part of the reality many global fashion brands face as a result of their business model. At the same time, garment factory work may provide women a rare entrypoint to the formal economy and a scarce opportunity for professional advancement. The picture is a mixed one.

Consumer-facing fashion brands in particular are sensitive to the need to safeguard their licence to operate. Many fast-fashion brands focus heavily on a female consumer base that is highly connected on social media, where news travels fast. To be effective, these brands need to develop an approach grounded in a gender-informed view on the human rights challenges women are unduly likely to face. In response to this shared challenge, fashion buyers and suppliers can collaborate with RISE, a workforce development programme focused on ensuring that SDG 5 is delivered in garment manufacturing supply chains. The initiative was designed in collaboration between Gap Inc. and four global NGOs with decades of expertise working with female garment workers.[1] When RISE was launched, these NGOs already had a track record of direct collaboration with 50 of the world's largest fashion retailers including Gap Inc., Inditex, Macy's Inc., Marks & Spencer and The Walt Disney Company. Currently active in factories in Bangladesh, China, Vietnam, Cambodia, Indonesia, India, Egypt and Pakistan, RISE is a collaborative response to a problem that is shared by brands, buyers and suppliers throughout the fashion industry: how to improve the health, skill levels and financial status of female workers on which their supply chain depends.

Rather than each company attempting to accomplish this – with limited prospect of success, if the industry track record is any indicator – RISE allows companies to pool resources, collaborate with experts and community workers, and deploy proven interventions to increase skill levels and financial services for women in their supply chains.[xlviii] Notably, this collaboration has also resulted in increased productivity, higher performance and better employee retention. In addition, it has reinforced companies' licence to operate and minimised their risk of enabling human rights violations in their supply chains. In this way, RISE's focus on SDG 5 has enabled companies to make credible improvement to gendered aspects of the social systems on which they impact and depend, reducing their risk.

The gains delivered by RISE on SDG 5 mean it is not simply corporate philanthropy or corporate social responsibility. Rather, it protects the social systems on which fashion houses currently rely to generate value and protects the companies themselves from risk. The persistence of global and pernicious violations of labour standards represents an archetypal case of a need for corporate leaders to take a systems view of the challenge: individual companies will be unable to secure human rights across their supply chains by working alone. Considering human rights at the system level offers you a view of the world in which your company is part of, and not separate from, ongoing challenges. For you as a

---

1   BSR's HERproject, P.A.C.E, CARE and Better Work.

leader, this means curiosity about how your own processes, business models and ways of working may perpetuate features of the system itself.

A final example drives home the point. Precisely because they are aspirational, the SDGs draw attention to aspects of social systems that firms might otherwise overlook, such as SDG 1 – ending poverty, in all its forms. The World Bank found that between 2011 and 2021, the percentage of adults across the globe with access to a bank or mobile money account increased from 51 per cent to 76 per cent, or from 37 per cent to 68 per cent for women in developing economies across the same period.[xlix] At the most basic level, access to banking services is a matter of financial inclusion that enables people to save, transfer funds safely and protect their earnings from theft or exploitation. Members of marginalised communities may lack essential items such as national identification cards or birth certificates, rendering them unable to transition into the formal economy. In many contexts, entire groups lack access to this provision.[l] By 2024, Mastercard had so far worked with governments, civil society and telecommunications providers to bring first-time digital financial services to 500 million people across the world.[li] The company works with governments to overcome administrative hurdles, which in turn strengthens social systems by overcoming systematic patterns of exclusion for specific people and communities.

This programme is not simply a 'nice to have' or an instance of corporate philanthropy. The initiative has strengthened the company's licence to operate in the eyes of governments. It has increased Mastercard's market, also generated knowledge about potential new markets, products and services, and increased the company's ability to be sought after as an expert on financial inclusion and innovative forms of finance across the globe. Some will argue that the existence of a profit motive makes such activity suspect – in this case, for example, is Mastercard deriving a business benefit from its work with some of the world's most financially disadvantaged communities? As with so much in the sphere of social systems, this is a topic worthy of debate.[lii] Returning, however, to our definition of sustainability: profit need not be at odds with value generation for social and environmental systems. While extractive models of profit making are indeed anachronistic, an embedded view of the firm within social systems means that it is appropriate for a company like Mastercard to have a transparent, strategic approach to its impact and dependencies on social systems, particularly regarding how they relate to its core value proposition, financial services. The SDGs can guide your company in defining what specific elements of social 'good' looks like, and how this applies to your business. This framework enables both internal and external audiences to assess efforts and draw conclusions about effectiveness.

It will come as no surprise to any corporate leader that the SDGs have limitations. They are complex and far reaching – to their detriment, some would argue.[liii] Equally unsurprisingly, they contain trade-offs within themselves. A goal in pursuit of better work may sit in tension with a goal to reduce consumption, and so on. From a leadership perspective, however, the presence of trade-offs is precisely the point: the SDGs, like human rights themselves, are aspirational. They signal the gap between the status quo and potential futures for social and environmental systems. For social systems, they are an imperfect but crucial guide to action.

Contributing to stronger social systems does not guarantee a quick win for your company. Far from it. Many social problems are non-linear in nature and costly to address. However, identifying the social systems on which your organisation impacts and depends is strategic time well spent. Such an approach enables you to have a clear view of what you can and cannot deliver, and why, and to allocate resources in a smart way. In addition, as the examples we have shared in this section demonstrate, an SDG lens can draw attention to areas where mutual benefit for your business and society might already exist. Because your company already impacts and depends on social systems, this scenario is more frequent than perhaps initially evident. With social systems, perhaps more than any other area, a shift in mindset is often necessary, along with adaptive leadership. When combined with leadership that embodies these qualities, the SDGs offer a credible framework for reviewing your company's activities and identifying new opportunities – not only for risk management but also for innovation and value creation.

Following the structure of the previous chapter, can now outline how social licence to operate and human rights can be re-framed, evaluated and acted upon for your business.

Re-framing business and social systems

At the framing stage, your task is twofold. The first is to identify pain points within social systems upon which your company impacts and depends. Where is there weakness, risk, waste, vulnerability, inefficiency or other avenues through which value is lost? Second, where can your business generate value? Given the expansive nature of potential corporate impact and dependencies on social systems, how can companies effectively frame their strategy in this area? In the previous chapter, we presented the process of framing as the task of identifying waste. We argued that companies can either create waste through their impact upon natural systems or else depend upon resources that are being wasted, or both. The intuition of framing corporate impact and dependency on social systems is not dissimilar.

First, a systems lens reminds us that your company's first task is to identify the social systems on which it impacts and depends. What social systems does the company impact directly as an employer, buyer, perhaps as an investor or as a vendor? Who does it employ, under which conditions and terms, how are goods procured, and with what level of insight into their origins? Which social systems are impacted by or crucial to its investments? What is its direct impact on consumers, including, for example, on their physical, emotional or financial health? When considering these questions for your own company, the SDGs provide a guide for what to pay attention to when framing impacts and dependencies on social systems. More importantly, they also provide a general standard against which to assess the health of social systems. Consider the Mastercard example: a major global financial services provider may or may not typically focus strategic attention on the issue of financial inclusion. But the lens on SDG 1 – ending poverty in all its forms – suddenly makes the issue evident. Extreme income poverty refers to surviving on less than $2.15 per person per day at 2017 purchasing power parity. It is an outcome with classic systemic causes, including poor access to social protections in the form of education and health services. The UN estimates that 55 per cent of the global population live without these social protections. Unemployment, social marginalisation, natural disasters and conflict are often confounding factors. At current rates, an estimated 7 per cent of the global is anticipated to remain in extreme poverty by 2030,[liv] a complex challenge requiring systems-level interventions.

Standard Chartered Bank, like most elite financial institutions, offers employees the possibility for well-remunerated work with significant scope for professional advancement. Consider that 80 to 90 per cent of persons with disabilities of working age in non-OECD countries are unemployed. In OECD countries, that figure is between 50 and 70 per cent.[lv] The economic irrationality, not to mention grave human rights failure, suggested by these statistics is jarring.

A simple glance at the SDGs is enough to suggest that this status quo is far from 'good' – SDG 8, decent work, for example, is clearly not being achieved at scale for people with disabilities across the globe. Standard Chartered has partnered with the International Labour Organisation to build its knowledge on how to better integrate people with disabilities into its workforce. Sign language classes, targeted career fairs and recruitment drives, flexible working options and tailored on-boarding processes are just a few of the initiatives the company has successfully deployed in this area via its global Employee Resource Groups.[lvi] These groups have a mandate not only to provide a collective voice and platform for coordinated activity across the bank's 55+ country locations, but also to deliver mentoring and education to break down stereotypes regarding people with disabilities throughout the organisation. The result is access to highly desirable careers for people from a group for which unemployment is globally endemic.

A systems view enables you to 'zoom out' from your employees, suppliers and customers and generate truly fresh strategic insights. Consider the PwC example: do workers all tend to come from a similar social background, racial or ethnic group, or gender? What risks or vulnerabilities might that introduce to your social licence to operate or indeed to your business directly? The examples of Mastercard and PwC raise an important point: in both cases, companies identified specific social systems on which they impact and depend and built strategy around these. In an area as potentially wide-ranging as social systems, this level of focus is crucial.

This kind of framing enables you to identify which social systems your company impacts and depends upon, and to ask what 'good' looks like in these systems. Framing also enables you and your teams to make clear choices about where to focus, and how to do so efficiently. This means going beyond reacting to events and outcomes to work at the level of root causes, as PwC has done with the basic step of offering new joiners a cash advance. As a professional services firm, it makes sense for PwC to start by asking 'where can our business generate value?' Once a set of possibilities is identified, the company is in a position to prioritise based upon business impact. In the case of PwC, addressing diversity within their talent pipeline makes business sense. Companies who undertake the framing process effectively come away with a well-defined view of the social systems upon which they impact and depend, what 'good' looks like for these systems, and strategic clarity on where they will allocate their resources.

Evaluating social systems and your business

Once you have mapped your company's impacts and dependencies on social systems, you can begin evaluation. As with evaluation of environmental systems, a degree of estimation is inevitable here and should not put you off.[lvii] Social systems are open to evaluation through multiple methods including quantitative metrics (gender-based wage gaps or demographic patterns in recruitment or promotions, for example) as well as qualitative methods (including insights from focus groups, journals and in-depth case studies). Central to the integrity of evaluation of social systems is an agreed normative framework against which to judge progress. Here the role of human rights is important as a common language. Equally central is the co-creation of measures of progress from first-person accounts by those affected. This latter step is remarkably easy to overlook. However, an emphasis on developing indicators and evaluations that reflect the choices and values of people within the social system in question is core to the integrity of your activities, and builds your licence to operate.[lviii]

Precisely because your company is neither a charity nor a civil society entity, it may be wise for you to partner with or seek expertise from collaborators with front-line experience with the social system in question. This may be a government entity or an NGO. To design their approach to employment and advancement for people with disabilities, for example, Standard Chartered learned from the International Labour Organisation as well as a range of NGOs with long experience working directly with the topic. For fashion brands, RISE offers the same. Companies who skip this step risk directing scarce resources to interventions that make no difference or even worsen the situation they sought to improve.[lix] As a first step to partnering on evaluation in a manner that is credible, mutually beneficial for the NGO or government agency and the company, and generates shared insights, companies can begin by working with partners to, for example:

1 Identify people or groups to interview about the context for the current situation and clarify what questions to ask.
2 Organise and begin to improve the quality of the information gathered from interviews or focus groups.
3 Develop a preliminary system of analysis of how different factors interact over time to reinforce existing realities in the social system.[lx]

An approach of this type has at least two benefits: it can generate valuable insights for the company and, when approached from a corporate posture of curiosity and learning, can build trust with partners. In his book *Net Positive*, former Unilever CEO Paul Polman recounts his experience with global NGOs critiquing the company's record on human rights and environmental abuses related to its sourcing of palm oil. The company's leadership perceived themselves to be something of pioneers on this issue, having founded an industry *Roundtable on Sustainable Palm Oil* some years earlier. Unilever, however, remained neither fully trusted nor credible due to its ongoing record on palm-oil related deforestation. Scathing reports and challenges from the NGO sector led to a meeting between Paul Polman and then-Greenpeace UK CEO John Sauven, and a process of knowledge sharing, increased understanding and action on the part of the company began.[lxi] In hindsight, Polman reflects, the experience resulted in a 'life changing moment' for those sourcing palm oil for Unilever and for the company itself. The company reassessed its sourcing efforts, cancelled contracts with suppliers found to be in violation of core standards and worked with other multinational buyers to improve transparency and accountability in the global palm oil supply chain.

The palm oil experience was a success for Unilever in many ways. And yet this is not a fairytale: the social and environmental concerns associated with the product remain acute. Globally, palm oil employs millions of people across more than 15 countries – these are not small numbers.[lxii] The industry remains hugely reliant on smallholder farmers who have limited agency over their livelihoods. Deforestation, often a result of poverty in communities, is far from eliminated. But the issue is no longer obscured, poorly monitored or treated as a corporate irrelevance. Companies like Unilever impact and depend on producer communities for palm oil and – if they so choose – are in a position today to evaluate these impacts and make strategic changes as a result. The implications are summarised as follows by Caroline Rees and Bob Eccles:

> *We should pay attention to indicators showing whether a company's business model, governance and leadership are designed to function in a way that is respectful of people's human rights. When risks to people are embedded into a business model, it's likely that people will be hurt – again and again. Similarly, when the actions of the board and a company's leaders are not geared toward fostering a culture that treats people with respect, it is predictable that vulnerable workers, communities, or customers will suffer negative consequences.*[lxiii]

As a step to robust evaluation, partnering with those with front-line expertise and first-hand experience with the social system in question is crucial. This leads us to a second task of evaluation of corporate impact and dependencies on social systems: learn about the whole system, not just the 'part' of the system you believe your company affects or is affected by. In the case of social mobility, efforts by a company like PwC will be more effective if they reflect the contributors to social exclusion that exist outside their recruits, i.e. the educational, social and access barriers that might prevent someone from a given socioeconomic background from even applying to a role at the company in the first place. The information you gather from interviews and focus groups, for example, can help enormously in this regard. As you organise and make sense of this information, steps to help understand the whole system include:[lxiv]

1 Listen for what is curious, confusing or contrary among interviewees. This is likely to be evidence of a systemic issue, something that lies behind what is going on but that might not be immediately evident.
2 Distinguish measurable data from how these data are interpreted. If there is a difference, then so too there are accepted norms and ways of understanding that belie an underlying reality, and possibly therefore a latent risk or opportunity.
3 Identify key variables, which social systems specialists sometimes call 'critical success factors' or 'key indicators'. You need to understand where any given action can realistically achieve change.
4 Stay alert to patterns in story lines or archetypes that emerge repeatedly. Change may require challenging existing accounts.

These steps, along with collaboration with partners, can go a long way to enabling your company to develop a deep strategic understanding of social systems on which your business impacts and depends, and of the intervention points that may be most effective.

As you progress in this work, remember that environmental systems and social systems interact. An example is the link between climate change and human health, which is increasingly compromised by extreme heat. Heat stress affects the safety, well-being and productivity of hundreds of millions of agricultural, construction, manufacturing and other workers worldwide each year. The International Labour Organisation estimates that by 2030 the equivalent of

2 per cent of total working hours globally will be 'lost' each year due to productivity decreases related to extreme heat, with serious implications for employers and investors, alike.[lxv] Similar climate change related impacts are evident in the area of health, where the World Health Organisation estimates that between 2030 and 2050, as many as 250,000 additional deaths will be due every year across the globe as a result of climate change related malaria, diarrhoea, malnutrition and heat stress.[lxvi] Food security, air quality, water scarcity and increased disease burden are all climate change related stressors that threaten the social systems on which companies depend.[lxvii] As a result, when you evaluate your corporate impacts and dependencies on social systems, it is essential to do so with a view on how social systems connect to the environmental systems we discussed in Chapters 3 and 4.

In fact, as you evaluate what 'good' looks like within the social systems on which your company impacts and depends, drawing a link between social and environmental systems can be a powerful tool to identify risk, opportunity and strategy. This is particularly salient given how the losses and gains from the transition to new forms of production and energy will be distributed, within and between countries. The International Labour Organisation defines the 'just transition' to mean 'greening the economy in a way that is as fair and inclusive as possible to everyone concerned, creating decent work opportunities and leaving no one behind'.[lxviii] In the context of today's social and geopolitical landscape, this remains a tall order. While it is true that current modes of production and consumption lead to biodiversity loss, pollution and create potentially catastrophic levels of risk for human life and the environment, we have also emphasised that they create employment, food, housing, transport, healthcare and financial security for many. There is a need to generate these goods – and more – via means that mitigate and adapt in light of the social and environmental risks we currently face. In the second decade of the twenty-first century, close to 30 per cent of the global population lacks reliable access to clean fuels for cooking. An estimated 10 per cent of the global population lacks access to electricity, and recent years have seen access become increasingly spotty and unpredictable even in major urban centres.[lxix] Such statistics are a sobering reminder that hundreds of millions of people live daily without a suitable source of energy to transition from.

The transition to more sustainable forms of production and consumption will create new economic opportunities for firms. At the same time, many industries will be unable to continue to operate in their current forms. Identifying the opportunities for innovation and value creation associated with a 'just transition' requires companies to proactively evaluate their impact and dependency on social systems through the lens of who stands to be affected by this momentous change.

In summary, our focus here is on guiding your company through a comprehensive evaluation of its impacts and dependencies on social systems. As a first step, we emphasise the importance of asking the right questions of the right people: for many companies, this means partnering with those with front-line expertise and first-hand experience within the social systems relevant to the company. Next, your evaluation of specific impacts and dependencies will be stronger if you work to build a broad perspective of the social system, rather than limiting your assessment to impact areas as they may be initially perceived. This leads to a third evaluative lens, which underscores the power and importance of asking how social systems on which your company impacts and depends affect, and are in turn affected by, environmental systems. Finally, we offer the 'just transition' as a lens through which you can proactively assess the shape of not just current but also future impacts and dependencies. Coupled with the framing processes we shared earlier in this chapter, these approaches to evaluation serve as a comprehensive guide for companies aspiring to evaluate their impacts and dependencies on social systems.

The framing process enables you to determine where to focus, and to identify gaps between the status quo and potential futures. Evaluation refines the scope of your approach and enables you to adjust course when needed. These steps enable you to identify key indicators of progress, and move towards action.

Action on social systems as a business

'If you really want to understand something, try to change it.'[lxx] For companies seeking to understand their impacts and dependencies on social systems, the maxim is apt. Moving from framing to evaluation brings you to the key step for your business: action. Here, you can build on your framing and evaluation work to start developing strategies and innovations.

An example of the kind of data point you might find revealing, and around which plan action, is the nature of the visas workers within your supply chain hold. For workers crossing international borders, visas that tie them to a single employer are commonplace. And yet these visas have been associated with high levels of worker exploitation. Examples from the agricultural, construction, manufacturing and domestic service sectors are rife, where workers may find themselves unable to leave their employer due to threats of debt repayment, loss of identity paperwork or similar. Hewlett Packard exhibited early awareness of this issue and became a pioneer in proactively upholding a human-rights based approach to recruitment and asking their suppliers to do the same. Aware of risks to social licence to operate and to their reputation, the company requires three things from all their suppliers: training on human rights for all workers, clear and accessible grievance mechanisms, and zero tolerance for intermediaries who require workers to pay recruitment fees, transport charges or other costs that result in worker indebtedness.[lxxi] This is a strong example of action based on a clear-eyed understanding of the social systems on which the company depends. As a result, Hewlett Packard has been recognised as an industry leader on human rights and is a standard-setter for others within and outside their industry.

In a similar vein, an approach known as worker-driven social responsibility (WSR) has gained increasing acceptance among corporate buyers seeking to de-risk their supply chains.[lxxii] In large-scale industries from US agriculture to UK fishing, it represents a powerful example of how smart companies are partnering to manage their impact and dependencies on social systems, and strengthening their businesses and these systems as a result. Originating in migrant workers in agricultural settings in the United States, WSR programmes now collaborate with some of the largest commercial food buyers in the USA via the Fair Food Programme,[lxxiii] a comprehensive effort to bring worker voice front and centre to buyers at the top of the industry. A partnership between growers, farmworkers and food company buyers has dramatically improved conditions for farmworkers and reduced supply chain risk for participating companies. The initiative works via peer-to-peer training on human rights and labour rights delivered at partner farms, a clear set of grievance mechanisms and support for class action lawsuits in case of abuse and direct hiring of workers from abroad without the use of recruiters.

UK seafood industry cracks down on exploitation of overseas crew

Two-year scheme sets new standards for pay and working conditions on British boats

By Antonia Cundy

The UK seafood sector has launched Europe's first "worker-driven" scheme to tackle the exploitation of migrant crew on British fishing boats by setting minimum standards for pay and working conditions.

The two-year pilot will be run by labour rights groups in partnership with the Seafood Ethics Action Alliance (SEA Alliance), a consumer group whose members represent 95 per cent of the UK seafood market and include Tesco, Asda, Morrisons and Whitby Seafoods.

The scheme gives workers a key role in establishing, monitoring and enforcing their own employment rights. It aims to address a lack of labour legislation for crew created by an immigration "loophole" that denies those who work in international waters the protection of UK employment law.

Chris Williams, fisheries expert at the ITF, said the project gives migrant fishers "a chance for greater protection and improved conditions at work, as well as the ability to shape their own working conditions".

The attempt to clean up labour standards comes after criticism of the seafood industry's systemic dependence on low-paid migrant crew and a series of labour abuse scandals that have rocked the sector in recent years.

Experts estimate that more than 1,200 overseas crew on British boats are employed through "transit visas", which in recent decades have been adopted by some employers seeking to evade UK employment law.

Transit visas give an individual a fixed period of time to enter and pass through the UK to a place outside the country and are intended for use by merchant seafarers, such as those boarding a cargo ship bound for another country.

A Financial Times investigation last year highlighted the mistreatment of vulnerable overseas crew under the system, which human rights lawyers have argued facilitates modern slavery.

The government has in recent years introduced legislation to crack down on boats misusing transit visas. The Nationalities and Borders Act 2022 requires employers to apply for skilled worker visas in order to hire migrant crew in UK waters.

But many boats are exempt because they fish beyond the 12-nautical mile territorial limit. The pilot programme promises to fill the gaps in legislation for this group of workers by guaranteeing minimum standards over pay, rest hours and grievance procedures.

> The programme will run out of two ports in north east Scotland in partnership with the Scottish White Fish Producers Association, the largest fish producer group in Europe.
>
> Unlike many voluntary corporate social responsibility schemes, the pilot programme is based on legally binding agreements between employers and buyers that incentivise adherence and are audited by an independent council.
>
> The agreements are expected to be in place by the second quarter of this year, according to a person close to the discussions.
>
> The programme has been launched by Focus on Labour Exploitation (Flex), a non-profit group, the International Transport Workers' Federation (ITF) and the Fair Food Programme.

Source: Antonia Cundy (2024) 'UK seafood industry cracks down on exploitation of overseas crew', Financial Times, 08 Jan. ©The Financial Times Limited 2025. All Rights Reserved.

When choosing pathways for action on social systems, your company cannot be all things to all people. However, you can incorporate human rights and the social licence to operate into the design processes for framing and evaluation, resulting in effective action. The current landscape reflects a growing appetite for strategic, creative, innovative corporate engagement with impacts and dependencies on social systems. Conversely, companies who are slow to act on their impacts and dependencies on social systems face risk and lost opportunity.

In summary, corporations are natural catalysts for social change due to their scale, resources and capacity for experimentation and innovation. By dint of their size and scale, it is unlikely that any substantial company can avoid having an impact on people and communities. The question, therefore, is not whether your company has impact and dependencies on social systems, but what the nature of these impacts and dependencies is. Your engagement with this question creates an awareness of risk and opportunity for your business, acting as a guide to strategy, resilience and value creation. Companies who do this well have powerful opportunities to lead.

Reflection questions

In this chapter, we have explored the connection between business and social systems. Social systems are influenced by, and in turn influence, natural and climate systems, highlighting the need for an integrated approach that considers these dimensions holistically rather than as separate silos. As you have been discussing with your team since the reflection questions we introduced the end of Chapter 3, each of these systems is crucial to the other and to the resilience of your business. The way a company interacts with communities, employees and social systems as a whole has implications not only for its social licence to operate but also for its ability to thrive in a rapidly changing world. By understanding what this means for your business in particular, you can uncover opportunities for innovation, leadership and growth.

As you conclude this chapter, take the time to consider the questions we have provided here. With your teams, use this moment to deepen your understanding of how social, natural and climate systems interact within the context of your business. This level of reflection will prepare you for Chapter 6, where we shift our focus to the practical aspects of measuring and reporting outcomes.

1. To what extent does your executive leadership team have a comprehensive understanding of the key social system impacts and dependencies of your company? What about your board?
2. How effective are your company's efforts to engage in this area?
3. What partnerships might there be outside the company to develop your strategy on social system level impacts and dependencies?
4. What steps could you take to strengthen your company's framing, evaluation or action on impacts and dependencies on social systems?

Recommended reading

Andreou, N. and Besharov, M. (2022) Rethinking How We Measure Companies on Social and Environmental Impact. *MIT Sloan Management Review*. Available at: https://sloanreview.mit.edu/article/rethinking-how-we-measure-companies-on-social-and-environmental-impact/.

Business & Human Rights Resource Centre (2024) KnowTheChain: Good Practice Guide 2024. Available at: https://www.business-humanrights.org/en/from-us/briefings/knowthechain-good-practice-guide-2024/.

IPCC (2022) IPCC Sixth Assessment Report: Impacts, Adaptation and Vulnerability – Summary for Policymakers. www.ipcc.ch. Available at: https://www.ipcc.ch/report/ar6/wg2/chapter/summary-for-policymakers/.

Polman, P. and Winston, A. (2021) The Net Positive Manifesto. *Harvard Business Review*, 1 September. Available at: hbr.org/2021/09/the-net-positive-manifesto.

Ruggie, J.G. (2013) *Just Business: Multinational Corporations and Human Rights*. New York: W.W. Norton & Company.

Sen, A. (1999) *Development as Freedom*. Oxford: Oxford University Press.

Shift (2024) Strengthening the S in ESG. 27 August. Available at: https://shiftproject.org/resource/strengthening-the-s-in-esg/.

Stroh, D.P. (2015) *Systems Thinking for Social Change: A Practical Guide to Solving Complex Problems, Avoiding Unintended Consequences, and Achieving Lasting Results*. White River Junction, Vermont: Chelsea Green Publishing.

Taylor, A. (2021) So Many Stakeholders. How Do Companies Choose Who to Satisfy? *Wall Street Journal*, 24 June, sec. Business. Available at: https://www.wsj.com/articles/so-many-stakeholders-strategy-11624308112.

United Nations (2011) Guiding Principles on Business and Human Rights Implementing the United Nations 'Protect, Respect and Remedy' Framework. Available at: https://www.ohchr.org/sites/default/files/documents/publications/guidingprinciplesbusinesshr_en.pdf.

Notes

[i] Murray, C. and Dempsey, H. (2023) Protesters vs Critical Minerals: Panama Copper Fiasco Shows Risks to Green Transition. www.ft.com, 18 December. Available at: https://www.ft.com/content/1d3e72fb-9c6d-48da-963d-31afd456850f?.

[ii] Alkire, S. (2008) *Valuing Freedoms: Sen's Capability Approach and Poverty Reduction*. Oxford: Oxford University Press.

[iii] Smyth, J. and Murphy, H. (2023) The Teen Mental Health Crisis: A Reckoning for Big Tech. *Financial Times*, 26 March. Available at: https://www.ft.com/content/77d06d3e-2b9f-4d46-814f-da2646fea60c.

[iv] Wilson, T. (2023) Shell Hit with Damages Claim by 11,000 Nigerians in UK High Court. *Financial Times*, 2 February. Available at: https://www.ft.com/content/7356e0c4-47eb-483c-9732-e3cd84d83a75.

[v] Hume, N. (2021) Rio to Form Indigenous Advisory Group after Rock Cave Blasts. www.ft.com, Autumn 3. Available at: https://www.ft.com/content/9759fb6b-9a75-4230-b6d4-235b87287f99.

vi   Botsman, R. (2018) *Who Can You Trust? How Technology Brought Us Together – and Why It Could Drive Us Apart*. UK: Penguin Business.

vii   Speed, M. and Louch, W. (2024) CVC Accused of Ignoring Kenyan Co-Operatives in Tea Estates Sale. www.ft.com, 3 April. Available at: https://www.ft.com/content/4d858b66-2321-46bd-a2e5-e99a21865f99.

viii   Gartenberg, C., Prat, A. and Serafeim, G. (2019) Corporate Purpose and Financial Performance. *Organization Science* 30, no. 1, January: 1–18. Available at: https://doi.org/10.1287/orsc.2018.1230.

ix   Gautier, K., *et al*. (2022) Research: How Employee Experience Impacts Your Bottom Line. *Harvard Business Review*, 22 March. Available at: https://hbr.org/2022/03/research-how-employee-experience-impacts-your-bottom-line.

x   Bellet, C., De Neve, J.-E. and Ward, G. (2023) Does Employee Happiness Have an Impact on Productivity? *Management Science*, 11 May. Available at: https://doi.org/10.1287/mnsc.2023.4766.

xi   Bartleby, (2018) The High Costs of Staff Turnover. *The Economist*, 20 September 20. Available at: https://www.economist.com/business/2018/09/20/the-high-costs-of-staff-turnover.

xii   Glaveski, S. (2021) Stop Sabotaging Your Workforce. *Harvard Business Review*, 27 May. Available at: https://hbr.org/2021/05/stop-sabotaging-your-workforce.

xiii   Business & Human Rights Resource Centre (2023) True Cost of Our Tea: Sexual Abuse on Kenyan Tea Farms Revealed. 20 February. Available at: https://www.business-humanrights.org/en/latest-news/true-cost-of-our-tea-sexual-abuse-on-kenyan-tea-farms-revealed/.

xiv   Hill, A. (2023) Apple Workers Deserve i-Dorms as Good as the Technology. www.ft.com, 15 December. Available at: https://www.ft.com/content/6f6e3e62-c06c-42b3-8b1b-a4dabbf2334c.

xv   Yang, Y. He Blew the Whistle on Amazon. He's Still Paying the Price. www.ft.com, 7 December. Available at: https://www.ft.com/content/de5fea12-2938-4c20-b394-10ca258a5fa1.

xvi   International Labour Organisation (2023) The Rana Plaza Disaster Ten Years On: What Has Changed? www.ilo.org, April. Available at: https://www.ilo.org/infostories/en-GB/Stories/Country-Focus/rana-plaza#footer.

xvii   Burton, A. and Confino, P. (2022) Refugees, Trafficking Survivors, and the Formerly Incarcerated Are at Center of Hilton's Hiring Strategy. *Fortune*, 14 October Available at: https://fortune.com/2022/10/14/

xviii hilton-is-widening-its-talent-pool-recruiting-refugees-and-embracing-second-chance-hiring/.
xviii Boo, J. (2022) World's Best Workplaces. Great Place to Work®. Available at: https://www.greatplacetowork.com/worlds-best-workplaces.
xix https://www.tent.org/resource/company-resources/.
xx van der Erve, L., *et al.* (2023) Intergenerational Mobility in the UK. IFS Deaton Review of Inequalities, intergenerational-mobility-in-the-uk. Available at: https://ifs.org.uk/inequality/intergenerational-mobility-in-the-uk
xxi PricewaterhouseCoopers (2023) PwC Announces New Steps to Support New Joiners and Prospective Recruits from Lower Socio-Economic Backgrounds. PwC, 3 December. Available at: https://www.pwc.co.uk/press-room/press-releases/corporate-news/pwc-announces-new-steps-to-support-new-joiners-and-prospective-recruits-from-lower-socio-economic-backgrounds.html.
xxii Leppert, R. (2023) A Look at Black-Owned Businesses in the U.S. Pew Research Center, 21 February. Available at: https://www.pewresearch.org/short-reads/2025/02/12/a-look-at-black-owned-businesses-in-the-us/.
xxiii BLK + GRN (2023) BLK + GRN – About. Accessed 14 December 2023 at: https://blkgrn.com/pages/new-about-2023.
xxiv Baboolall, D., *et al.* (2022) Black Representation in the Beauty Industry. McKinsey, www.mckinsey.com, 10 June. Available at: https://www.mckinsey.com/industries/consumer-packaged-goods/our-insights/black-representation-in-the-beauty-industry#:~:text=Black%20brands%20make%20up%20only.
xxv Unnikrishnan, S. and Blair, C. (2019) Want to Boost the Global Economy by $5 Trillion? Support Women as Entrepreneurs. BCG Global, 30 July. Available at: https://www.bcg.com/publications/2019/boost-global-economy-5-trillion-dollar-support-women-entrepreneurs.
xxvi International Labour Organization (2022) Global Estimates of Modern Slavery: Forced Labour and Forced Marriage. www.ilo.org, 12 September. Available at: https://www.ilo.org/global/topics/forced-labour/publications/WCMS_854733/lang--en/index.htm.
xxvii Business and Human Rights Resource Centre (2022) Closing the Gap: Evidence for Effective Human Rights Due Diligence. Available at: https://knowthechain.org/wp-content/uploads/2022-KTC-mHREDD-brief.pdf.

xxviii Murray, S. (2023) So You Think You Know Your Supply Chain? *Financial Times*, 24 March, sec. Moral Money. Available at: https://www.ft.com/content/687c2a10-403b-4a93-85c0-3ede41af5d09.

xxix https://globalfishingwatch.org.

xxx https://altana.ai.

xxxi Stengel, G. (2022) A Wearable Device Company That Protects against Heat Injury Finds Its Product-Culture-Talent Fit. *Forbes*, 30 March. Available at: https://www.forbes.com/sites/geristengel/2022/03/30/a-wearable-device-company-that-protects-against-heat-injury-finds-its-product-culture-talent-fit/.

xxxii Norges Bank Investment Management (2017) UNICEF and the Fund Establish Children's Rights Network. https://www.nbim.no/en/news-and-insights/the-press/press-releases/2017/unicef-and-the-fund-establish-childrens-rights-network/.

xxxiii Murray, S. (2023) So You Think You Know Your Supply Chain? *Financial Times*, 24 March, sec. Moral Money. Available at: https://www.ft.com/content/687c2a10-403b-4a93-85c0-3ede41af5d09.

xxxiv Hamdani, K.A. and Turner Ruffing, L. (2015) *United Nations Centre on Transnational Corporations: Corporate Conduct and the Public Interest*. Abingdon, Oxon: Routledge.

xxxv Ruggie, R. (2008) *Protect, Respect and Remedy: A Framework for Business and Human Rights*. Human Rights Council, New York: United Nations, 7 April.

xxxvi United Nations (2011) Guiding Principles on Business and Human Rights: Implementing the United Nations 'Protect, Respect and Remedy' Framework. Available at: https://cfnhri.org/wp-content/uploads/2020/01/GuidingPrinciplesBusinessHR_EN.pdf.

xxxvii Davies, P. (2022) Ending Human Rights Abuses in Which Companies and States Are Complicit. blogs.law.ox.ac.uk, 5 April. Available at: https://blogs.law.ox.ac.uk/business-law-blog/blog/2022/04/ending-human-rights-abuses-which-companies-and-states-are-complicit.

xxxviii Hancock, A. (2024) Climate Change Failings Violate Citizens' Rights, European Court Rules. www.ft.com, 9 April. Available at: https://www.ft.com/content/2f65a1b9-ba6c-4f09-8e66-96a1e06ad5b6.

xxxix United Nations Office of the High Commissioner on Human Rights, OHCHR and Business and Human Rights. OHCHR, n.d. Available at: https://www.ohchr.org/en/business-and-human-rights#:~:text=About%20business%20and%20human%20rights&text=Even%20if%20States%20do%20not.

xl Sandström, V., et al. (2018) The Role of Trade in the Greenhouse Gas Footprints of EU Diets. *Global Food Security*, Vol. 19, December: 48–55. Available at: https://doi.org/10.1016/j.gfs.2018.08.007.

xli Ritchie, H. (2022) Dairy vs. Plant-Based Milk: What Are the Environmental Impacts? *Our World in Data*, 19 January. Available at: https://ourworldindata.org/environmental-impact-milks.

xlii Schmitz, R. (2023) In the Netherlands, a Farmers Party Taps into Widespread Discontent with Government. NPR, 21 September. Available at: https://www.npr.org/2023/09/21/1199431374/netherlands-farmer-citizen-movement-bbb-dutch-elections.

xliii Abboud, L. (2019) Can British Farmers Achieve Net Zero Carbon Emissions by 2050? www.ft.com, Autumn 7. Available at: https://www.ft.com/content/7d522ad8-abb4-11e9-8030-530adfa879c2.

xliv How to Achieve Gender Equality in Global Garment Supply Chains. (2023) www.ilo.org. Available at: https://www.ilo.org/infostories/en-GB/Stories/discrimination/garment-gender#the-global-garment-industry-a-bird.

xlv Nilsson, P. (2021) Pandemic Deprives Asia's Garment Workers of Almost $12bn in Wages. www.ft.com, 18 July. Available at: https://www.ft.com/content/22007eb9-440d-48c7-b3dc-fce62c735e1e.

xlvi International Labour Organisation (2023) How to Achieve Gender Equality in Global Garment Supply Chains. webapps.ilo.org, March. Available at: https://webapps.ilo.org/infostories/en-GB/Stories/discrimination/garment-gender#voice.

xlvii Hyde, P. (2023) Rags, Not Riches: Why Ghana Is Fast Fashion's Dumping Ground. www.forbesafrica.com, 18 January. Available at: https://www.forbesafrica.com/fashion/2023/01/18/rags-not-riches-why-ghana-is-fast-fashions-dumping-ground/.

xlviii Svarer, C. and Cramer, A. (2023) Accelerating Equality for Women Workers in Global Garment Supply Chains through New Initiative RISE. Blog, Sustainable Business Network and Consultancy, BSR. www.bsr.org, 8 March. Available at: https://riseequal.org/about-rise/.

xlix World Bank (2021) The Global Findex Database 2021. World Bank. Available at: https://www.worldbank.org/en/publication/globalfindex.

l Advancing Financial Inclusion to Help Thrive in a Digital Economy (2021) www.mastercardcenter.org, 3 October. Available at: https://www.mastercard.com/news/perspectives/2024/when-financial-access-isn-t-enough/.

li   Prosperity | Priceless Causes | Mastercard. Mastercard Financial Inclusion, accessed 29 March 2024. Available at: https://www.mastercard.co.uk/en-gb/vision/priceless-causes/prosperity.html.

lii   Dolan, C. and Johnstone-Louis, M. (2011) Re-Siting Corporate Responsibility. Focaal 2011, no. 60, 1 June: 21–33. Available at: https://doi.org/10.3167/fcl.2011.600103.

liii   Pilling, D. (2023) Why the SDGs Are a Bad Idea. www.ft.com, 31 December. Available at: https://www.ft.com/content/ceedd447-a6d1-4773-9a8a-e3b25a50645c.

liv   United Nations (2015) Goal 1: End Poverty in All Its Forms Everywhere. United Nations Sustainable Development, United Nations. Available at: https://www.un.org/sustainabledevelopment/poverty/.

lv   United Nations (2019) Disability and Employment | United Nations Enable. Un.org, United Nations. Available at: https://www.un.org/development/desa/disabilities/resources/factsheet-on-persons-with-disabilities.html.

lvi   Miller, C. (2023) Standard Chartered Bank. The Valuable 500. Available at: https://www.thevaluable500.com/companies/standard-chartered-bank#:~:text=We%20want%20to%20be%20a.

lvii   Rees, C. and Eccles, R.G. Quantify Your Company's Impact on People. *Harvard Business Review*, 8 September. Available at: https://hbr.org/2020/09/quantify-your-companys-impact-on-people.

lviii   Sen, A. (1999) *Development as Freedom*. Oxford: Oxford University Press.

lix   Stroh, D.P. (2015) *Systems Thinking for Social Change: A Practical Guide to Solving Complex Problems, Avoiding Unintended Consequences, and Achieving Lasting Results*. White River Junction, Vermont: Chelsea Green Publishing.

lx   Questions adapted from Stroh, D.P. (2015) *Systems Thinking for Social Change: A Practical Guide to Solving Complex Problems, and Achieving Lasting Results*. White River Junction, Vermont: Chelsea Green Publishing.

lxi   Polman, P. and Winston, A.S. (2021) *Net Positive How Courageous Companies Thrive by Giving More than They Take*. Boston, Ma: Harvard Business Review Press.

lxii   Ritchie, H. and Roser, M. (2020) Palm Oil. *Our World in Data*, December. Available at: https://ourworldindata.org/palm-oil.

lxiii Rees, C. and Eccles, R.G. (2020) Quantify Your Company's Impact on People. *Harvard Business Review*, 8 September. Available at: https://hbr.org/2020/09/quantify-your-companys-impact-on-people.

lxiv Questions adapted from Stroh, D.P. (2015) *Systems Thinking for Social Change : A Practical Guide to Solving Complex Problems, Avoiding Unintended Consequences, and Achieving Lasting Results*. White River Junction, Vermont: Chelsea Green Publishing.

lxv International Labour Organisation (2019) Working on a Warmer Planet. Available at: https://www.ilo.org/wcmsp5/groups/public/---dgreports/---dcomm/---publ/documents/publication/wcms_711919.pdf.

lxvi World Health Organization Climate Change. World Health Organization, WHO, 12 October. Available at: https://www.who.int/news-room/fact-sheets/detail/climate-change-and-health.

lxvii Forum for the Future (2023) Climate and Health Toolkit. *Forum for the Future*, 4 December. Available at: https://www.forumforthefuture.org/climate-and-health-toolkit.

lxviii International Labour Organisation (2021) Just Transition. www.ilo.org, 22 October. Available at: https://www.ilo.org/topics-and-sectors/just-transition-towards-environmentally-sustainable-economies-and-societies.

lxix Ritchie, H. and Roser, M. (2019) Energy Access. *Our World in Data*. Available at: https://ourworldindata.org/energy-access.

lxx The quote is attributed to social psychologist Kurt Lewin in Stroh, D.P. *Systems Thinking for Social Change : A Practical Guide to Solving Complex Problems*, p. 91, though there is some debate about the original source and phrasing.

lxxi Schultz, J. (2022) Boldly Dedicated to Upholding Human Rights. Hpe.com, *Hewlett Packard Enterprise*, 9 December. Available at: https://www.hpe.com/us/en/newsroom/blog-post/2022/12/boldly-dedicated-to-upholding-human-rights.html.

lxxii https://media.business-humanrights.org/media/documents/files/documents/What_is_WSR_0.pdf.

lxxiii https://fairfoodprogram.org.

CHAPTER 6
HOW AND WHY TO EMBED SUSTAINABILITY INTO CORPORATE REPORTING

Companies have long been encouraged to report on their environmental and social impacts, not least since the Global Reporting Initiative (GRI) was created in 1997. As Figure 6.1 suggests, corporate social responsibility (CSR) and other sustainability reports have proliferated. Yet such reporting has too often remained disconnected from corporate strategy and capital allocation decisions, while also being mostly voluntary and therefore discretionary and partial in content.

This is now changing. Sustainability reporting is becoming central to corporate communications, as important in explaining current and prospective business performance as reporting on market strategy or product development. Sustainability reporting is also becoming mandatory, across jurisdictions including China, the EU, the UK, Japan, Singapore, Nigeria, Brazil and elsewhere. This aligns with the corporate reporting of financial accounts, which has long been mandatory, and for which International Financial Reporting Standards (IFRS) are the established global norm.[i] Set by the International Accounting Standards Board (IASB), these standards are mandatory in more than 140 countries worldwide. As mentioned in Chapter 1, the 2021 COP 26 in Glasgow saw the IFRS foundation announce the creation of the International Sustainability Standards Board (ISSB), to sit alongside the IASB, addressing investor demand for integrating sustainability reporting with existing financial reporting.[ii] 'Financial' and 'sustainable' are now part of the same conversation.

In this chapter, we put these developments in context, setting out what business leaders need to know about this rapidly changing landscape. To do so, we build on previous chapters. In Chapter 2, we explored the traditional concept of the

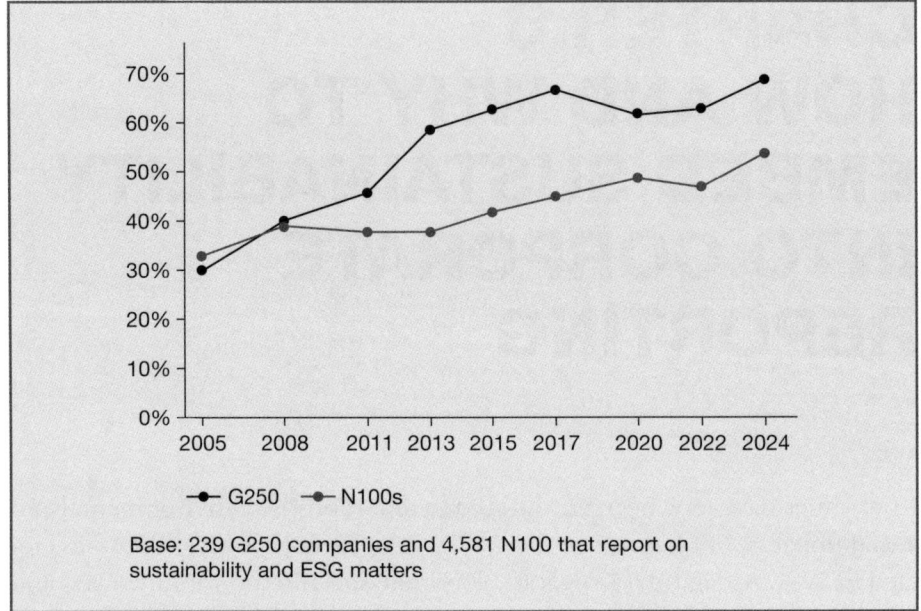

Figure 6.1 Global sustainability reporting rates (1993–2022)

Note: G250 refers to the world's 250 largest companies by revenue based on the 2021 Fortune 500 ranking. N100 refers to the top 100 companies in 58 countries, territories and jurisdictions, compiled by KPMG.

Source: 'The move to mandatory reporting. Survey of Sustainability Reporting 2024' by KPMG International. ©2024 Copyright owned by one or more of the KPMG International entities. All rights reserved.

corporation being run for its shareholders, with the aim of increasing financial capital while, in subsequent chapters, we showed how the corporation depends upon, and impacts, both natural and social systems. In this chapter, we extend the analysis to consider how the corporation is held to account for its performance in adapting to dependencies and mitigating impacts. This raises issues of governance and reporting which, in the spotlight of public disclosure, call upon business leaders to explain how the business is being run, what they are trying to achieve and how successful they have been and are likely to be. In turn, this shapes strategic direction, operating targets and, for business leaders themselves, executive compensation and career progression.

Corporate governance is traditionally concerned with mechanisms to ensure that financial capital is invested effectively. Given that shareholders invest their capital but then cede control to management, the question is how they ensure that management is sufficiently focused on generating financial return on capital. To that end, shareholders want to understand how management thinks strategically about the business, how it evaluates risks and opportunities,

6 HOW AND WHY TO EMBED SUSTAINABILITY INTO CORPORATE REPORTING   173

what targets it sets and why and, in due course, how it performs against those targets. Such information is the substance of corporate reporting.

We first explore these issues from an investor perspective and we then extend the analysis to include the interests of other stakeholders. We identify that corporate sustainability reporting is demanded by both investors and other stakeholders, albeit that the substance of the reporting differs somewhat between these two demands. As a business leader, your challenge is to understand where these demands come from and how best to respond to them.

Financial accounting

Corporate reporting has its origins in disclosing financial performance to investors in the form of financial accounts. Yet these disclosures have only ever been a part of the information that investors would ideally like to receive.

Consider the decision made when an investor buys shares in a company. There is an immediate cash outflow, in exchange for the right to receive cash inflows (dividends) that are expected to arise in the future.[1] While the amount of the outflow is known, the timing and amount of the future inflows are uncertain. Investors would ideally like to know how much they are likely to receive and also how much risk to attach to that expectation. Armed with such information, investors can place a value on their investment. Formally, they can create a valuation model, comprising estimated future cash flows, along with a process by which those cash flows are valued less highly ('discounted') to the extent that they arise later in the future and/or are perceived to carry higher risk.

But where do these expectations of future cash flows come from? A valuation relates to events that are expected to happen in the future. Valuation is therefore highly subjective, an estimate of something that hasn't happened yet and that is therefore inherently unknowable.

This is where accounting comes in. In practice, companies do not provide forecasts of future performance but instead they provide accounts of the past.

---

1 The purchase of shares could be directly from the company or instead from another shareholder. If the former, the company is issuing new shares and the cash flows directly into the company (this is a 'primary market' transaction). If the latter, the cash is transferred from one shareholder to another, and the financial position of the company is unchanged (this is a 'secondary market' transaction).

Profit is a measure of the financial surplus created by the company in the most recent financial reporting period. From an investors' perspective, it provides information on the effectiveness of the board and management team. At the risk of oversimplifying, the investor question that companies are answering is this: 'what have you done with my money over the course of the past year?'

Why, though, would investors be satisfied with information about what the company has done in the past when the economic value of that company depends upon what it is expected to do in the future? In this valuation context, financial accounting provides useful input, even though it does not (and cannot) provide an answer to the question of what the future financial performance of the company will be. Valuation involves forecasting the future profits that the company is expected to make. These forecasts cannot simply be picked out of the air. They must come from somewhere. And the most natural starting point in estimating future performance is the evaluation of past performance. It is (in principle) possible to account for past transactions and events with a degree of accuracy, given that those specific activities have actually occurred, and so can be observed, measured and audited. This helps to ground the accounting system in reliability. It is because accounting is a system of measurement, and not of speculation, that it differs from valuation, which is concerned with estimating an unknown future. Yet the two are related. The process of valuation is one of estimation, projection and risk adjustment; it is not a record of what has happened. Yet by recording how effectively a company has been able to create value in the past, financial accounting provides the foundation for estimating how it will create value in the future.

To see how this works, recall the balance sheet that was introduced in Chapter 2. A balance sheet aims to capture, at a specific point in time, the outstanding ownership and obligation relationships of the reporting company. Assets are reported on one side of a balance sheet, liabilities and equity on the other. In the balance sheet, a company records an asset if, and only if, it has both control over the resource and the expectation of economic benefit from it. And so, too, for a liability, which is an obligation on the reporting company to transfer economic benefits; in substance, liabilities are claims on the company's assets, and they correspond to beneficial rights, typically contractual, that are held by parties external to the business. Mechanically, the 'double-entry' system of accounting ensures that the balance sheet always balances. Conceptually, balance is maintained because the total claims on the assets of a company – i.e. the sum of liabilities and equity – must be equal to the value of assets controlled by the company; while a corporation may be a 'person' in a strict, legal sense, it cannot be independently wealthy, and all of its assets must, ultimately, belong to someone.

While the balance sheet captures ownership claims at a particular point in time, the income statement records change between one balance sheet and the next. If, for example, a company receives money, having provided a service, its cash balance increases. This increase in assets corresponds, on the other side of the balance sheet, to an increase in equity. And that increase in equity is profit. The logic is surprisingly straightforward.[iii] Financial capital measures the shareholders' claim on the (net) assets of the company. If the value of those (net) assets goes up, then financial capital goes up, and that increase is the amount by which shareholders have become better off, which by definition is profit.

An important feature of this accounting system is that there is a single bottom line. Disparate transactions and events are all represented in monetary terms, which is the basis for measuring exchange value in a market economy. This applies to straightforward cases such as receiving cash for selling a product or paying wages to an employee. It also applies to more complex cases, for example in estimating the liabilities that arise from unexpired product warranties or unsettled lawsuits or fines. To illustrate, take the example of a fine, let's say of £1 million for a breach of an environmental regulation. When the company receives the fine, the environmental authority is, in effect, asserting a claim on that company's assets, which the company itself recognises as a new liability. The effect is that financial capital (equity) goes down, because £1 million of the company's assets that were previously owned by shareholders is now claimed by the environmental authority. In the income statement, the company reports a loss of £1 million. The simple intuition is that the company having to pay a fine to a third party makes the shareholders worse off.

If monetary measurement is universal, then all transactions and events can be compared directly with one another. A fee of £1 million charged by a service provider is recorded as 'equal' to 8,000 hours of employee labour at £125 per hour, and equal also to £1 million paid for breaching environmental regulation. Formally, this monetisation enables all amounts reported in the accounting system to be added together, thereby allowing summary, aggregate metrics such as total assets or profit, or ratios such as return on capital employed.[2]

---

2   Return on capital employed is a percentage rate of return, defined as income from an investment divided by the amount of capital invested.

Profit, in particular, is the defining output of the accounting system. It is a measure of how much value the company is able to add in a given period of time. It captures all of the revenue that the company is able to generate, in other words all of the buying power that customers are willing to cede to the company in exchange for its products or services. And it deducts from revenue all of the buying power that the company itself cedes to its employees, suppliers and others. The surplus of revenue over expenses is profit, which measures how well the company is positioned in its competitive environment. If it has a strong brand, intelligent product design, loyal consumers, aligned employees and efficient operations, then it will likely have higher output and a higher margin between the value of its output and the cost of its input.[3]

It is because of the economic importance of profit that its measurement is tightly regulated. Only if different businesses measure their performance against the same standards can investors effectively compare one business against another. Take, for example, an environmental clean-up cost, where a company plans to operate a site for the next 20 years, after which it has a legal obligation to restore the site. An accounting question here is whether, during the life of the operation, the company has a liability. The answer to the question is not immediately obvious, yet the development of best practice through an agreed standard helps to ensure that all companies answer the question well and in the same way. Financial information is thereby complete (all companies report all liabilities whenever they have them), there is consistency in measurement and disclosure (clean-up costs are not reported in different ways by different companies) and there is a benchmark of quality in reported information.

Beyond these benefits in having comparable information, mandatory reporting requirements form part of a broader system of corporate governance. Corporate executives are not allowed discretion in the measurement of profit. Instead, they are legally required to apply IFRS (or an equivalent set of standards) in measuring and reporting their financial performance, and they are also required to have their financial statements audited. Accounting is about accountability. And corporate governance is about ensuring accountability.

---

3 Notice that it doesn't actually matter whether or not 'assets' such as the company's brand, or its operational know-how, are captured on the balance sheet. Either way, the financial benefits that they bring are reflected in the profit that the company earns.

Corporate governance

Corporate governance is a general term referring to the mechanisms designed to ensure that business leaders do what they are 'supposed to do', by serving the interests of the corporation and its shareholders. The need for these mechanisms arises because shareholders sit 'outside' the company, as we detailed in Chapter 2. They do not have direct access to financial information. They also do not have managers' understanding of what that information means and neither do they have direct control over what the business is doing or plans to do. Instead, shareholders depend upon management to operate the business and to report information about it. Yet that dependence is problematic because, in combination with their various informational advantages, managers are also likely to have incentives that differ from those of shareholders.

In practice, there are several corporate governance mechanisms and they work in combination. They might be contractual, for example linking executive compensation to share price performance. There might also be direct shareholder engagement with the company, not least through shareholder resolutions, which might be backed up by implicit threats of shareholder litigation or of relieving current management of control by means of acquisition of the company through the stock market. Governance mechanisms also include other legal rights of shareholders, such as the appointment of independent directors, who can act as the eyes and ears of the shareholders within the company. These directors exercise control over the remuneration committee and the audit committee of the board. They also appoint external auditors, whose job it is to verify to shareholders that the reporting of financial performance adheres to mandatory standards.

Effective governance also requires reporting *about* governance. This includes locating responsibility within the organisation in the form of a description of the governance body (board, committee, etc.) or the individual charged with oversight of a given area. It also includes explanation of how that responsibility is discharged. This means disclosing such things as: how responsibilities for the governance body are reflected in its terms of reference; how the body ensures that it has the appropriate skills and competencies; how and how often the body is kept informed and how, in turn, this information feeds into oversight of the company's strategy, risk management, target setting, performance evaluation and remuneration policy.

Why sustainability reporting matters

We have seen that 'useful' information for shareholders is more than just the financial statements. They also need other types of information. They need reassurance that the company has in place an effective system of corporate governance and they need information that complements the financial statements in the form of access to the insights and interpretations of management. In both cases, shareholders demand this information because they are making investment decisions in the face of uncertainty. They want to know about the past and the present, but only in so far as this informs their evaluation of the future.

In this regard, there are two reasons why the amount of profit that a company has made in the past does not reliably predict how much it will make in the future. Both of these are particularly important in the case of sustainability. First, the profit reported in any given year might include one-off or unusual events arising, for example, from a news story that shakes the reputation of the company or a major restructuring or litigation. In practice, companies and stock market analysts alike will typically adjust the actual profit reported by companies to take out any of these 'unusual' items that are unlikely to recur and that are therefore not relevant in forecasting future profit. If, for example, a company reports a profit of £25 million, yet included in that number was one-off gain of £12 million from disposing of a business unit, then the adjusted profit would be £13 million. Second, a company's future sources of profitability will differ from those available at present. There will be variation with the development of new technologies and markets, with the natural ebb and flow of the economic cycle and with competitors of differing strengths coming and going. In the auto industry, for example, it might have been the case historically that sales of internal combustion engine vehicles dominated, while the less-established technology of electric-powered vehicles was loss-making in its early years of production. Yet changes in regulation, consumer demand and production costs are reversing this position, meaning that expectations of ongoing profitability cannot be based upon a simple extrapolation of activities reported in the accounts. Sustainability leaders are keenly alert to this reality. In contrast, 'greenwashing' is symptomatic of an instinct to cling on to the past, to pretend to oneself and to others that a changing economic reality can wilfully be ignored.[iv]

There is nothing new in shareholders demanding information beyond the financial statements. There has always been a need for managers to communicate whether, and how, profit might be generated differently in the future than in the past, for example because of product innovation. Increasing awareness of businesses as embedded in natural and social systems, however, is changing the picture considerably, making financial statements increasingly insufficient. In this section, we identify five sustainability-related issues that drive investor demand for information over and above that which is provided by the financial statements. These issues define the need for reporting on how sustainability-related issues are affecting the business.

First, as previous chapters describe, the world has changed. Issues of sustainability have economic consequences they did not previously have because the systems on which economic activity depends are increasingly under strain. As we have seen, natural systems provide food and other materials and will continue to do so for as long as we can maintain such things as a temperate climate, healthy soils and a regular supply of fresh water.[v] Likewise, sustainable economic activity relies upon the maintenance of social systems in the form of legal and social institutions and social stability and cohesion. If, however, these systems become strained, then the capacity of the corporate sector to create value is diminished. The unavoidable implication, in particular for high-emitting sectors such as agriculture, extractives, transport and heavy industry, is that business models in the future must differ from those in the past, making it increasingly unhelpful to adopt the 'business as usual' approach of using past profitability as a guide to the future.

Second, sustainability-related targets are in a sense predictable, even if long term, which implies that relatively reliable and useful information can be provided about them. Science-based targets are increasingly widely understood and accepted for natural systems, and they set the parameters for future business activity. In this sense, corporate net zero commitments are closer in nature to regulatory requirements than they are to business targets or forecasts. Instead of the inherent uncertainty of 'what will our sales be several years from now?' there is a specific target of operating at net zero by a future date. Yet this 'knowable' future transition is also long-term, uncertain with respect to changes in technology and other enabling factors and (in varying degrees) highly disruptive to existing business models. This certain-yet-uncertain, long-term commitment is essentially new territory for corporate reporting and it calls for extended disclosure of governance, strategy, risk management, metrics and targets.

Third, financial accounting is in general not well equipped to anticipate the disruption of climate change and other sustainability challenges. To illustrate, consider the UK's Climate Change Act (2008), which sets legally binding targets to reduce greenhouse gas emissions in the UK to net zero by 2050, from 1990 levels. Suppose that a company subject to the Act owns and operates buildings that are insufficiently energy efficient to meet the 2050 target and that will therefore need to be retrofitted with additional insulation and replacement heating systems. Suppose further that this will involve phased, costly shutdowns and that none of this work would be done in the absence of the Act. Finally, suppose that the company is entirely committed to operating in these buildings beyond 2050 and therefore also entirely committed to the expenditure required to satisfy the Act. All of this might suggest that the company has a liability for its committed expenditure. Yet this is unlikely in practice. The company only has the obligation to have met the target by 2050, not for that target to have already been achieved by any date before 2050; the target relates to the future, not to the past. The company will pay for the retrofit in the future, not now. And that future expense will be just one of many operating costs that 'belong' in the future and that will be offset against future revenue in calculating future profit. The bottom line is that not much currently hits the bottom line. Accounting is a record of the past, not an anticipation of the future. And if business-as-usual faces some major future shock, the accounts are unlikely to be the place to find evidence of it. It is for this reason that ISSB disclosure requirements require that a company looks forward, explaining to investors what it plans to achieve.

Fourth, the financial statements account for the company itself, yet sustainability-related risks and opportunities are likely to arise elsewhere in the value chain. The scope of sustainability reporting is broader than that of financial reporting. Information in the financial statements is based upon assets that are directly controlled by the company and liabilities which the company is directly responsible for settling. In contrast, sustainability-related risks and opportunities for the company are likely to arise in all sorts of ways that are beyond its direct control. This applies in upstream activity, where the carbon footprint is in the hands of suppliers. And it applies downstream, in a product's use and end-of-life treatment. It applies also in the broader environment. In addition, and unlike financial reporting, the scope of sustainability reporting includes current externalities of the business. While these – by definition – do not affect profit as currently reported, they are likely to be a good proxy for the challenge that the company faces in its licence to operate, and therefore in its capacity to continue to profit from its existing business model. Such information on the value chain is material to investors. It is also largely new territory for the companies doing the reporting. We can expect rapid development in the amount, quality and auditing of information provided by suppliers and others to reporting entities. For the time being, however, a practical issue is that the institutional structure of sustainability reporting is very much in its infancy in relation to financial reporting, including data systems, novel techniques such as scenario analysis, and regulatory and assurance requirements.

Fifth, and finally, sustainability issues vary by industry. While financial accounting has essentially the same structure for all companies – with all information summarised in a balance sheet and an income statement – sustainability reporting varies more widely, because different sustainability issues provide more or less material information across different sectors. It is for this reason – and in response to investor demand – that the ISSB requires sector-specific disclosures, which by design focus on sustainability-related issues that are typically material for any given type of business activity.

A common theme in all of the above is not to be fooled by the past, by taking business-as-usual as a guide to the future. Sustainability is inherently disruptive.[vi] The future will not be the same as the past, and the later we recognise this the more difficult and costly it will be to adapt. That said, however, sustainability reporting shares with financial accounting an anchor in past performance. It is important, for example, to disclose the GHG emissions of the reporting period and to compare progress against previously stated targets. This form of quantified, assurable information on current business performance is needed to separate truth from fiction, so to speak; the reliable reporting of past performance provides accountability for speculative claims about future transition. Yet sustainability reporting is also concerned with looking ahead, with the help of science-based targets, climate transition pathways and scenario modelling, and with working backwards from a future target in order to define and disclose interim targets and transition plans. In contrast with the financial statements, much of this information is neither monetary nor historical, and it might be either qualitative or quantitative, for example either a description of likely shifts in consumer demand, or a target schedule for phasing out the sale of diesel cars.[4]

---

4 To illustrate how this works, we will consider the obvious example of climate-related reporting. While this example is sufficient to illustrate what investors need to know about how the depletion of natural capital creates both risks and opportunities for corporations, you should note that the logic of the approach applies to any sustainability issue, whether plastic, water, diversity, living wage or anything else.

To illustrate these issues, consider the example of the US movie industry. In early 2025, unprecedented wildfires spread across large areas of Los Angeles, California. The precise location of the fires was difficult to predict, yet (consistent with climate science and with the associated 'availability' of combustible resource) their presence was not a surprise. Damage has been estimated at around $150 billion, making unavoidable the association between the sustainable and the economic. In this context, imagine a company operating in the movie industry, with a Hollywood studio that has just burned down. Its latest financial statements are silent on this news because they capture events from last year. The financial statements for the current year will include large write-offs, reducing both assets and profits, though these will not be published until after the year ends. Anyway, there will also be other information that investors will want to understand. If the plan is to rebuild the studio, will the banks be willing to provide finance and, if so, at what price? Would a new studio be insurable? If so, at what cost? For local employees, if issues of finance and insurance force them to live elsewhere, will the studio still be able to operate and, if so, how will it be affected by the reduced availability of talent? In general, how will management factor future climate-related risk into its decision making? Note that, on all of these issues, this is not sustainability as a 'nice to have' but instead as core (even existential) to the financial viability and success of the business.

Top financial watchdog warns climate change set to trigger market panics

By Martin Arnold and Lee Harris

The world's financial stability watchdog has warned that disasters caused by climate change are increasingly likely to trigger broader panic in financial markets.

The world breached 1.5C of warming above preindustrial levels for the first time last year, raising the prospect of more environmental disasters.

The Financial Stability Board said the financial damage of climate shocks such as floods, droughts, fires or storms could cause a broader pullback in lending and downturn in investor confidence.

"Banks could reduce lending, including for recovery to already vulnerable households and corporates," the body, which brings together the world's central bankers, ministers and regulators, said. "There could also be an abrupt, broad-based repricing of climate-physical risk, as the expectation of larger future losses are incorporated into current prices and impact sectors and jurisdictions not currently directly affected by disasters."

The report comes amid broader concerns about the capacity of the insurance sector to cover losses associated with climate change following devastating fires in Los Angeles that are estimated to have caused tens of billions of dollars' worth of damages.

The Californian crisis has put the spotlight on how some major companies have been pulling out of the state, leaving about 10 per cent of residences without home insurance and many others reliant on a non-profit insurer of last resort.

Leading reinsurance groups are also paring back their exposure to natural catastrophe risks, while US lender Wells Fargo believes insurance payouts for the Californian fires could reach $30bn.

The Basel-based FSB said its research also found climate change was making insurance less available and more expensive, while also risking higher property losses and wider market stress.

"There are indications that insurance premiums have been rising in certain vulnerable areas to reflect expected or realised increases in physical risks, with some insurers withdrawing from markets that are deemed too risky," the FSB said.

Without specifically mentioning the California fires, the FSB warned that this kind of disaster could lead to higher losses for banks and other firms, triggering broader stresses in financial markets by pushing up government borrowing costs and causing cross-border spillovers.

Pointing out that 62 per cent of the global losses from natural disasters were uninsured in 2023, the FSB warned: "Risks that are opaque and not well-managed could create correlated shocks whose impact is magnified as they propagate through the system."

Some US lawmakers, meanwhile, have warned the fires, which have destroyed more than 12,000 structures and killed at least 25 people, could cause a permanent increase in insurance costs and require more state support to fill gaps in coverage.

"The California fires may be the trigger for an accelerated collapse in insurance markets," said Senator Sheldon Whitehouse, until recently chair of the senate budget committee.

"The industry is looking at an entirely new and unpredictable risk profile for homeowners' insurance . . . driven by climate factors that are worsening. This isn't a fiscal blip of some kind that you recover from," he added.

Regulators around the world are worried about falling levels of insurance cover for natural catastrophes.

> A group of EU authorities last month called for the bloc to create a taxpayer-backed reinsurance scheme to fill the growing gap in cover against climate change-related disasters, such as last year's floods in the Spanish region of Valencia.
>
> The FSB's report provides "an analytical framework and toolkit" to help regulators assess climaterelated vulnerabilities.
>
> Sarah Breeden, deputy governor for financial stability at the Bank of England, who chaired the FSB group that produced its new framework, said it "provides a forward-looking approach to be able to capture the unique aspects of climate risks while staying rooted in traditional financial stability analysis".
>
> Nellie Liang, under-secretary for domestic finance at the US Treasury department who also worked on the report, called it "a welcome addition" to financial markets surveillance.

Source: Martin Arnold and Lee Harris (2025) 'Top financial watchdog warns climate change set to trigger market panics', Financial Times, 16 Jan. © The Financial Times Limited 2025. All Rights Reserved.

The change in mindset required by this evolution in financial reporting, of this expansion beyond financial accounting, should not be underestimated. We expect the sun to rise tomorrow because it always has done so in the past. We expect forests to remain because they have always been there. Our instinct is to think in the same way as the turkey in Bertrand Russell's thought experiment, which is fed every day at 9 am, and finds itself expecting to be fed at 9 am on Christmas Eve when, in fact, it will form part of the Christmas dinner.[vii] For those currently in senior business leadership positions, most of their corporate experience has been gained without accounting for the nature and scale of corporate impacts and dependencies on environmental and social systems. As Figure 6.2 illustrates, they have not needed to think about it. They have acquired skills, experience, job security and vested interest in current business models, and they typically have power over incumbent industries, as opposed to being personally and financially invested in innovative, future industries that will, in due course, create value and grow. For those at an early stage in their careers, the position is dramatically different.

The effects of climate change, and of other systemic depletions, are really only starting to be felt and it can be tempting for leaders to play them down, to extrapolate business as usual. In this regard, it is both easier and more feasible to evaluate costs and benefits arising currently than those arising in the future. Yet this is problematic. The benefits from GHG emissions have been enjoyed by current and past generations, in the form of inexpensive and plentiful energy,

6 HOW AND WHY TO EMBED SUSTAINABILITY INTO CORPORATE REPORTING

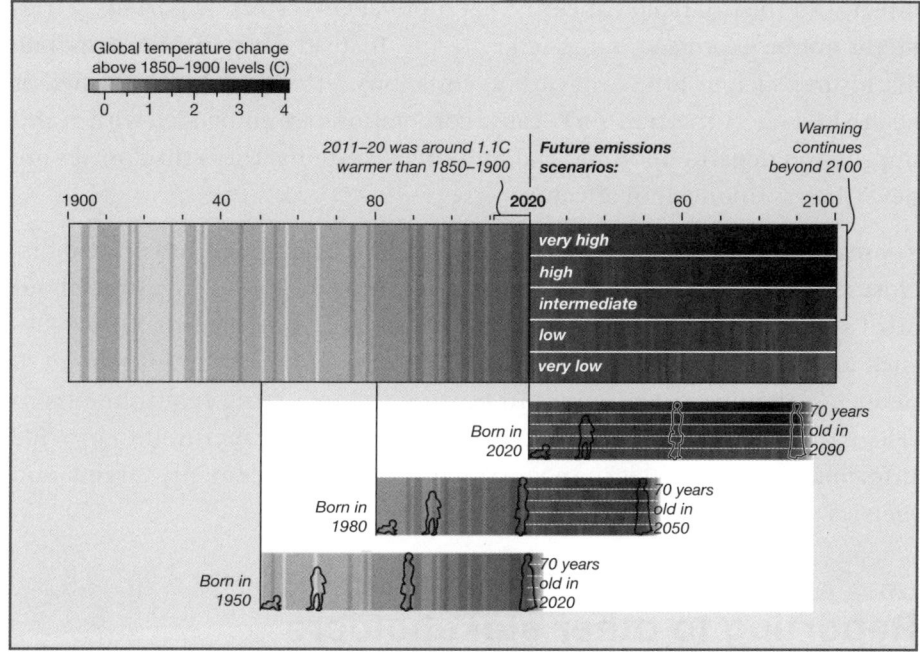

Figure 6.2 How future generations will experience global warming[viii]
Source: Synthesis Report of the IPCC Sixth Assessment Report. ©FT

while the costs are likely to be borne by future generations. At the risk of oversimplifying, it has proved too easy for society to place excess weight on readily experienced benefits and too little weight on relatively uncertain and remote costs, and especially so when wishful optimism about the distant future cannot evidentially be refuted and when examples such as fires in Los Angeles indicate that the future is in part already here.[ix]

These issues are important to investors because they are relevant to financial returns on investment and they affect the performance and stability of capital markets. Sustainable economic activity relies upon natural and social systems. Corporations are supplementing financial accounting with sustainability reporting because they recognise that investors are more likely to invest when they understand sustainability-related risks and opportunities. Such risks and opportunities affect financial prospects, including the expectations of future cash flows and the cost of capital at which potential holders of equity and debt are willing to invest. In this regard, sustainability reporting is a component of 'financial' reporting because it relates, more or less directly, to the financial concerns that motivate investors. Reported metrics might not be expressed in monetary terms. Instead, they include disparate disclosures such as tonnes of carbon emissions, litres of water consumed or health and safety metrics. Yet because corporations are embedded within and impact and depend upon natural and social systems, these disclosures are nevertheless financial in effect.

These considerations have led the ISSB to require sustainability-related disclosures that focus on providing material information to investors about all of a company's risks and opportunities arising from sustainability issues such as climate change, natural resource depletion or the management of people. Appendix 6.1 provides in outline the reporting requirements in IFRS sustainability disclosure standards, which are structured to provide information about governance, strategy, risk management, targets and metrics.

Reporting to other stakeholders

Meeting investors' demands for sustainability reporting contributes to the broader, societal demand for a sustainable economy, as expressed in the United Nation's Sustainable Development Goals (SDGs). Given the scale of economic activity that falls within the control of investors and corporations, it is unrealistic to imagine that the SDGs can be realised without capital markets being aligned. To that end, it is essential that investors are fully informed of sustainability-related risks and opportunities and that corporations are thereby directed towards the effective mitigation of those risks and the effective exploitation of the opportunities. Moreover, because corporations are embedded in, not separate from, the same natural and social systems as anyone else, there is significant overlap between the sustainability-related risks and opportunities faced by corporations and the sustainability challenges of society at large. Greenhouse gas emissions make this point clearly. The corporate disclosure of these emissions provides material information to investors, even though their economic impact is typically not felt directly (for example via taxation) by the corporation, nor by those in its value chain, but instead the impact is indirect, via global warming, on society at large and on future generations. There is material information for investors not least because a company's current carbon footprint signals the extent of the transition it is likely to have to make, with consequences for the capital and operating expenditures associated with that transition, and for changes in business models and therefore in future sources of revenue and expense.

Yet this alignment between investors' information needs and those of other stakeholders should not be overstated. The interests of investors are not those of society as a whole. Externalities persist and, as we have discussed, it would be naïve to think that economic self-interest in financial markets is a sufficient mechanism to make them go away. Returning to our definition of sustainability, which calls for profitability 'while also strengthening natural and social systems', there is therefore a need for companies to report not just on the financial performance and prospects that are material to investors but also on impacts on environment and society that are material to all other stakeholders. In this regard, corporate reporting is not 'purely' economic. It is also concerned with asking 'what sort of society do we want?' This might, for example, raise issues of human rights, equity or social inclusion that do not always relate directly to financial value but that might nevertheless create expectations of corporate performance.

Multi-stakeholder reporting is the domain of the widely adopted standards of the Global Reporting Initiative (GRI). These are not concerned directly with the sustainability-related risks and opportunities that affect the reporting business but instead with the environmental and social impacts imposed by the business on society. To be clear, and picking up on a consistent theme in this book, risk and opportunity are not independent of impact, not least because corporate impacts might affect dependencies, making them important from an investor's perspective. Yet to the extent that investors are concerned with a company's financial prospects, while other stakeholders are concerned with how they are impacted by the activities of the corporation, the information needs of these two groups will be distinct. This is the notion of 'double materiality' – information not just for investors but also for all other stakeholders affected by business activity.[x] In Europe, through various legislative acts, companies are increasingly being required to adopt sustainable business practices. By enactment of the Corporate Sustainability Reporting Directive (CSRD), companies are required to follow the European Sustainability Reporting Standards (ESRS), which are designed around the concept of double materiality.

Transition plans

Whichever materiality perspective is applied, the reality of economic transition calls for a plan. From an impact perspective, a transition plan is essential for business leadership if the activities of the business are not currently sustainable but if a target has been set to make them so. From an investor perspective, a transition plan can be understood as a business case for transition, setting out the company's economic self-interest in achieving any given environmental or social target. The context is that business exposure to sustainability-related risks[xi] and opportunities[xii] leads to changes in strategy and business model. A transition plan explains how the management understands the value created by these changes and how it seeks to implement them. While, in this way, the primary concern of investors is the financial effects for them of adaptation to a different economic reality, for other stakeholders the primary concern is mitigating the effects on them of corporate externalities. Appropriate reporting might therefore differ depending upon whether the audience is investors or other stakeholders.

A transition plan is inherently forward looking.[xiii] Unavoidably, it is therefore also speculative and conditional upon future events and conditions that are as yet unknown. Effective reporting about transition planning must accommodate this uncertainty. A credible transition plan provides evidence – to the extent possible – of how the plan is determined, whether it is realistic, how it will be evaluated over time and how it affects stakeholders in the entity.

The question of how a plan is determined is closely related to whether it is realistic. Setting a target is easily done. Setting a target that can realistically be achieved is less easy. Setting a credible target is therefore an iteration between what the entity would like to achieve and what it feels it can achieve. Effective disclosure therefore covers a range of issues. Investors (and/or other stakeholders) want to understand how targets are set, including the extent to which they cover all of an entity's value chain. For environmental targets (not least on GHG emissions), a relevant issue is the extent to which the company's targets are guided by, and consistent with, science-based targets.

Perhaps more important is how the company plans to meet its targets. The underlying issue is how the entity makes a business case for transition, reconciling environmental and social outcomes with operationally and financially viable courses of action. In evaluating a transition plan, it is important to be wary of empty 'win–win' rhetoric, of unsupported claims that what is good for society is good for the business. Look instead for granular evaluation of changes to business models, sources of funding, credible discussion of business opportunity and candid acknowledgement of where a business case is not currently achievable. A related issue is how confident the entity is in meeting its targets and of how much investors and others can therefore rely upon the expectations that the targets create. In this, it is important to be aware of any conditionality in the assumptions that the company is making about the future. For example, it might be relying upon uncertain future technologies, transition pathways that are highly contingent, expected changes to supply or demand that might be more wishful than realistic, or the emergence of industry partnerships and government subsidy (rather than disruptive competitors and tighter government regulation). Given the systemic, connected nature of sustainability issues, this co-dependence of assumptions is particularly important, making publicly-available transition pathways critical in building a collective norm, built on consistent projections.

Look also for a clear distinction between short-, medium- and long-term information. The reality of business planning (and of inherent uncertainty about the future) is that these phases each correspond to different levels of confidence, for example with the short-term being baked into approved investment decisions but with the long-term being a source of great uncertainty. It is unavoidable, of course, that disclosures are, to a degree, estimated and uncertain. The need is to be realistic, for a company to report as well as it can.

Different transition pathways for the economy as a whole will be associated with different risks, opportunities and impacts for the corporate sector. Compare a swift transition to a low-carbon economy with a delayed transition. In the former, the company's exposure to transition risks is faced sooner, with less time to respond. Correspondingly, however, physical risks are minimised with a swift transition because global warming is relatively effectively contained. The impact on other stakeholders is minimised. In contrast, a delayed transition increases physical risks while pushing transition risks out to a later date. It is the role of an entity's risk management systems to capture these combinations of risk exposures and to support leaders in ensuring the resilience of the business to whatever the future might hold.

In this regard, transition planning provides a coordinating structure to consider sustainability as a core business issue in a way that would not otherwise emerge from evaluating business as usual or from within any existing leadership roles. In addition, and because the issues are cross-cutting across all aspects of the business, transition planning requires different stakeholders to engage with one another, both within and outside the business. For these reasons, a transition plan is not simply an external representation of what the business is thinking and doing. It is in itself constitutive of what the business thinks and does. The act of preparing a transition plan calls for a different way of thinking and operating. It is a chance to exercise leadership.

A transition plan is also anchored in existing systems of corporate accountability. In monitoring progress against the plan, sustainability reporting connects back to familiar accounting territory. The analogy is that the future profit a company expects to make will, ultimately, be compared with the actual profit it achieves. So, too, expectations in the form of sustainability-related targets will be measured ultimately against actual performance. This calls for consistency, in that the scope and method of measurement must be the same in the projection as it is in the performance measurement. Consistency is also required in order to compare one company against another. Resource allocation decisions are always a matter of choice between competing alternatives and so a core requirement of investors, policy makers and other users is for information that is directly comparable. This is where intensity metrics are useful because they normalise data from entities or activities of different sizes. This is also why global standards are so important, whether from the ISSB, GRI, the GHG Protocol or (across a range of specific business activities) the International Standards Organisation (ISO). This is also where sector-specific metrics can be particularly important because these allow comparison of performance across activities that face much the same sustainability-related issues.

By means of transparent disclosure of its transition plan, and thereby the provision of useful information to investors and other stakeholders, a company is likely to be in a better position than it would otherwise be. This holds however challenging the transition. To see this, consider that a science-based target might not be economically viable. If a company adopts such a target, in effect it would be communicating 'here's what we feel obliged to claim' as a desired or 'necessary' target, rather than 'here's what we are actually capable of achieving'. Yet informed investors will reward transparent disclosure in this regard. Compare a company that offers a credible transition plan with one that does not. The former has gaps. It has identified where there is a business case for transition and where – on plausible assumptions about such things as regulatory policy – there is not. The latter claims to be free from such gaps. Such 'win-win' rhetoric means either that the company has not done the analysis that identifies the gaps, or that it has but is unwilling to disclose its findings, or that (least likely) there really are no gaps and the business can authentically aspire to becoming fully sustainable. Faced with evidence that a company is either itself uninformed or instead unwilling to inform its investors, it becomes a riskier investment. Investors would therefore be less willing to invest and the share price should fall in relation to the company that reports a credible transition plan. This might seem counter intuitive. The company declaring that (desirable) sustainability targets are beyond reach is worth more than the company offering reassurance that 'all will be OK'. But consider an example. One company plans to produce an energy-efficient vehicle which, while not carbon neutral, is a deliverable improvement on current technology. Another company blindly assumes that future technology will come along that resolves any need to worry about carbon neutrality, making it possible to make a zero emissions commitment now. Which company do you trust to be more likely to make a successful economic transition, and in which would you therefore rather invest?

Evaluate sustainability reporting in your own business

Consider now your own company. Look at the sustainability metrics and other disclosures that your company generates and provides, internally and externally, and ask yourself: who is supposed to be using these numbers?

There are three scenarios. The worst-case scenario is that they are compliance data, that they are provided either because the company has no choice or else because it otherwise feels obliged to put data out there. They are not really used by anybody. They are not intended to be used by anybody. Similarly, it could be that the data are provided for marketing purposes, for example so that the company is 'understood' by its customers to be acting on climate change, plastic pollution, social inclusion or similar, or maybe so that the company gets to be included in a sustainability index. Again, if it is done for those purposes, then there isn't really an intended use, or at least not one that corresponds to meaningful strategy or implementation. You should be alert to the possibility of this worst-case scenario. It is common in practice. You should ask difficult questions, challenge assumptions, consider what is *not* being covered in your reporting and why.

The medium-case scenario is that data are provided primarily to investors, or to other stakeholders, to communicate the sustainability performance of the business. Here, the company's position is: 'You say you would like to understand our environmental and social impact; well, here are some data that will help you to do that.' In that sense, the data are simply descriptive, they give a picture of the way the business is, such that investors and others can use that information in whatever way they feel is useful to them. The data are used by stakeholders, but not by the company itself. They are not articulated as a business case, not mainstreamed in the strategic narrative.

The best-case scenario is where the ultimate users are the leaders of the company themselves. In this scenario, the report is setting out how and why the company is addressing sustainability-related issues. The reason for reporting the metrics externally is that management is holding itself to account to the company's stakeholders, in much the same way that it does in reporting profit. There is a meaningful connection between the data that are reported and the way in which the business is run.

In order to distinguish between these scenarios, you can find evidence in a number of ways. You can look for meaningful stakeholder engagement. In putting the data together, and in the way in which the data are communicated, is there very clearly a stakeholder involved at the other end of that communication? Another question is whether the data are related to management performance targets. Are there key performance indicators (KPIs)? Is there management compensation attached to those metrics? In which case you can assume that they are being used.

You might also ask whether the company's targets and plans are 'serious', in the sense that they can genuinely address the sustainability challenges that the company faces. For example, are the metrics related to science-based environmental targets or to comparable benchmarks for human and social capital? Is 'Scope 3' included for all aspects of environmental and social performance, keeping in mind that transition might mostly be required outside the conventional boundaries of corporate responsibility? And, if all Scope 3 activities are included in this way, does the company have reliable data? Are targets and commitments connected, through a granular process of planning and resource commitment, to meaningful business transition? Is the company reporting incrementally on some degree of improvement on past performance or is there instead a vision of where the company needs to be in the future, which is worked backwards into substantial yet realistic corporate transition? Is the company preoccupied with peer group comparison, with relative performance and with intensity metrics, or does it instead have absolute performance targets? Finally, is your company drawn towards telling a story of 'positive impact' – for example that it contributes to economic well-being and invests in training and community projects – with the effect that is glosses over negative impacts that it would rather not have to acknowledge or discuss?

A good indicator of where a company lies on this spectrum is whether it demonstrably has transition plans in place and whether these are credible – both in the sense of being technically feasible and also in there being a business case for the company, giving reason to believe that the company can and will pursue the targets it has set.

A critically important test is whether the company is focused on what really matters. Do not assume that a lengthy sustainability report is a good one. On the contrary, if it opines at length on issues that are not particularly important, or if it works hard to convince you of all of the positive impacts that the company is having, then it probably obscures a reality that insufficient attention is being given to where it is most needed. Remember that, in most cases, impact will be outside the boundaries of the company and you should be especially wary of reporting that provides detailed disclosure on own operations, yet that fails to convince on taking value chain impacts and dependencies seriously.

In this regard, effective reporting is not only a descriptive summary of impacts but also an explanation of why these matter for the business and of what management is doing about them. For example, investors are not directly interested in carbon emissions themselves. Instead, their concern is for the effects on the company of climate-related risks and opportunities, for which the disclosure of emissions is a proxy for the business transformation that lies ahead. From an investors' perspective, it matters to understand such things as the extent to which the existing assets of the business are exposed to economic obsolescence, the likely capital expenditure required to meet net zero commitments, the effects on revenue from likely growth in carbon-neutral products and services and likely decline in those that are carbon-intensive, the effects on operating expenses if the supply chain faces transition, shock or strain, and changes in the terms on which the company is able to finance its operations, for example whether green bonds provide attractive rates of interest and, if so, whether the company is eligible to secure these. Reporting is not an end unto itself. It is a tool to guide decision making, essential to leading your company through a credible sustainability transition – the subject of our final chapter.

Reflection questions

Sustainability reporting is not a compliance exercise. It follows directly from your company's purpose, which we explored in Chapter 2, and it becomes an essential tool as you work to understand the impacts and dependencies of your business on the natural and social systems we describe in Chapters 3 through 5. This highlights the interrelated nature of this book's content, guiding you step-by-step from defining your company's core aims to developing the specialised knowledge needed to craft strategies that create sustainable value.

The goal of measurement and reporting is not simply to meet the growing demands of regulatory requirement, but to provide a framework for tracking progress, identifying areas where improvement is needed, and showcasing the outcomes of your efforts to both your business and your stakeholders alike. Done well, sustainability reporting becomes highly relevant to investors by improving their understanding of risks and returns. This perspective offers a valuable test: assess your company's sustainability reporting from an investor's standpoint. Does the information presented feel disconnected from the decisions an investor needs to make? If so, keep in mind that alignment is critical to initiating and maintaining the transformative changes discussed throughout this book. As you and your teams reflect on what you have learned so far and craft an Action Plan tailored to your business, keep the following questions in mind. These will help sharpen your strategy, complementing the steps we will outline in Chapter 7, in which we focus on leading change.

1. In turn, consider each of the disclosure categories ISSB sustainability reporting provides: governance; strategy; risk management; and targets and metrics.
   a) How well does your company disclose on each of these? What can be improved?
   b) How well does this disclosure translate into action? What can be improved?
2. Consider your key stakeholders. How effectively does your company's reporting enable each of them to understand your company's impacts? What insight does it provide into the credibility of your company's plans in the light to address those impacts? (Note: A critical eye on the business case is especially important here because the absence of such a case

signals a (most likely unstated) conflict between the interests of the company (and its investors) and those of one or more of its stakeholder groups.)

Recommended reading

Barker, R. (2011) *Cambridge Short Introductions: Accounting*. Cambridge, UK: Cambridge University Press.

Barker, R. (2023) Get Ready for More Transparent Sustainability Reporting. *MIT Sloan Management Review*, 12 December. Available at: https://sloanreview.mit.edu/article/get-ready-for-more-transparent-sustainability-reporting/.

Howard-Grenville, J. (2021) ESG Impact Is Hard to Measure – but It's Not Impossible. *Harvard Business Review*, 22 January. Available at: https://hbr.org/2021/01/esg-impact-is-hard-to-measure-but-its-not-impossible.

IFRS S1 (2023a) IFRS S1 – *General Sustainability-related Disclosures*. London: International Financial Reporting Standards Foundation.

IFRS S2 (2023b) IFRS S2 – *Climate-related Disclosures*. London: International Financial Reporting Standards Foundation.

TCFD (2023) *The Use of Scenario Analysis in Disclosure of Climate-related Risks and Opportunities*. Available at: https://www.tcfdhub.org/scenario-analysis/.

TPT (2023) *TPT Disclosure Framework*. London: Transition Plan Taskforce.

Appendix 6.1 Overview of IFRS Sustainability Disclosure Standards

The ISSB requires an entity to disclose information about all sustainability-related risks and opportunities that could reasonably be expected to affect the entity's cash flows, its access to finance or cost of capital over the short, medium or long term. Such information is useful to investors because an entity's ability to generate cash flows over the short, medium and long term is inextricably linked to the interactions between the entity and its stakeholders, society, the economy and the natural environment throughout the entity's value chain. Together, the entity and the resources and relationships throughout its value chain form an interdependent system in which the entity operates. Specific disclosure requirements are structured as follows.

Governance

The objective of disclosures on governance is to provide information on the processes, controls and procedures an entity uses to monitor, manage and oversee sustainability-related risks and opportunities. This includes information about the governance body responsible for oversight of sustainability-related risks and opportunities, including terms of reference, appropriate skills, frequency and basis of decision making, links to remuneration policies, controls and procedures to support the oversight of management.

Strategy

Strategy disclosures concern the sustainability-related risks and opportunities that could reasonably be expected to affect the entity's prospects, including the effects of these on: the entity's business model and value chain; its strategy and decision making; its financial position, financial performance and cash flows (in the reporting period and over the short, medium and long term); and its resilience. In the specific case of climate change, the company must report a transition plan (if it has one) and it must also use a scenario analysis, whereby it models its possible risks and opportunities, drawing upon a generally accepted understanding of how the economy as a whole might plausibly transition to meet a target level of global warming. The entity must identify exposure to physical risks, whereby the value of a company's assets might be directly impaired, for example by flooding or extreme temperature. There are also transition risks, because a company's potential revenues and expenses might be affected by changes in government regulation or taxation, consumer preferences, labour market conditions, or raw material prices. These might be triggered by social movements, perhaps where an NGO organises coordinated action against a carbon-intensive corporation. And there are also opportunities, as attested by growth markets such as solar and wind power, carbon capture, electric vehicles, recyclable materials, low-carbon steel, non-dairy milk and meat substitutes. Investors need to understand what these sustainability-related risks and opportunities are, and how business leaders are responding to them. The company should disclose information about current and anticipated mitigation and adaptation efforts, plans to achieve any sustainability-related targets, including its transition to a lower-carbon economy, critical assumptions the company has made and dependencies it has identified and how it is currently resourcing, or plans to resource, its transition. It should also disclose current and anticipated financial effects, arising for example if the value of an asset is at risk of being written down because of a climate-related event, or if the entity has current and committed investment plans, requiring capital expenditure to decarbonise its operations.

Risk management

It is useful for investors to understand the processes an entity uses to identify, assess, prioritise and monitor sustainability-related risks and opportunities, including whether and how those processes are integrated into and inform the entity's overall risk management process. Disclosure requirements therefore include information about the inputs and parameters the entity uses in its risk management, how scenario analysis informs its identification of sustainability-related risks, how the entity assesses the nature, likelihood and magnitude of the effects of those risks, whether and how the entity prioritises sustainability-related risks relative to other types of risk and how the entity monitors sustainability-related risks.

Metrics and targets

The importance of metrics and targets is in understanding an entity's performance in relation to its sustainability-related risks and opportunities, including progress towards any targets the entity has set, and any targets it is required to meet by law or regulation. An entity is required to disclose the metrics used to set target and to monitor progress towards reaching targets, the specific quantitative or qualitative targets set, the base period from which progress is measured, milestones and interim targets, performance against each target and an analysis of trends or changes in the entity's performance, and any revisions to the target and an explanation for those revisions. These requirements apply both to cross-industry metric categories and industry-based metrics, where the former are applicable to entities regardless of business models, economic activities and other common features that characterise participation in an industry.

In the case of climate, the entity must disclose (when material) all of its Scope 1, 2 and 3 GHG emissions. Of greatest interest are metrics used by the board or management to measure progress towards the targets set for the purposes of mitigation or adaptation. The entity must include absolute targets and can also add intensity targets, explaining the objective of the targets (for example mitigation, adaptation or conformance with sector- or science-based initiatives), whether it applies to the company in its entirety or to only a part of the company (for example specific business units or specific geographical regions), how the latest international agreement on climate change (including jurisdictional commitments that arise from that agreement) has informed the target, whether the target and target methodology has been validated by a third party, the period over which the target applies, the base period from which progress is measured, any milestones or interim targets, the company's processes for reviewing the target, performance against the target and an analysis of trends or changes in the company's performance, and any revisions to the target and an explanation for those revisions. The company must also explain its planned use of carbon credits to offset emissions, including whether these will be subject to a third-party offset verification or certification scheme, whether the underlying offset will be nature-based or based on technological carbon removals, and so on.

Notes

[i] As of June 2025, 30 jurisdictions have decided to use or are taking steps to introduce ISSB Standards in their legal or regulatory frameworks, representing nearly 60 per cent of global GDP, more than 40 per cent of global market capitalisation and more than half of global greenhouse gas (GHG) emissions: Progress on Corporate Climate-related Disclosures—2024 Report. Available at: https://www.ifrs.org/content/dam/ifrs/supporting-implementation/issb-standards/progress-climate-related-disclosures-2024.pdf; IFRS Foundation publishes jurisdictional profiles - https://www.ifrs.org/news-and-events/news/2025/06/ifrs-foundation-publishes-jurisdictional-profiles-issb-standards/

[ii] O'Dwyer, M. (2021) New Body to Oversee Global Sustainability Disclosure Standards. *Financial Times*, 3 November. Available at: https://www.ft.com/content/3fb80e89-4ce6-4cc8-8472-ae4c8c99b12d.

[iii] For an expanded, though concise, discussion of how the financial accounting system works, see Barker (2011).
[iv] Bryan, K. and Georgiadis, P. (2024) Dutch Court Rules KLM Ads 'Misleading' in Greenwashing Case. www.ft.com, 20 March. Available at: https://www.ft.com/content/5169410d-427e-4156-ba08-f17284c477ca.
[v] Rininsland, A. (2023) How Will Global Warming Affect the Crops That We Grow?. *Financial Times*, 20 July. Available at: https://www.ft.com/content/e758a83b-efa0-4203-8305-7d71ad17e2e0.
[vi] Mychasuk, E. (2023) Climate Change Turns up the Heat on Supply Chains. *Financial Times*, 21 July. Available at: https://www.ft.com/content/20096903-5523-42ff-9d95-e9ca3d5e72b0.
[vii] Russell, B. (1912) *The Problems of Philosophy*.
[viii] Hodgson, C., et al. (2023) How an Era of Extreme Heat Is Reshaping Economies. *Financial Times*, 21 July. Available at: https://www.ft.com/content/4ca7ac75-ab0a-4808-9b6b-d6695cd333c4.
[ix] Burn-Murdoch, J. (2023) What We Get Wrong When We Talk about Global Warming. www.ft.com, 21 July. Available at: https://www.ft.com/content/de449d0d-0558-48da-90b9-5bb4fe809dab.
[x] Ross, A. (2023) Why Fast Fashion Is Still Not Available in Green. *Financial Times*, 21 April. Available at: https://www.ft.com/content/8fed1e01-f685-4752-adc5-422b06493eee.
[xi] Nilsson, P. (2024) German Car Parts Suppliers Plan Job Cuts amid Costly EV Transition. www.ft.com, 18 January. Available at: https://www.ft.com/content/ceefa6bb-a7db-4f36-ae1e-04a5c4f6cb09.
[xii] Nilsson, P. (2024) How Germany's Steelmakers Plan to Go Green. www.ft.com, 25 February. Available at: https://www.ft.com/content/8bf86419-e749-46d1-9cd9-5a72bc306fdc.
[xiii] Transition Plan Taskforce (2024) Build Your Transition Plan | the Transition Plan Taskforce. Transition Taskforce, accessed 15 April 2024. Available at: https://www.ifrs.org/sustainability/knowledge-hub/transition-plan-taskforce-resources/.

CHAPTER 7
HOW TO BUILD YOUR SUSTAINABILITY ACTION PLAN AND LEAD CHANGE

Introduction

Throughout this book, we present your company as an entity that impacts and depends on social and environmental systems to create value. We make the case that a clear understanding of corporate impacts and dependencies on environmental and social systems is crucial to ongoing strategy and innovation in your business. Our key point is this: sustainability is core, not adjacent, to business now and in future. Following the definition we have used in this book – that a *sustainable corporation creates profitable products and services as it strengthens natural and social systems* – we conclude that evaluating your company's position vis à vis climate, nature and social systems enables you and your teams to pinpoint specific systems on which your company impacts and depends and build strategy accordingly.

We ended Chapter 1 by offering four questions on which to reflect as you read this book with your company in mind. Now, as you build your Action Plan, you can use these to guide your thinking:

1. How well is sustainability integrated into your corporate assessments of risk *and* opportunity?
2. Given your understanding of risks and opportunities, is your approach to governance and strategy fit for purpose?
3. Does your organisation (targets, processes and culture) enable you to demonstrate leadership in how you deliver on your strategy?
4. Do your reporting and accountability mechanisms demonstrate leadership in sustainability?

These questions are not designed to provoke a simple 'yes' or 'no'. Rather, they are a set of high-level checks to which you can refer on an ongoing basis as you build and implement your Action Plan. In this final chapter, we offer guidance to accompany you as you bring your plan to life. To that end, we draw from our respective work with senior leaders and from participants of Oxford *Leading Sustainable Corporations*, our online teaching programme that has trained more than 6,000 leaders from multiple sectors and more than 60 countries to date. Recurring themes that we observe from this experience is the need to maintain a vision of a sustainable business, while distinguishing in everyday decisions between trade-offs and paradox. Finally, we outline three steps that your Action Plan will need to include and offer examples from organisations that have brought these to life in practice. These three steps are: collaborating with stakeholders to define priorities; setting ambitious yet achievable goals (including identifying the levers of change available to you); and communicating the vision to drive organisational change. Together, they form the foundation of your Action Plan.

In Chapter 1, we emphasised that this book was not designed for passive readership. It is an invitation to you as a leader to act. Every reader who engages with this book will be navigating a unique phase in their organisation's sustainability transformation. Your own company may be deep into a change process that is well understood, widely accepted and appropriately resourced. More likely, your company may be grappling with how to begin, where to draw boundaries around the work that lies ahead, or how to keep momentum in the face of significant headwinds. This chapter is about action, and our aim is to offer a guide that enables every reader to find a place in this process. The scale of the sustainability transition means that risks and opportunities exist in every company and industry. Regardless of your starting point, this chapter provides you with guidance to design an Action Plan for yourself, your team and your organisation.

Maintaining vision while rethinking the trade-off mindset

Corporate impacts and dependencies on social and environmental systems are fundamental to business. Leaders who pick their priorities well today have the potential to innovate new ways to generate value and even remake their industries. Your task as a leader, at any level in your organisation, is to make the case for sustainability transition and enable delivery of the change that is required. Because this transition may require substantial, even fundamental, shifts in business models, this is a significant leadership challenge. While the business potential for leading sustainable corporations is strong, 'sustainability' is habitually perceived as a trade-off; either costly, risky or too long-term to matter to the decisions a business faces today. Short-term profits versus long-term viability of the business, returns for shareholders versus stakeholders, or financial gains versus environmental or social good are familiar tropes in the corporate sustainability landscape. Too often, these tropes become roadblocks to the mindset shifts that sustainability transformation requires. It is also commonplace for incumbent stakeholders to perceive change as a threat. At the same time, your competitors may be the ones with this perception. This introduces a window of opportunity for your company to gain competitive advantage if you can bring your organisation onside.

As we set out in Chapter 1, a trade-off is a decision between competing alternatives, typically between those that are currently, practically available. Examples include your ability to invest in R&D for environmentally friendly packaging versus meeting profit targets *this quarter*, to make the capital investments required to reduce the carbon footprint of your operations in one market versus another *this financial year* with a *specific investment partner*, or to upskill your work force on sustainability at scale *with existing training technology*. Trade-offs are often taken for granted as a standard feature of business. However, the key is that trade-offs are not always what they appear. A shift in parameters, time horizons or re-examination of assumed constraints may reveal that an apparent trade-off is not quite so black and white, thus expanding the set of solutions available to you.[i] In the sustainability 'trade-offs' above, for example, a change to timelines, a new investment partner or an advance in technology could expand the set of possibilities.

This leads us to the concept of paradox. In Chapter 1, we introduced paradox as the 'interdependent, persistent contradictions'[ii] inherent in dilemmas we face. Living with paradox involves a perspective shift, i.e. a challenge to underlying logic. While the language of trade-offs is familiar in business, paradox is in fact ubiquitous to corporate life. Consider any large firm's need to be both global *and* local, to foster employee well-being *and* operational efficiency, to encourage innovation *while* delivering on business-as-usual. The list goes on. No company can succeed if it consistently pursues just one aspect of these dyads at the expense of the other: companies must and do pursue both. Sustainability, we argue, is no different.

Why is paradox so core to building your Action Plan as an outcome of reading this book? The answer is grounded in our understanding of what sustainability means. If we define a sustainable corporation as one that strengthens natural and social systems while generating profitable products and services, then any apparent trade-off between profit and sustainability is cause for leadership attention towards alternative solutions. Too often, businesses assume that pursuing sustainability will inevitably come at the expense of financial performance. However, in many cases, the parameters contributing to this perceived trade-off are unclear, unexamined or poorly defined.

Take fast fashion, an industry we have referenced several times. The industry is associated with high levels of pollution and human rights abuse in the supply chain, but consumers demand cheap clothing, generating a clear apparent trade-off for retailers. However, a closer look at the parameters behind this 'trade-off' reveals at least one significant assumption: that technology is static. Once identified, this assumption can be contested, opening the possibility to move beyond a trade-off mindset. When the trade-off is understood as a paradox, it becomes clear that innovation leading to cost reductions in sustainable materials, supply-chain efficiencies and increased visibility for violations are key strategic considerations for fast fashion. This insight can then guide corporate decision making, spotlighting the business case for investment in technology and innovation. In just one example from the sector, it is notable that EcoVero, an innovative lower water-use material made from sustainable wood pulp and fibres that would otherwise go to waste, emerged in 2017 as a niche sustainable fabric. As fashion brands understood its benefits, it has become mainstream.[iii]

Another example comes from the fishing industry, worth more than US $300 billion annually across the globe.[iv] The apparent trade-off is this: consumers demand seafood at a low price and, therefore, companies who do not pursue the lowest-cost fishing methods will lose out to competitive pressure. A closer look at this argument reveals at least one important assumption: fishing stocks will remain available for commercial use. This assumption is shaky at best. In an accelerating trend, more than 30 per cent of global fishing stocks have already been overfished to the point of collapse.[v] A shift in time horizon reveals the fallacy of what today appears to be a trade-off. In a classic paradox, fisheries must simultaneously exploit and protect fishing stocks. In this industry, a trade-off mindset, left unchallenged leads to bad strategy. Conversely, industry collaboration on sustainable fishing can prevent supply collapse and associated higher costs. Investing in traceability and responsible sourcing future-proofs the supply chain. In your Action Plan, remain alert to the false simplicity of a trade-off mindset. In fashion as in fishing, challenging a trade-off mindset reveals a paradox when the full set of risks and opportunities are considered. In your own industry, you are likely to find examples of the same.

The move from a trade-off to a paradox mindset is powerful. The reason for this is deeply practical but easily overlooked: parameters such as time horizons, investor preferences, advances in technology or operations, social licence to operate and the regulatory landscape all affect what appears to be a trade-off. And yet these parameters are rarely static. They contain a high degree of uncertainty; the future will likely be different from the past. What appears to be a trade-off might instead be understood as a paradox, thereby opening the space for sustainability and value creation to align. This is why it is so crucial for you and your teams to become adept at identifying the parameters contributing to a perceived trade-off. When these parameters are made explicit, you give yourself and your teams the ability to assess whether you are indeed facing a trade-off or whether a shift could reveal a paradox that opens new strategic possibilities.

Of course, trade-offs do exist, particularly in the short term. Parameters cannot always be immediately altered. The question for you, in your Action Plan, is whether you have done the analytical work to interrogate apparent trade-offs before accepting them tacitly. If a trade-off persists despite careful examination, and no paradox emerges, then the underlying issue may be a feature of the business model itself. As we discussed in Chapter 2 (Figure 2.4 A sustainable corporation?), a model that repeatedly forces a choice between financial returns and the health of environmental or social systems is ultimately not viable. Such business models are common, notwithstanding that they will become less so as environmental or social systems become increasingly strained.

But, as we set out in Chapters 3, 4 and 5, it is also common for business to lack a holistic understanding of its impacts and dependencies on social and environmental systems. Investigating what appear to be intractable trade-offs offers you the chance to scrutinise your business model in new ways. You will identify trade-offs you cannot immediately overcome. When this happens, use this insight to note priority areas for your sustainability transition, and continue to revisit. This can be quarterly, annually or as market conditions change. Repeated over time, and without backsliding to a default trade-off mindset, this process allows you to develop an understanding of why trade-offs persist and where paradox might be preset. The iterative process of challenging yourself and your teams to better understand the drivers of apparent trade-offs positions you to prioritise interventions that transition your business, towards one in which environmental and social systems are understood to be integral drivers of performance.

Your ability to sustain vision, differentiate between trade-offs and paradox and enable others to do the same is essential to your Action Plan. Leading sustainable corporations is a trajectory, not a fixed state. The key is for you to draw attention to the connection between sustainability and value creation again and again. Your approach to building this link in your organisation will depend on the existing understanding of sustainability in your company. One leader we know in the built environment sector recently moved from a company with a strong understanding of the strategic importance of sustainability to a firm that was at a much earlier stage. At the new firm, this leader noticed that, while sustainability was mentioned in almost every leadership meeting, it was typically shunted to the final slides of a presentation. The implicit message to the organisation was that sustainability was an afterthought and largely independent of the company's core strategy. This leader made a straightforward change: in their own presentations, they mentioned sustainability first, drawing attention to specific sustainability-related risks and opportunities for the company. The result was a clear message that sustainability was core: a simple change that enabled this leader to begin to communicate vision. Changes like this matter to the success of your Action Plan.

As you maintain vision, it goes without saying that you cannot change your company overnight. Along the way, identify and prioritise which changes you are willing or able to make over which time horizons and under which conditions. Greenwashing and ineffective sustainability plans are characterised by a lack of clarity around resource allocation and project timelines. On the contrary, a strong and credible plan proactively identifies where trade-offs currently exist and how they will be monitored while maintaining vision and commitment to change across the organisation. With vision, a trade-off may be re-evaluated as a paradox, increasing the set of solutions available to you, your teams and your company.

As you translate the insights from this book into action, your key leadership task is to maintain vision and commitment to sustainability while enabling your organisation to differentiate between trade-off and paradox. The former signals a need to more closely examine the impacts and dependencies of your business model. The latter suggests your business may have more opportunities for innovation than you might initially expect.

Long-term orientation and adaptive leadership

Leading a sustainability transition means equipping an organisation to challenge a trade-off mindset, recognise the drivers of apparent trade-offs and, whenever possible, identify how a paradox mindset opens new strategic possibilities. Because this process is iterative, the ability to lead with vision on what may be a significant journey of change over time is essential. While vision and moving from a trade-off to a paradox mindset will set your Action Plan in good stead to deliver results, your experience of leading a sustainability transition is unlikely to be smooth. This is because you are leading a shift from the familiar to the unfamiliar, in many cases, introducing complexity that necessitates a re-evaluation of core business logic for some or all of the organisation. Individuals and teams will find this challenging.

The demands of this kind of endeavour require at least two core leadership traits. First, long-term orientation. As with many examples we have shared throughout this book, businesses thriving in the present may sow the seeds of their own decline through a failure to reflect their impact and dependency on social and environmental systems in their strategy. A long-term view can help to make this omission evident. Furthermore, perceived tension between profitability and sustainability can be illusory when time horizons are stretched beyond the immediate or new strategic considerations are introduced, as in the illustrative example of overfishing.

Indeed, a long-term orientation will often help you to distinguish between trade-off and paradox. Examples across industries abound. Aviation engineering firms find themselves playing a costly game of catch-up with regulators and public scrutiny as they make investments in sustainable aviation fuels and greener aircraft. A firm that had initiated substantial R&D in these areas

20 years ago would today find itself a clear industry leader. US, European and Japanese car manufacturers, slow to transition to electric vehicles, today find themselves in danger of losing substantial market share to fast-emerging competition from manufacturers based in China.

Such unrealised potential contrasts with the experience of energy company Ørsted, which famously moved their core business from fossil fuels to renewables, profitably and ahead of schedule.[vi] Formerly Danish Oil and Natural Gas Energy, Ørsted was one of Europe's key players in coal. The company alone was responsible for an estimated one third of Denmark's carbon emissions. Their leadership picked up early signals of scrutiny of rising emissions from regulators and the public and took note of the up-and-coming renewable energy sector. A long-term horizon enabled the company to envision a world in which environmental impact sharply increased risk to their business. They also spotted an opportunity. In 2008, the company committed to reverse their energy production from 85 per cent fossil fuels to 85 per cent renewable energy by 2040. Through a combination of the sale of fossil fuel assets and large-scale investment in technology and renewable energy projects, the company reached economies of scale that enabled them to meet their target in 2019 – 21 years ahead of schedule. The company is now a global leader in renewable energy.

Ørsted's investments, perceived by some as an example of 'trade off' in the early 2000s, paradoxically held the potential to future-proof the business. The key was a shift in time horizon. What counts as 'long term' inevitably varies by company and industry. In many industries, planning cycles of three to five years is standard. You may have experience with firms for which a focus beyond annual or even quarterly results is counter cultural. Regardless of the specific timeline, maintaining your focus on a *longer time horizon than is the company norm* could what enables you to lead.

To stand out from the company norm itself requires a second key leadership trait: adaptability. 'Adaptive leadership'[vii] emphasises that the leader's role is to 'assist people in moving beyond the edge of familiar patters into unknown terrain'.[viii] While this description is self-evidently suited to leadership in general, adaptability is a distinctive hallmark of effective sustainability leadership due to the complex and emergent nature of corporate impacts and dependencies on natural and social systems. In this context, an adaptive leader keeps a strong emphasis on the 'known' focus of value creation for the business, while creating space for the organisation to adapt its understanding of potential new areas for value creation and how these can be realised.

To do this well requires the ability to identify social and environmental dependencies in incumbent business models and, through a paradox mindset, enable the organisation to think in an adaptive manner about risk, market and investor demand, and competitive advantage. An example of such leadership comes from IKEA, the world's largest furniture retailer. IKEA's CEO took note of the company's decision to stop selling incandescent lighting while the business case for doing so still appeared 'terrible'.[ix] This early adoption of LED light bulbs led IKEA to be a market leader and burnished its emerging sustainability credentials, which it now sees as a significant competitive advantage. IKEA's 'sustainable living' offerings now are the company's fastest-growing business. A design-led approach to 'make it easy' for consumers to buy products made from re-used or re-cycled materials has become a key feature of IKEA's strategy, making sustainability a default part of everyday life through innovations in manufacturing, product and operations.[x]

Cases of companies on successful adaptive journeys are increasingly commonplace: Mars Incorporated, for example, a global firm with more than US $50 billion annual revenue, is famously associated with its confectionery and snack food products. With such products under scrutiny for their impact on human health, among other concerns, the company's leadership has sought to build on their core competencies by increasing their investments in pet care, reducing their exposure to the confectionery and snack market. This process, which over time saw the company build relationships with pet health providers, farmers and a range of stakeholders across the petcare ecosystem, saw 60 per cent of the company's revenues come from pet care as of 2023. The company is now the largest vet provider in the United States. While Mars is still heavily invested in processed food for human consumption, this adaptive move by their leadership has, over time, strengthened the company's value proposition relative to their traditional product offerings and enabled them to chart a credible path forward for a more diversified future. In addition, Mars has made important investments in the farming ecosystems required for key commodities including rice and cocoa, aware of the need to transition their supply chains to sustainable approaches to ensure future supply.

In another industry, VELUX, the Danish pioneer of roof windows to introduce light and ventilation into buildings, made a similar adaptive move as their leadership became increasingly aware of the emissions associated with their supply chain. The raw materials behind windows – steel, glass and aluminium – are highly energy intensive. Understanding this as a challenge across the built environment sector led VELUX to offer themselves as a customer for their suppliers to test new, lower-emissions materials. Partnerships with their steel supplier led to the development of a viable product with a significantly lower emissions footprint. Similar partnerships were struck with suppliers to develop lower-carbon aluminium. In this way, VELUX saw themselves not only as solving a technical challenge to increase their own sustainability and competitive advantage but as creating demand for products that did not exist and needed to be developed. In this way, the company decreased its emissions, differentiated itself and enabled its supply chain to adapt.[xi]

Finally, a word on complexity: adaptive leaders work to maintain vision in the face of complexity and equip their teams to do the same. This ability will be necessary as you bring your Action Plan to life in your organisation. As individuals and teams move towards a more comprehensive understanding of how your organisation interacts with social and environmental systems, complexity is introduced. If, as is likely, some individuals and teams feel unable to reconcile complexity (sustainability and financial performance, for example) one response is to cognitively separate the two. This may take the form of downplaying your company's impact and dependency on social or environmental systems, simplifying the issue by not seeing it, as for example in the case of real-estate investments whose valuation does not consider risk from flood, fire or other extreme weather events, a situation that has caused some analysts to argue that key property holdings are overvalued by hundreds of billions of dollars.[xii] A second version is presuming financial returns to be inherently incompatible with sustainability goals, in other words, remaining constrained by a trade-off mindset rather than spotting the opportunity in paradox. As you deliver your Action Plan, remember that a company that denies (or otherwise fails to demonstrate curiosity about) its impacts and dependencies on social or environmental systems is unlikely to build a compelling sustainable value proposition. And neither is a company likely to build such a proposition if it engages only at a level of corporate philanthropy or CSR, without a clear understanding that there is financial value to be generated from social and environmental systems. Either pathway is strategically disadvantageous.

Promising technological or process solutions to well-known challenges including emissions, waste and natural resource degradation often remain niche or sub-scale for reasons unrelated to their technical viability. Rather, they stay blocked as a result, at least in part, of organisational or institutional resistance, an inability to reconcile the company's past value proposition with a future that may look quite different. Your task is to maintain an adaptive, long-term vision in the face of such a response. To do this, you will need to work effectively with your teams to build strategies and value propositions that work with and reinforce strong social and environmental systems. You will need to become relentlessly curious and inspire curiosity in your teams. You, and they, need to become deep and effective observers of your business, able to draw connections and to spot value hitherto untapped.

Building your Action Plan: three steps

With a clear understanding of the primary challenges and leadership competencies required, we now turn our attention to practical steps you can take to implement change. Step 1 is to work with stakeholders inside and outside the business to identify a clear set of priority areas on which to focus. Step 2 is to set goals and identify and test the levers of change available to you to achieve them. Once you and your teams have thereby developed a clear view of the strategic connection between value creation and corporate impacts and dependencies, you share ownership of Step 3: communicating this vision and enabling the organisation to change.

It is worth emphasising this third point. A sustainability transition will require endurance from you and your teams. The mindset shift it demands can be profound, potentially reframing what your company needs to do to create value in a complex, dynamic environment. Leading a sustainable corporation may offer some quick wins. It also, by definition, requires that you create conditions for an enduring change agenda. The need to reiterate and reframe your vision to stakeholders will be ongoing. As you lead in this manner, you will find yourself positioning and repositioning your approach to your levers of change to ensure stakeholders understand and embrace adaptations to their mindsets, roles and daily work.

Step 1 Stakeholders and priorities

In the face of a significant change project, it can be tempting to resort to command-and-control forms of leadership. But, as you identify your priorities, it is essential that you consult with stakeholders to unearth new knowledge rather than working unilaterally or only with an existing team. This is likely to extend beyond direct consultation with stakeholders to include those who speak on their behalf, e.g. data-driven conservation groups equipped to speak on behalf of nature or community organisations with an established record of representing marginalised groups. The fact remains that very few companies today possess a comprehensive understanding of the full scope of their impacts and dependencies on climate, nature and social systems and how these link to strategy. Even if your understanding is well developed in some areas, it is wise to review with an open mind and with our definition of sustainability as a guide to your level of ambition.

We recommend starting with a set of internal and external consultations, designed to include a wide set of stakeholder perspectives, to gain a holistic picture of where your company's impacts and dependencies on social and environmental systems may be. Ensure that these consultations are framed as core to the company's strategy and business objectives, not as an add-on. Awareness of risk and opportunity, and where fresh value can be created, is often latent within existing stakeholders who simply need an invitation to tap their understanding in a serious and meaningful way. In one example, a UK agricultural supplier, operating in regions with high unemployment, identified a potential forced labour risk during such stakeholder consultations. Combining this with insights from government and NGO partners, the company subsequently implemented two key recruitment strategies: prioritising local hiring, and partnering with local charities to reintegrate long-term unemployed individuals into the workforce. Both approaches have bolstered the company's' social licence and reduced labour-force risk. In addition, recognising their position as a lower-tier supplier with limited direct influence over their customers, the company has leveraged its findings to advocate for improved labour policies within the entire sector.

To achieve outcomes like this one, create channels to enable a wide range of stakeholders to directly share their views as you build strategy. You may do this through surveys, focus groups or live polls at key company or community events. You may wish to use impartial outsiders to solicit feedback, as stakeholders themselves might be unlikely to voice to a company representative. When we ourselves conduct diagnostics as part of the design of sustainability education for large corporates, we frequently find that managers are willing to be candid with us precisely because we are 'outsiders' to the company. They

7 HOW TO BUILD YOUR SUSTAINABILITY ACTION PLAN AND LEAD CHANGE 213

are more than ready to offer valuable insight on opportunities and risks, yet they may not feel comfortable sharing with leadership and often also doubt the authenticity of a top-down, internal ask. Academics, NGOs and consultants all have the potential to play this role if they are well briefed.

Whatever means you choose, provide at least one channel through which stakeholders know that their views will remain anonymous. Internally, ensure your efforts go beyond engaging the usual suspects, i.e. include those who do not currently have 'sustainability' included in their job description. Ask directly for examples of where they see risk and opportunity in their roles. Broaden the scope of your engagement by asking about aspects of natural and social systems because insight might be lost by raising only issues that stakeholders currently perceive to be sustainability-related. One firm in the extractives industry recently led a comprehensive consultation of this type. Through this process, it became evident that operational leaders across the globe perceived that leadership expected worker health and safety to be their primary social priority. Essential, to be sure, but it overlooked the knowledge these operators had of the risk to social licence due to an entrenched track record of poor engagement with some local communities in which they worked. This was taken-for-granted knowledge for many operators but had not been clearly articulated to management in the context of the company's strategy. Discovering this allowed the company to expand their operators' understanding of their role and provide training to equip them to better deliver value.

In many companies, a process of canvassing stakeholders to identify priority areas is accomplished through something called a 'materiality assessment.'[1] This is a structured process designed to identify the relative importance for the company of specific areas of sustainability. Inputs for materiality assessments include internal and external sources of data on key sustainability topics, desk-based research including social media, traditional media and NGO sources, as well as stakeholders including investors, customers, employees and suppliers. These are assessed considering existing business goals, company values and corporate risks. The output from this exercise is often presented in the form of a materiality matrix mapping the level of significance of sustainability topics

---

1 The term 'materiality' can be a source of confusion because it carries different meanings in different contexts. In Chapter 6, the term refers to financially material aspects of a company's sustainability disclosure, i.e. information useful to investors. Here, the term refers to information that enables you to identify and assess the relative importance of sustainability topics to your business.

to stakeholders against their level of importance for the financial prospects of the business.

Today, materiality assessments are increasingly a standard exercise among corporates. They can have enormous value, and it is prudent to build up internal expertise or hire external providers to ensure that your company benefits from the value of this tool. In addition, your challenge and opportunity as a leader is to ensure that materiality assessments, and similar efforts, are linked to action. As the sophistication and scope of sustainability reporting requirements increases, the motivation for companies to develop a deep understanding of their impact and dependencies on social and environmental systems becomes stronger. This is a benefit. To leverage this exercise fully, ensure you create space for a sufficient diversity of internal and external voices in the process, link the process clearly to strategy, and put mechanisms in place to govern the risks and opportunities that materiality assessments identify.

To ensure the link between information and action, do what you can to create ongoing mechanisms for substantive engagement between your leadership and the natural and social systems on which you impact and depend. In many cases, executives and board members may need to experience the impact and dependency of their company first-hand to grasp their significance. One executive of a listed UK company recently shared with us their reflections of visiting a rural area of Europe whose produce is a key input to one of the company's most popular consumer products. Speaking with farmers who had experienced the threat to their crops due to soil degradation from overly intensive farming methods, this leader gained a deep appreciation for, and interest in, supporting the company's innovation in sustainable and regenerative agricultural practices throughout their supply chain. With a first-hand understanding of how such approaches could mitigate risk to the company, this executive became an eloquent internal and external advocate for the strategic opportunities such approaches present. This leader now chairs the company's executive team working group on sustainability and championed a company-wide commitment to halve Scope 3 GHG emissions by 2030, an ambitious target compared to industry peers.

Materiality assessments and similar efforts are powerful inputs to strategy. As part of your Action Plan, you might ask how the impacts and dependencies you have prioritised for your company might reflect the status quo in the industry. The chocolate retail industry offers strong examples of such an approach. Because the supply chain remains dogged by modern slavery and child labour, several companies have prioritised this issue in their strategy, operations and brand, enabling them to secure reputational benefits and a premium price for their products. One of these – currently one of the world's fastest growing chocolate companies – recently raised equity to launch a data-driven B2B company, enabling other firms to source cocoa according to its ethical principles. The initiative quickly secured interest from major retailers, significantly reducing supply chain and reputational risk for these companies.[xiii] In the face of increased supply chain transparency – scrutiny from regulators, and social media activity that quickly amplifies negative stories – companies taking these steps are protecting their businesses.

This raises an important final point: your company may not have mechanisms in place to govern the risks and opportunities materiality assessments identify. You might not be in a position to change your governance but, as you select your priorities, you need to have a clear understanding of the kind of commitments your company is placed to deliver and that are out of scope for the governance mechanisms you have. Considering your governance in this manner provides an important way to stretch and test your thinking as you consider the viability of your plan over the long term. One striking example comes from a prominent global extractives company whose operations created severe violations of human rights within indigenous communities. Notably, the board of this company now includes dedicated representation for human rights concerns. Such innovations emphasise how such structures can be wielded to foster sustainable leadership that integrates into the company's strategy long term.

Step 2 Goals and levers of change

Leading a sustainable corporation entails a shift from a known present to a less well-known future. As with any change process, well-chosen goals enable you to focus energy and resources and track progress. A key element of determining which goals to select, and the timelines you attach to them, is developing a clear understanding of the levers of change available to you. Here, 'levers of change' refers to the processes, structures and systems whereby your company's impact or dependency on specific social or environmental systems can be better aligned to value creation. Importantly, in this context, 'goals' is not about a rigid plan, but about setting key milestones and priorities within an emergent strategy – one that stays agile, responsive and remains adaptable to change while keeping a clear focus on the core aim of sustainability transformation.

Identifying goals of this nature, and activating levers of change, will require you to create space for innovation and experimentation by your team. This will help ensure that your goals are realistic, potentially avoiding untold frustration for you, your stakeholders and your teams. As you begin to test goals and the levers of change you would need to achieve them, inevitably, you will identify levers you can access directly, those you can access indirectly or with stakeholder support, and those you cannot – or cannot yet – access but that may, nevertheless, be significant.[xiv] The latter often concern issues of policy or regulation, i.e. the rules of the game, which affect not just you but your sector. Keep note of these levers that initially may appear out of reach. In due course, they may form the basis for a systems-level goal you can pursue with others.

Building on the work you did in Step 1 on stakeholders and priorities, the goals to which you commit in Step 2 should be 'transparent and explainable'.[xv] It is self-evidently easier to gain support if you are clear about what you want to achieve, and about how and why each goal matters. Also unsurprising is that interim goals will keep you, your teams and wider stakeholders engaged and on track. Credible and compelling goals will also help you to communicate authentically, which is crucial to success in Step 3. As with other projects you have experienced, the goals themselves need to have time-bound criteria. Teams perform best when goals are realistic, have clearly defined indicators for progress (which can be qualitative or quantitative) and allow for the need to course correct in the face of unintended consequences.[xvi] Remember that social and environmental systems are connected and that, for example, a shift to a more environmentally friendly production method may have significant impact on jobs and communities, which can have a profound impact on the business' reputation and licence to operate.

Keep in mind that your resources and those of your teams and stakeholders are finite, especially as business-as-usual imperatives do not disappear during a sustainability transition. To keep energy and focus, it is crucial to enlist mentors and champions across the organisation. Your resilience will erode without delegation to an empowered team. It is also important to prepare the organisation for perceived 'failure' when new ideas are being tested. As we have emphasised from the outset of this book, the transition to sustainability is the biggest innovation challenge and opportunity of our time. Consequently, a core element of delivering your plan is an adaptive mindset that embraces the potential for paradox and thus enables the organisation to experiment and prototype.[xvii]

7 HOW TO BUILD YOUR SUSTAINABILITY ACTION PLAN AND LEAD CHANGE

This adaptive mindset is crucial when asking an organisation to move from the known to the unknown. In one company we know well, we observed a sustainability change process that initially lacked this characteristic. In this firm, leadership set forth an ambitious approach to sustainability transition. While this senior-level buy-in was powerful, it was also articulated using language that made many within the organisation feel there was zero room for error. In many cases, the result was paralysis and low levels of ownership across the organisation. Internal stakeholders with significant potential to influence outcomes told us that they would wait to be told what to do before acting – not a good sign. Vision and ambition alone did not rally the organisation because it was not matched by acknowledgement that iteration would be an inevitable part of the change process. For a time, it seemed inertia would reign. Executive leadership picked up on this tension and adjusted its approach, wisely creating channels for experimentation and learning. When leadership course-corrected, engagement with and ownership for the vision increased across the firm's global operations.

As you consider the levers of change available to you, remember that your company's current strategy for creating value, current ways of understanding its impact and dependencies, current corporate culture, and current reporting regimes are just a few of the factors that combine in very real ways to 'create' the current reality of your business. You and your teams have choices about how you operate and the choices you make. It is the job of leading sustainable corporations to make strategic choices explicit. This may be both challenging and countercultural within the organisation, but it is crucial to selecting goals with the right level of vision and ambition. For example, for value chain goals to be realised, change is typically required in more than one single company. Multiple buyers making the same requests from their suppliers, whether around carbon emissions, waste reduction or working conditions is essential. Likewise, systems-level goals typically require sector-wide collaboration as well as work with governments or civil society actors. Identify advocates across your company and partners within your industry, perhaps in the form of those who face similar transition challenges.

An example of a collaborative initiative is the Leather Working Group (LWG), a 'cross-competitor consortium' founded by buyers of leather goods, including Timberland, Nike and IKEA, as an 'impartial body to develop and maintain a protocol to assess and rate the environmental performance of leather tanneries', which are extremely emissions-intensive.[xviii] Of the experience, Timberland's chief operating officer reflected that, 'The scale of competing brands working together engendered sustainability advances that no single brand could achieve on its own.'[xix] Better still than this collective effort in damage limitation would be innovation across the industry to move beyond a high-emissions source of materials. In the case of LWG, it is possible that the first step in working across the industry will itself enable the second. In such cases, system-level goals gain momentum because they address a shared problem. The case of LWG, and the RISE programme we introduced in the context of industry-wide human rights concerns in Chapter 5, are good examples of this.

Regardless of whether you are focused on operations, the value chain or a system, your goals should be both ambitious and achievable. This may seem self-evident but, as the example of corporate net zero pledges demonstrates, getting the balance right between vision and pragmatism is key to delivering on the core task of transitioning to a sustainable corporation. In our teaching, we have seen individuals from all corners of organisations develop and implement successful change plans including with their teams, direct reports and even colleagues. Levers of change are not confined to executive leadership. As you measure a goal's progress, continuously refer to your priorities and stakeholders from Step 1. If there is a lack of alignment, identify what needs to change. At this stage, it is also prudent to consider how you will communicate progress and the outcomes of experiments, to whom, and how often. This leads us to Step 3 of your Action Plan: communication.

Step 3 Communication

Once your priorities, stakeholders, goals and levers of change are clear, it may feel that your work is almost done. However, sustainability transitions require special ongoing attention to communication. Because sustainability is so often perceived as a cost rather than an investment or strategic benefit, all or part of your Action Plan may be met with disinterest, scepticism, resistance or even derision. The ability of you and your team to influence through communication is key, as is your command of the facts behind your priorities and goals. As part of identifying goals and levers of change in Step 2 of your Action Plan, you will have developed a keen understanding of the internal and external barriers you face. Your work on priorities with stakeholders in Step 1 provides you with the grounding to stay committed to the reasons motivating your plan. The ability to persist with influential, compelling communication will make you and your teams more effective.

Because you operate within a specific corporate culture, embodying pre-existing expectations from a range of stakeholders, you will need to identify and cultivate internal fellow travellers. Blending existing champions with opportunities for peer learning and internal recognition can be powerful. Whenever possible, our experience is that including peer working groups in your Action Plan is wise. We know several companies who created company-wide innovation challenges, inviting submissions from across the company of possible solutions to sustainability goals and priorities. This can be motivational and a powerful tool for communicating the importance of the work and raising awareness and buy-in.

As you build your Action Plan, remember that this will not be a one-off communication job, and resource accordingly. Prepare for an exercise in ongoing positioning and repositioning the case for your work. You will likely need to continually reframe the company's approach to value creation and its relationship to social and environmental systems, identifying wins along the way that reinforce evidence of direction of travel. A key skill is to make the issue familiar to others, for example by using the kind of data they will find credible or language they find recognisable. Internally, you need to communicate in a manner that invites ownership across the organisation. By these means, your colleagues will ideally see for themselves the merits of a sustainable business plan, without this feeling imposed. For internal and external stakeholders, you need to be able to use data and communication to account for progress on goals to establish and build credibility.

Crucially, do not overpromise. Companies that overstate their claims are vulnerable to reputational risk and (increasingly) to litigation. It is better to be clear on your priorities and confident in why you have chosen them through a stakeholder-informed process, than to fall into the trap of promising 'everything, all at once'.[xx] The latter is a recipe for loss of trust, accusations of greenwashing, purpose-washing or similar[xxi] and – most importantly – a missed opportunity for innovation and value creation.

Delivering your Action Plan will entail a change process with many steps. Stakeholders have multiple opportunities to affect the outcome of the effort. An isolated or disengaged stakeholder can build internal resistance.[xxii] Their input is also lost to the change project. When an internal stakeholder is unconvinced of the value of the work, it is sensible to ask what the most generous (and generative) interpretation of their concerns might be. Is there anything you and your team can take from their perspective that will genuinely improve your work? Importantly, how can you keep the dialogue open, demonstrating the value the change brings to the company? How can you create an environment that diminishes fear of failure and generates the psychological safety required for creativity, innovation and risk-taking? Remember that communication is two-way, and this openness to feedback is an important aspect of your communication plan.

Fundamentally, your communication should aim at increasing ownership and engagement. This means you will need to build in time and mechanisms to stay alert to stakeholder concerns that may be driving resistance to change. Whenever possible, involve others in generating solutions. Resistance to change may also relate to inertia. Incumbent systems remain because they bring benefit to some within the system. This is where the key task of vision comes to the fore. In Step 3, your aim in communication is to make the costs of the status quo and benefits of change clear, with the aim of enabling sceptics to make an explicit choice, rather than a passive acceptance of business-as-usual. One global professional services firm we know recently developed an AI-generated film outlining several future scenarios of environmental systems, some catastrophic and some optimistic. As part of a company gathering, they invited leaders from across the firm to 'experience' these realities and discuss the connection between the business' activities and these potential outcomes. The effect was powerful: beyond traditional 'communication', this experiential approach generated significant interest in the company's sustainability transition. In short, your communication plan should include diverse cohorts of advocates from across the business who actively contribute to the change plan. These individuals and teams need to be equipped to communicate in a simple, persuasive manner to a range of audiences. They need to anticipate pushback and maintain a strong vision of the value the change generates.

Critically, the degree of change required for a sustainability transition often means you will need to balance vision with the fact that you cannot meet everyone's expectations at once. One sustainability leader we know well shared that one of their biggest communication challenges is that they frequently need to say 'no' – or, more accurately, 'not yet' – to worthy ideas that sit outside the strategic priorities set for the organisation's sustainability transformation. Your Action Plan needs to be visionary and yet focused. This can be challenging to hold in tension, yet essential to deliver on the Action Plan you have set out with stakeholder support.

Conclusion

In this chapter, we set out the 'why' of the uniqueness of sustainability leadership: that a core challenge is to maintain vision and ambition while challenging a trade-off mindset. We also highlight the 'what' of sustainability leadership: a long-term orientation and adaptive leadership, two traits that will equip you to deliver the required change. Finally, we set out the 'how': three steps you will need to take to design and deliver an effective change plan: first, stakeholders and priorities, second, goals and levers of change and, finally, communication.

The approach we put forth in this chapter is intentionally not formulaic or 'tick box' in style. Rather, our objective is to provide you with a guide onto which you can map the realities of your own company and industry, and your own team and leadership style. Our hope is that you will design and deliver an effective plan of action in your organisation because of your engagement with this book.

Thankfully, this is a journey with many starting points. Regardless of where you and your company are today, you can consider afresh how your company can create value and strategically approach its impacts and dependencies on social and environmental systems. The opportunity you have before you – to build a strong business in stronger systems – is immense. The work is in identifying the impacts and dependencies of your business on social and environmental systems, and building a comprehensive strategic view of how this impacts your ability to create value. As you build your cohort of internal and external stakeholders in the change process, the key lies in articulating specific goals and identifying levers of change you can action together. This will not be 'everything, all at once' and one of your most important tasks is working with stakeholders to identify clear priorities. Also with your stakeholders, you will test and evaluate as you calibrate to identify the right balance between ambition and expediency, testing your thinking as you go to identify where you could be even more ambitious in creating value through sustainable business.

We have already noted that delivering on this project will require resilience from you and your teams. Among sustainability professionals, burnout is commonplace.[xxiii] Understanding the true impacts and dependencies of your business on social and environmental systems can be technically complex. For many leaders, the scope and scale of challenges faced by social and environmental systems can be jarring, even overwhelming. Coupled with the pressure to deliver financially for shareholders and employees as well as meet the expectations of the public, putting your head above the parapet with an ambitious and visionary sustainability transformation is demanding of you and your organisation, even of those not in a 'sustainability' role. The complexity of the task, and attendant stressors, is something to watch for as you and your teams pursue your change project.

Fortunately, resilience is not an inbuilt, static trait – it can be cultivated. As you embark on your Action Plan, it is crucial to understand the importance of resilience to sustained change processes and to communicate resilience as a skill that can be developed. Research-backed strategies for building resilience include clear boundaries around ownership and scope of tasks, reflection practices and maintaining a balance between work and personal life.[xxiv]

While the task of leading sustainable corporations is urgent, the challenges and opportunities faced and presented by impacts and dependencies on social and environmental systems are longer term in nature than the typical tenure of an executive or even a board member. An assessment of your company's ability to deliver on its commitments over time, and how to pass the baton effectively, is a key consideration. The challenges and opportunities you identify may be complex and take time to map fully. Remain relentlessly curious. The frontiers of knowledge about the social and environmental systems on which companies impact and depend are expanding rapidly. Geopolitical shifts mean that taken-for-granted ways of doing business are changing rapidly. Social media continues to profoundly impact the way in which we understand and consume information. Technological change, cultural shifts and new ways of working mean that leaders are in a position of constant learning, even about their own organisations.

With change as the constant facing you and your teams, the tools you build through leading a sustainable corporation are the tools contemporary organisations require. Understanding how your business creates value – and can create even more – from environmental and social systems is time well spent, and places you and your teams in one of the most exciting leadership positions in a generation: that of shaping not only today, but also tomorrow.

Kicking off your Action Plan

The purpose of this book has been to empower you to build resilient businesses within strong natural and social systems. Beginning with a clear understanding of the corporation and its purpose (Chapter 2), we explored the interdependent relationships between business and climate systems (Chapter 3), natural resources (Chapter 4) and social systems (Chapter 5). In Chapter 6, we provided approaches for measuring and reporting on sustainability.

At the start of your reading (Chapter 1), we encouraged you to identify individuals and teams in your own organisation with whom to discuss the reflection questions provided at the end of each chapter. Our aim throughout has been to enable you to workshop the material in real time within your corporate context. The guidance we offer here in this final chapter is intended to build on the cumulative work you have done together. By this stage, alongside the individuals and teams with whom you have engaged with throughout this process, you are equipped to design an Action Plan for your work. In that spirit, we invite you to reflect on the following:

1. With your teams and stakeholders, consider:
   a) What do you want to achieve by leading this change process?
   b) Why are these aims important to the business?
   c) Which internal and external stakeholders need to contribute to setting goals for this change process?
2. Which stakeholders do you need to engage to deliver your goals? How will you engage, persuade or incentivise them?
3. What will be different in your company because of this change process in six months? In a year? In five years?
4. What is your level of confidence in your ability to manage the personal challenges associated with spearheading a change process within your company? What strategies and resources will you use to boost your resilience along the way?

Our goal in writing this book has been to enable you to drive meaningful change within your leadership and organisation. This final chapter is not an endpoint, but a launching pad. Equipped with the insights you have gained, you and your teams are well positioned to design the Action Plan the future of your business requires. As you move forward, remember that building a sustainable business is not a solitary effort. It requires collaboration and a commitment to continuous learning. Together, you and your teams can shape a resilient future for your business and the systems on which it impacts and depends.

Recommended reading

Alexander, J. and Conrad, A. (2022) *Citizens: Why the Key to Fixing Everything is All of Us*. Canbury Press.

Bertels, S. and Dobson, R. (2020) Embedded Strategies for the Sustainability Transition Setting Priorities and Goals Aligned with Systems Resilience. The Embedding Project. Available at: https://doi.org/10.6084/m9.figshare.12071769.

Heifetz, R. and Laurie, D. (2001) The Work of Leadership. *Harvard Business Review*, December. Available at: https://hbr.org/2001/12/the-work-of-leadership.

Love, C. and Eccles, R.G. (2022) How Leaders Can Move beyond Greenwashing toward Real Change. *Harvard Business Review*, 25 January. Available at: https://hbr.org/2022/01/how-leaders-can-move-beyond-greenwashing-toward-real-change.

Smith, W., Lewis, M. and Edmondson, A.C. (2022) *Both/and Thinking: Embracing Creative Tensions to Solve Your Toughest Problems*. La Vergne: Harvard Business Review Press.

Whelan, T. (2024) Research: Boards Still Have an ESG Expertise Gap – but They're Improving. *Harvard Business Review*, 18 April 18. Available at: https://hbr.org/2024/04/research-boards-still-have-an-esg-expertise-gap-but-theyre-improving.

Notes

[i] Anthony, S.D. (2023) The Hidden Opportunity in Paradoxes. *MIT Sloan Management Review* 65, no. 2, 12 December. Available at: https://sloanreview.mit.edu/article/the-hidden-opportunity-in-paradoxes/.

[ii] Smith, W., Lewis, M. and Edmondson, A.C. (2022) *Both/and Thinking: Embracing Creative Tensions to Solve Your Toughest Problems*. La Vergne: Harvard Business Review Press.

[iii] Canopy (2024) Next Generation Solutions: Innovating for the Future. Canopy Planet. Canopyplanet.org. Available at: https://canopyplanet.org/next-generation-solutions.

[iv] World Wildlife Fund (2025) Overfishing. World Wildlife Fund. Available at: https://www.worldwildlife.org/threats/overfishing.

[v] World Wildlife Fund (2025) Overfishing. World Wildlife Fund. Available from: https://www.worldwildlife.org/threats/overfishing.

[vi] EACD (2020) From 90% Fossil Fuels to 90% Renewables: The Ørsted Transformation Story. EACD, 26 May. Available at: https://eacd-online.eu/from-90-fossil-fuels-to-90-renewables-the-orsted-transformation-story/.

7 HOW TO BUILD YOUR SUSTAINABILITY ACTION PLAN AND LEAD CHANGE

[vii] Heifetz, R.A., Grashow, A. and Linsky, A. (2009) *The Practice of Adaptive Leadership: Tools and Tactics for Changing Your Organization and the World*. Boston, Mass: Harvard Business Press.

[viii] Daloz Parks (2005), p. 9.

[ix] Vereckey, B. (2024) IKEA CEO: 3 Ways to Gain Competitive Advantage with Sustainability. MIT Sloan, 28 October. Available at: https://mitsloan.mit.edu/ideas-made-to-matter/ikea-ceo-3-ways-to-gain-competitive-advantage-sustainability.

[x] Vereckey, B. (2024) IKEA CEO: 3 Ways to Gain Competitive Advantage with Sustainability. MIT Sloan, 28 October. Available at: https://mitsloan.mit.edu/ideas-made-to-matter/ikea-ceo-3-ways-to-gain-competitive-advantage-sustainability.

[xi] Thanks go to COFRA, PwC, Mars and VELUX for support with codifying these examples.

[xii] Gourevitch, J.D., *et al.* (2023) Unpriced Climate Risk and the Potential Consequences of Overvaluation in US Housing Markets. *Nature Climate Change* 13, 16 February: 1–8. Available at: https://doi.org/10.1038/s41558-023-01594-8.

[xiii] Tony's Open Chain. Available at: https://www.tonysopenchain.com.

[xiv] Oxford *Leading Sustainable Corporations Programme* (2024) *Defining the Goals of Your Change Process*. University of Oxford.

[xv] Bertels, S. and Dobson, R. (2020) Embedded Strategies for the Sustainability Transition Setting Priorities and Goals Aligned with Systems Resilience. The Embedding Project. Available at: https://doi.org/10.6084/m9.figshare.12071769.

[xvi] Senge, P.M. (2006) The Fifth Discipline: The Art and Practice of the Learning Organization. London: Random House Business (1990; repr.).

[xvii] Stroh, D.P. (2015) *Systems Thinking for Social Change: A Practical Guide to Solving Complex Problems, Avoiding Unintended Consequences, and Achieving Lasting Results*. White River Junction, Vermont: Chelsea Green Publishing.

[xviii] United Nations Industrial Development Organisation (2017) Leather Carbon Footprint: Review of the European Standard. Available at: https://leatherpanel.org/sites/default/files/publications-attachments/leather_carbon_footprint_p.pdf.

[xix] Pucker, K.P. (2024) Companies Are Scaling Back Sustainability Pledges. Here's What They Should Do Instead. *Harvard Business Review*, 20 August. Available at: https://hbr.org/2024/08/companies-are-scaling-back-sustainability-pledges-heres-what-they-should-do-instead.

xx   Taylor, A. (2021) So Many Stakeholders. How Do Companies Choose Who to Satisfy? *Wall Street Journal*, 24 June, sec. Business. Available at: https://www.wsj.com/articles/so-many-stakeholders-strategy-11624308112.

xxi   Love, C. and Eccles, R.G. (2022) How Leaders Can Move beyond Greenwashing toward Real Change. *Harvard Business Review*, 25 January. Available at: https://hbr.org/2022/01/how-leaders-can-move-beyond-greenwashing-toward-real-change.

xxii   Miller, D. and Oliver, M. (2015) Engaging Stakeholders for Project Success. www.pmi.org, 1 January. Available at: https://www.pmi.org/learning/library/engaging-stakeholders-project-success-11199.

xxiii   Hicks, R. (2024) Chief Sustainability Officers Are Burning Out. Has the Role Become Unsustainable? *Eco-Business*, 14 May. Available at: https://www.eco-business.com/news/chief-sustainability-officers-are-burning-out-has-the-role-become-unsustainable/#:~:text=Acre.

xxiv   Fernandez, R. (2016) 5 Ways to Boost Your Resilience at Work. *Harvard Business Review*, 27 June. Available at: https://hbr.org/2016/06/627-building-resilience-ic-5-ways-to-build-your-personal-resilience-at-work.

INDEX

Accenture 138
actio popularis claims 144
action
    on nature as a business 126–8
    on social systems as a business 158–61
Action Plan
    Step 1 Stakeholders and priorities 211–15
    Step 2 Goals and levers of change 215–18
    Step 3 Communication 218–20
activity data 73
adaptation (dependency) 66
adaptive leadership 11, 207–11
additionality 82
Adecco 138
advertised emissions 111
Agboka, Ofori 138
Agreena 117
agricultural land 111
air pollution 14
Airbnb 137
airline industry 66
Allbirds 113
Alpro 120
Altana AI 140
Amazon 52, 136, 137–8
'Amazon dieback' 99, 100, 107
Amazon Web Services 138
Ambienta 50, 51, 52
Apple 136
ArcelorMittal 62
Arla Foods 146–8
Asda 160
ASN Bank 103
Astanor Ventures 118
atmospheric aerosol loading 98

Attenborough, David 95, 111
Australian government: nature positive plan 104
auto industry 3, 80, 178, 208
aviation 80
aviation engineering 207

B Corp 39, 40
Bachmann, Peter 95
balance sheet 174, 175
Bank of England 184
bees 103
Bell, Amy 143
benefit corporations 38
Benetton 136
Berkshire Partners 139
Bernard, Steven 58
Better Business Act campaign 40
Biden administration 62
biodiversity finance 95
biodiversity loss 4, 97
biodiversity "no net loss or net gain" 104
biological cycle 126
biosphere integrity, loss of 97
BlackRock 10, 11, 67
BLK + GRN 139
BloombergNEF 95
Blue Marble 14
BMW 120
Borrelli, Silvia Sciorilli 49
Boston Consulting Group 140
BP 145
Breeden, Sarah 184
British Academy 39, 40
Buontempo, Carlo 59
Burgess, Samantha 59, 60
'business as usual' 11, 12, 179

'business ethics' 13
Business for Nature 102, 105

California Department of Insurance 68
Californian wildfires 67-9, 183, 185
Capasa, Carlo 51
carbon capture 82
carbon credits 81
carbon dioxide equivalents 85-6
carbon emissions 50, 70-8
    climate change and 64-70
carbon footprint 3, 7, 70, 78, 79-80
carbon sink 91, 99, 101, 102, 109
carbon tax 65, 67
Carrefour 105
Chatzimichalakis, Fotis 95
chemical pollution 97
China: electric vehicles 63, 119-20
Chobani 137
circular economy 115, 120
ClientEarth 144, 145
climate change 4
Climate Change Act (2008) (UK) 179
climate change adaptation 57
climate change mitigation 57
climate transition 83
Cobre Panama mine, Panama 133, 145
Coca-Cola 127
coffee 14
Cofra 137
Colorado River, United States 91
common pool resources 107, 108
Companies Act (2006) Section 172 40
construction industry 80, 96
control of corporation 36-41
Copernicus 59, 60
corporate balance sheet 35
corporate capitalism 42-3
corporate commons 42
corporate governance 177
corporate purpose 39
corporate reporting 171-95
corporate social responsibility (CSR) 13
corporation
    climate change and 64-70
    control 36-41
    as legal structures 31-6
    what can go wrong? 41-5
cotton production 5
COVID-19 pandemic 93, 137
'cradle to cradle' value proposition 6
'cradle to grave' model 6, 115
CreditNature 121
critical success factors 156

Dalberg 119
Danish Oil and Natural Gas Energy 208
Danone 43, 117
Darwin, Charles 47
Dealroom 117
definition
    of sustainability 8, 12-15
    of sustainable corporation 2, 13, 45-53
    of trust 136
deforestation 4, 91, 121, 122
degradation of natural systems 100-11
dependency 64, 65
Digital Product Passport 51
digital tagging 140
directors
    acting 'in good faith' 38
    control 36
    duties of 37
double counting 76
double-entry system of accounting 174
double materiality 187
downcycling 127
downstream emissions 77, 79, 80
Durno, Mark 117, 118
'duty to promote the success of
    the company' 37

Eccles, Bob 155
ECHR 144
Eco-Age 50
economic efficiency 46
EcoVero, 204
Edison International 69

El Niño 59
electric vehicles (EVs) 3, 9, 63, 119–20
  see also auto industry
electricity generation 3
Ellen MacArthur Foundation 59
emergent properties 6
emissions: decision relevance 78–80
Employee Resource Groups 153
Environment Act (2021) (UK) 95
Environment Bank 95
Environmental Defense Fund 68
environmental degradation, economic expansion and 92
'ESG' (environmental, social, and governance) 12–13
European Central Bank 96
European Centre for Medium-Range Weather Forecasts 59
European Climate Foundation 101
European Council on Foreign Relations 63
European Court of Human Rights 142
European Fashion Alliance (EFA) 51
European Sustainability Reporting Standards (ESRS) 187
European Union
  Corporate Sustainability Reporting Directive (CSRD) 94, 187
  Green Deal 51, 118
  Net-Zero Industry Act 62

Fair Food Programme 159, 161
Fairr 103
fashion industry 49–52, 148, 204
fast fashion see fashion industry
fast-food chains 121
Federal Home Loan Mortgage Corporation 68
feedback mechanisms 6
fertiliser industry 118
Fidelity International 102, 103, 105
fiduciary duty 34
final products 78
financial accounting 173–6

financial capital (equity) 175
First Quantum Minerals 133
Firth, Livia Giuggioli 50, 52
fishing industry 204
Focus on Labour Exploitation (Flex) 161
food sources, environmental impact of 110
forced labour 140
Forest Stewardship Council 124
Fournier, Louise 143, 144
framing 153, 158
Frandsen, Martin 94
freshwater 91, 98
Friedman, Milton 20, 46, 47–8, 49
FSB group 183, 184

Gap Inc. 149
garment sector 5, 49
  see also fashion industry
gender discrimination 136
Generali 138
GHG emissions 64, 65, 67, 184, 214
  1.5 degree target 60
  historical experience 109
  by sector 70, 87
GHG Protocol 71, 72, 73, 78, 190
  corporate value chain standard 76, 77
Giller, Ken 118
Global Biodiversity Framework Fund, 94
Global Fishing Watch 140
Global Footprint Network 92
global green subsidy race 62–4
global metric [for] diversity 104, 105
Global Reporting Initiative (GRI) 171, 187
global risks 4
global warming 3
Goldman Sachs 136
Google 137, 140
green ammonia 118
green premium 47
greenhouse gas emissions
  see GHG emissions
Greenhouse Gas Protocol (GHG Protocol) 70

Greenpeace International 144
Greenpeace Norway 144
Greenpeace UK 155
Greensphere Capital 94
greenwashing 24, 105, 106, 145, 178, 206, 219
Gresham House 95
GRI 190
GSK 105, 106

H&M 51, 106, 136
Haldrup, Simon 117
heat stress 156
Heijn, Albert 113
Hewlett Packard 159
Hilton Hotels 137–8
human rights 134, 139, 141–6
human trafficking 137
Hydro (Norway) 3
hydrological cycle 98

IKEA 121, 209, 217
illycaffè 14
impact 64, 65, 66
Impax Environmental Markets plc 95
income statement records 175
Indeed 138
Inditex 149
Industrial Revolution 109
Inflation Reduction Act (2022) (US) 62
insurance 4, 10–11, 14, 66, 67–9
integrity 7
Intergovernmental Panel on Climate Change (IPCC) 58
intermediate products 78
International Accounting Standards Board (IASB) 171
International Financial Reporting Standards (IFRS) 8, 20, 171, 176
  Accounting Standards 4
  Sustainability Disclosure Standards 4, 195–8
    governance 196
    metrics and targets 197–8
    risk management 197
    strategy 196–7
International Labour Organisation 140, 153, 154, 156, 157
International Standards Organisation (ISO) 190
  ISO 14025 87
  ISO 14040 86
  ISO 14044 86
International Sustainability Standards Board (ISSB) 8, 20–1, 171, 180, 181, 186, 190
International Transport Workers' Federation (ITF) 161
Invesco 62
ISS 137
Italy
  fast fashion in 49
  insurance against climate-related threats 66

Jaguar cars 79
Jevons Paradox 66
Johnson, Mike 63
Junk (documentary series) 50
just transition 157, 158

Kalra, Rishi 103
Kapin, Leslie 118
Katapult Ocean 94
Katz, Joshua 105
Kellogg 15
Kenzen 141
key indicators 156
key performance indicators (KPIs) 193
Kin + Carta 39
KlimaSeniorinnen 143, 144

La Niña 59
Laboratory for Climate and Environmental Sciences 101
Lambertini, Marco 101, 102, 104, 106
land system change 98
leadership and sustainability 8–12

INDEX   231

Leather Working Group (LWG) 217, 218
Lenton, Tim 59
Liang, Nellie 184
licence to operate 38
lifecycle analysis 80–1, 86
limited liability 34
linear economy 6, 21, 57, 115
Lipton 136
Long-term orientation 207–11
LVMH 106
LWG 218

Macy's Inc. 149
Mallone, Federica 50, 51, 52
Manley, Richard 20
ManpowerGroup 138
Marks & Spencer 149
Maron, Martine 102, 104
Marriott 137
Mars Incorporated 15, 209
Marzotto 49
Mastercard 150, 153
materiality assessment 213
Mayer 53
McDonald's 136
McGuire, Patrick 59
McKinsey 105
McMahon, Paul 103
microplastic fibres 50
Mielle Organics 139
milk, daairy and non-dairy 4, 112
Milner-Gulland, EJ 104, 105
Miteni 49
mitigation (impact) 66
mitigation hierarchy 121
Montreal Protocol 97
Mooney, Attracta 58
Moral Money 67
moral responsibility to shareholders 48
Morgan Stanley 69, 117
Morningstar Sustainalytics 94
Morrisons 160
Murray, Sarah 141

National Interagency Coordination Center (US) 68
Nationalities and Borders Act (2022) (UK) 160
natural capital 98–100
natural selection 47
Nature Conservancy 102, 106
Nature Positive Initiative 101, 104
'nature positive', being 101–6
negative externalities 5
Nestlé 14, 106, 117
net zero 61, 81–3
Net Zero Asset Managers alliance 67
Net Zero Banking 67
net zero corporate commitments 179
Nike 217
Nio 63
nitrogen flow 98
non-renewable resources 100

Oatly 120
Ocean 14 Capital 94
ocean acidification 98
OECD 113
Oertel, Janka 63, 64
off mindset 202–7
Ofwat 48
Ogallala Aquifer 107–8
Olam Food Ingredients 103
operational boundary 71
operational risk 136
organisational boundary 71
Ørsted 208
Oxford *Leading Sustainable Corporations* 1, 202

palm oil 103, 155
pandemic risk 4
Paris Agreement on climate change (2015) 58, 67, 101, 114
Patagonia 127
perfluoroalkyl and polyfluoroalkyl substances (PFAS) 49
permanence 82

PG Tips 136
pharmaceutical industry 80
phosphorus flow 98
planetary boundaries 4, 97
plastic 113, 119
  single-use 5
polar ice caps, melting of 96
polluter pays principle 113
pollution 4
  air 14
  chemical 97
  water 49–50
Polman, Paul 42
  Net Positive 155
Porsche 3, 120
Pratty, Freya 116
precautionary principle 97
primary data 76, 77
Principal Asset Management 94
Procter & Gamble 61, 139
profit 174, 176
proportionality principle 20
PwC 138, 153, 156

Rana Plaza, Bangladesh 136
Randstad 138
Ranghino, Fabio 50, 51, 52
Rawnsley, Jessica 93
recycling rates 100
Rees, Caroline 155
re-framing business
  and nature 115–23
  and social systems 151–3
regenerative agriculture 116–18
regenerative economy 115
Rent the Runway 121
reputational risk 136, 148
responsible business 13
return on capital employed 175
rice farming 15
right of control 33
right to benefit 33
Rimar 49
RISE 149, 154, 218

risk-oriented funds 94
Rockstart 117
role of business 111–13
Ruggie, John 142
'Ruggie Report' 142
Russell, Bertrand's thought
  experiment 184

S&P Global 1200 96
Saleh, Firas 68
SAP 137
Sauven, John 155
Savafe, Susannah 101
SBTi FLAG 124
Schinas, Margaritis 138
Science Based Target Network 106
Scope 1 emissions 72, 73, 76, 77, 123
Scope 2 emissions 72, 73, 77
Scope 3 emissions 73–6, 77, 78, 79, 80,
  123, 193, 214
Scottish White Fish Producers
  Association 161
Seafood Ethics Action Alliance (SEA
  Alliance) 160
secondary data 76
second-hand clothing 4
Senge, Peter 12
Setzer, Joana 143, 145
Shahbazian, Gayaneh 94, 95
share capital 34
share ownership 33
shared value 13
shareholder capitalism 47
shareholder investment 33
shareholder ownership 33–5
shareholder primacy 37
Shein 51
Siddi, Marco 63
slavery 140
SLM Partners 103
Smith, Adam: 'invisible hand' 46
'social licence to operate' 134, 135–41
social media networks 6
social sustainability 133–62

soil 109
solutions-focused funds 94
sphere of influence 142
stakeholder capitalism 39
Standard Chartered Bank 152, 153, 154
Starbucks 137–8
State Farm 4, 68
State Street 67
Stellantis 62
strategic asset 135
stratospheric ozone depletion 97
Sundial Brands 139
sustainability, definition 8, 12–15
sustainability agenda 119
sustainability efforts 15–17
sustainability reporting 178–86
    in your own business 191–3
sustainable corporation, definition 2, 13, 45–53
Sustainable Development Goals 146–53
    SDG 1 (ending poverty) 150, 152
    SDG 5 (gender equality) 148, 149
    SDG 8 (decent work and economic growth) 147, 153
    SDG 15 (life on land) 147

Taco Bell 136
'take, make, use and lose' model 6
Tan, Jenn-Hui 102, 103, 105
tariff proposals 64
Taskforce on Nature-related Financial Disclosures 94, 105, 106, 124
Tauschinski, Jana 58
technical cycle 126
Temple-West, Patrick 62, 67
Temu 51
TENT 137
Tent Partnership for Refugees 137
Tesco 160
Tesla 3, 63
textile waste recycling 50
Thomas, Helen 39
threats 66
Timberland 217

'tipping point' effects in natural systems 96
tracking systems 140
trade-off 7, 8, 202–7
tragedy of the commons 106, 107, 110, 127
transferable shares 33
transit visas 160
transition plans 188–91
'triple bottom line' 13
tropical rainforest 113
Trump, Donald 59, 63, 64
Tubiana, Laurence 101

UK seafood industry 160–1
UK Social Mobility Commission 138
Ulukaya, Hamdi 137
Unilever 42, 117, 139, 155
United Nations Brundtland Commission 8
United Nations Convention on Biological Diversity
    COP15 (2022) (Montreal) 94, 114
    COP16 (2024) (Colombia) 94
United Nations Environment Programme 95
United Nations General Assembly 141
United Nations Global Compact (UNGC) 17, 134, 146
United Nations Guiding Principles on Human Rights 142
United Nations Human Rights Commission 145
United Nations Sustainable Development Goals (SDGs) 15–16, 42, 136, 186
Universal Declaration of Human Rights (UDHR) (1948) 141
upstream emissions 77, 79, 80
US Business Roundtable (BRT) 7, 42, 43
US hurricanes (Helene and Milton) 10
US movie industry 182
US tariffs 64

value chain emissions 75
value creation 7

value on biodiversity 93–5
Vectura 40
VELUX 209, 210
Vestas 64
Vinted 121
visas 159
Volkswagen 120
von der Leyen, Ursula 62–3
VUCA landscape (volatility, uncertainty, complexity and ambiguity) 18

Walmart 136
Walt Disney Company 149
Ward, Matteo 50
waste textiles 6
water
   drinking 112
   fresh 91, 98
   pollution 49–50
   UK 48
Weiss, Adam 144, 145
Wells Fargo 183
Whitby Seafoods 160
Whitehouse, Senator Sheldon 183
Williams, Chris 160
wind power 64
Wironen, Michael 102, 104, 106
Wm Morrison 40
worker-driven social responsibility (WSR) 159
World Bank 150
World Business Council for Sustainable Development (WBCSD) 70
World Economic Forum (2024) 4, 96, 102
World Resources Institute (WRI) 70
World Wildlife Fund 101
WRÅD 50
WWF 109
WWF Living Index 91

Zabey, Eva 102
Zara 51, 136
'zero impact factories' 120